Y0-BWW-230

WINNING YOUR NEXT PROMOTION IN ONE YEAR
(OR LESS!)

Also by Lawrence D. Schwimmer

How to Ask for a Raise Without Getting Fired

Lawrence D. Schwimmer

WINNING YOUR NEXT PROMOTION IN ONE YEAR (OR LESS!)

PERENNIAL LIBRARY

Harper & Row, Publishers, New York,
Cambridge, Philadelphia, San Francisco, London,
Mexico City, São Paulo, Singapore, Sydney

WINNING YOUR NEXT PROMOTION IN ONE YEAR (OR LESS!). Copyright © 1986 by Lawrence D. Schwimmer. All rights reserved. Printed in the United States of America. No part of this book may be used or reproduced in any manner whatsoever without written permission except in the case of brief quotations embodied in critical articles and reviews. For information address Harper & Row, Publishers, Inc., 10 East 53rd Street, New York, N.Y. 10022. Published simultaneously in Canada by Fitzhenry & Whiteside Limited, Toronto.

FIRST EDITION

Designed by Ruth Bornschlegel

Library of Congress Cataloging-in-Publication Data
Schwimmer, Lawrence D.
    Winning your next promotion in one year (or less!)
    1. Promotions.   2. Success in business.   I. Title.
HF5549.5.P7S37   1986   650.1'4   85-45660
ISBN 0-06-055006-6
ISBN 0-06-096071-X (pbk)

86	87	88	89	90	MPC	10	9	8	7	6	5	4	3	2	1
86	87	88	89	90	MPC	10	9	8	7	6	5	4	3	2	1

Contents

Acknowledgments

I want to sincerely thank the many friends and colleagues whose suggestions, input, and experiences helped me in the writing of this book. And I want to particularly thank Jody Brown, a very special woman in my life—who can no doubt look forward to a career of winning many promotions.

In addition, I would like to extend my heartfelt appreciation to Beth Kuper for encouraging me to write this book and for faithfully supporting my goals and dreams. Her tireless dedication in editing the manuscript for over a year and a half has been invaluable in making this book a reality.

My literary agents, Michael Larsen and Elizabeth Pomada, also have my gratitude for their valuable guidance and encouragement during the publishing process.

Finally, I want to acknowledge the thousands of talented business and professional people with whom I have had the pleasure of working throughout the country. My sincere wish is that you all win the promotions you so richly deserve.

Introduction

My interest in the "hows" and "whys" of winning promotions started when I was in line for my first promotion. I began to watch the actions of "fast track" stars who rapidly advanced in the company—versus other employees who seemed to stagnate "on the vine." Then, as I progressed in my career, working for different companies, I began analyzing which factors upper management seemed to consider when they gave or withheld promotions. Later, as president of a multimillion-dollar foods company, I was responsible for these same management decisions on whom to promote and whom to pass by.

It was my firsthand experience in the corporate and organizational world that led me to develop courses which I taught at Northwestern University and the City Colleges of Chicago. Later, I offered public seminars to business and professional people on such career advancement topics as "Developing Your Management Style," "Power, Politics, and Productivity," and "Executives on the Fast Track."

To date, more than 25,000 people have attended my seminars. In addition, I have personally counseled and provided mentorship guidance to hundreds of promotion-minded individuals. These people have been a wonderful laboratory for me as a "business and social" scientist to observe and draw conclusions on how to win promotions. It is from this vantage point that I have written *Winning Your Next Promotion in One Year (or Less!)*.

Let's face it: Just about everyone who works in a company or organization is interested in winning promotions and salary increases. Some people are less ambitious and would be content to win only an occasional promotion. Others will not stop in their quest for promotions until they reach their goal of becoming company president. Thus, information on getting ahead and advancing one's career receives a great deal of attention from career-oriented people.

Over the years, I have eagerly read many books that advise promotion-bound individuals. While there are excellent books on this topic, most of them do not tell the reader *how* to implement the information presented. So, I resolved to write my own book with specific step-by-step methods on winning promotions.

Obviously, if all it took to get ahead were to read books and acquire information, few people would be frustrated over stagnating careers. Unfortunately, many well-qualified business professionals have failed to gain the promotions they deserve—and can't understand why.

To win promotions, you must not only have talent, ability, and knowledge, but you must also have a risk-taking mindset. As Chapter 1 explains more fully, whenever you expose yourself to uncertain situations or conflicts with people at work, you are taking a risk. Yet most people are afraid to engage in these uncertain situations. They don't realize that taking risks can be the very means of *advancing* their career and breaking through the barriers that have stopped them in the past. Therefore, in order to apply the information, techniques, and skills presented in this book, you will be *required* to take risks.

Chapter 1 will be valuable in making you conscious of the many work situations in which you are indeed taking risks, whether you've ever thought so or not. It will show you how to become a *calculated* risk taker, furthering your career by specifically designed strategies. Best of all, it will show you how risk taking will build your confidence level. These factors will ultimately lead you to win many promotions in your career.

Chapter 2 discusses the importance of understanding the hidden rules vital to playing and winning the game of business. Skill, competence, and experience are not enough to advance you, so I will show you how to understand better the *politics* of your organization in order to get ahead.

The cornerstone of winning promotions is your ability to deal with people, especially aggressive and difficult people. Chapters 3 and 4 present communication techniques you can use to face conflict situations, motivate people for higher productivity, and position yourself better for promotional opportunities.

At work, everyone faces the manipulation and pressure tactics of others. How would you handle a situation where you are being intimidated by the senior vice president? You would definitely be at risk. Poor handling of such a situation could not only interfere with future promotions, but it could also result in your abrupt termination. Because of such weighty consequences, Chapter 5 discusses specific ways in which you can protect yourself from the manipulation tactics of others.

Have you ever thought of yourself as being charismatic? You will, after reading and implementing the strategies discussed in Chapter 6. As a charismatic individual, you will gain greater cooperation from your coworkers and customers and find yourself in management's spotlight as a prime candidate for leadership positions.

Chapter 7 focuses on using your manager and your staff to help you win promotions. For example, do you know the seven key questions you should ask your prospective manager *before* you accept a new position? Do you know how to motivate your staff to produce results that make you look like an outstanding manager? The right answers can spell the difference between career momentum and career stagnation.

Chapter 8 on delegation will be vital to enhancing your skill in assigning your work load, even if you don't presently have a staff. This chapter will show you *how* to delegate work and *whom* to delegate it to. The ability to delegate is one of the most important criteria others will use in evaluating your suitability for promotions.

Publicizing yourself and your accomplishments within your organization may seem like bragging. Many people consider it too risky to publicize a new idea, for fear that it might not turn out well. Yet advancing your career is often based on letting others know about your noteworthy accomplishments. Chapter 9 will show you the best ways to gain publicity and receive the recognition you deserve for your performance and achievements. This visibility will translate into promotions throughout your career.

Chapter 10 will show you how to manage, motivate, and influence others through the use of memos, especially when you need to "cover your ass" on decisions you didn't make but for which you will be held responsible. Memos can also help you accomplish projects successfully, present your ideas, manage people, gain cooperation, and earn recognition that will lead to promotions.

Many people are uncomfortable with being powerful or with dealing with powerful people. Chapter 11 focuses on the various kinds of power available to you and how you can use power to get things done and establish your leadership position.

Chapter 12, on selling yourself and your ideas, is written especially for people who hate the notion of selling. After you see the clear connection between successfully selling your ideas and winning promotions, you will be motivated to learn the persuasion skills presented. These skills will help you succeed at winning support for your projects, proposals, and salary raises.

Another important part of winning promotions is developing a support system. For this purpose, Chapters 13 and 14 show you how valuable mentors and networks can be in revealing promotional opportunities and specific strategies for getting ahead.

Chapter 15 will show you how to create a "perfect" job. This information will be extremely valuable to those of you who are not sure what you really want to do "when you grow up." The chapter examines the psychological, personal, and material factors you should consider in order to get a more accurate idea of the kind of job that will make you feel most fulfilled and give you the greatest opportunities for promotions. And Chapter 16 will show you how to create a ten-year plan that will take you straight to the top—if that is your goal.

I have put these two chapters at the end of the book because I believe you ought to know what is involved in being promotable and advancing your career *before* you plan your future promotional moves. I have not attempted to write a Pollyannaish book promising that everyone can be promoted to president or executive director because not everyone is cut out for or disposed to doing what is necessary to win that position. But I do promise that however far you have decided to climb the ladder in your organization, you'll climb faster and farther if you implement the ideas, skills, and techniques in this book.

Before you begin reading, here are a few more notes to assist you in implementing the suggestions in this book:

- I believe that repetition is the mother of memory. Thus I often discuss certain definitions, skills, and concepts more than once. (You will thank me for this 30 days after you've read this book.)

- Many chapters have exercises and assignments that will allow you to experience the ideas presented. This is important because you probably won't want to try a new idea or skill without some practice in a safe environment. After all, you wouldn't enter a race without warming up first. Take the exercises and assignments in this book seriously. Doing them will result in the promotions you are striving for; not doing them will result in your being an also-ran.

- If you have no ambition to be promoted, this book will be useful because you will be working with many people who *do* want to win promotions. It is in your best interest to understand these people and form alliances with them that could benefit you in the future.

- Some of you, in such positions as chairman of the board, president, owner of the business, or at the top of your job category, are perhaps beyond being concerned with promotions. For you this book will be valuable in helping you determine which individuals to promote and what to look for in your organization's rising stars. It will also give you fair warning as to who's coming after your job!

I hope you will keep this book in your office as a handy reference to the ideas, actions, and strategies that you will want to implement in your quest for future promotions. Keep in mind that this information is not based solely on my personal experiences in winning promotions but, just as important, on the promotional successes of talented people I have worked with and counseled. All I ask is that you read and practice what is discussed in this book. Then, please write me after you win your next promotion—I am eager to hear about your accomplishments. Who knows, I may put your success story in my next book!

Lawrence D. Schwimmer

P.O. Box 159
Mill Valley, CA 94941

WINNING
YOUR
NEXT
PROMOTION
IN ONE
YEAR
(OR LESS!)

chapter 1

Becoming
a Successful
Risk Taker

SITUATION

You are sitting in an important executive staff meeting. You have
been with the company for only one month, but you have a suggestion
that you think may remedy one of the company's long-standing problems. So you decide to make your suggestion in front of the group.
No sooner do you get the last words out of your mouth than the vice
president turns to you and in front of everyone contemptuously snaps,
"That's a totally ridiculous idea. It will never work!"

Everyone is now looking at you. They want to see what you,
"the new kid on the block," will say or do. Standing up to this intimidating vice president could be the first and last risk you ever take
with this company. How would you handle this situation?

SITUATION

You have been working very hard on a research project for the last
several months when your rather nonassertive manager informs you
that he will be turning your project over to another executive. You
thought you were doing a great job. Your manager agrees but has
decided that it's time for a change. Despite your obvious disappointment, your boss says he's too busy to discuss it further. "Don't worry,
there will be other projects."

What do you say?

SITUATION

You have just been promoted to supervisor in charge of other staff. They still remember you when you were their peer, and one of the staff in particular is being uncooperative and sarcastic. She thinks your new promotion has made you "power crazy." You need her cooperation to ensure that the department operates at peak efficiency.

How do you assert yourself?

Most people are very uncomfortable in typical conflict situations such as these. In fact, people are much more used to avoiding risky situations or being indirect when one presents itself. Many people resort to manipulation tactics or playing politics to avoid the risk of standing up to a person or situation.

To implement the ideas, strategies, and techniques that I discuss in each chapter, it will be necessary for you to take risks. This is why it is important for you to be familiar with the nature of risk taking and to develop an authentic risk-taking mindset.

Just what is risk taking? And why is it so important to your career advancement?

Risk taking means confronting uncertain situations, making decisions, and asserting yourself—whether it's standing up to an aggressive boss or speaking up for an idea or project you believe in. It means having the courage to take advantage of the many opportunities, big and small, that come your way every day. It is an inevitable part of doing business, managing people, and moving on to higher leadership positions. The ability to take risks confidently is the key factor to winning promotions. Risk takers make things happen. They face situations that directly or indirectly affect their future promotability. Yet fear of risk taking is the greatest single deficiency in today's working professional.

RISK: to expose oneself to a situation whose outcome is uncertain and may involve danger or hazard but which offers the possibility of ultimate gain.

Have you ever seriously considered whether or not you are a real risk taker in your job? Taking risks is essential to climbing the ladder and advancing your career. While it is a popular notion for business and professional people to claim to be risk takers, the truth is that most people are afraid to engage in or expose themselves to situations where the outcome is uncertain and may involve danger or hazard—for two simple reasons:

1. Ignorance of which situations require risk taking.
2. Fear of failure.

I am not referring to strategic risk taking, such as whether or not to introduce a new product line or open up a new company plant or whether to go into business for yourself. There are plenty of books that discuss that kind of risk taking.

I'm talking about a much more personal side to risk taking: your ability to take interpersonal risks with people on the job, whether they are coworkers or clients. There are many work situations that you may not even have recognized as being risky, yet handling those situations skillfully and confidently is the secret to creating success in any job you are in.

TAKING RISKS

Consider each of the following work situations and the potential risks involved in resolving them.

1. One of your staff has no qualms about going over your head and breaking the chain of command.
2. A colleague continues to take credit for your ideas.
3. Your manager belittles you publicly by making disparaging or humiliating remarks about you at meetings.
4. A boss or colleague persists in making remarks to you with heavy sexual overtones.
5. You need to take a stand on an issue that you know will make you unpopular in the organization.
6. You believe that your boss's boss is intimidating you so that you will take on his own pet project.
7. You want to publicize your talents without people thinking you are a braggart.

8. You want to know which political hidden agendas you must observe in order to climb the ladder in your organization.

9. You're not sure of the kind of memo you should use to protect yourself on a decision you didn't make but will be held responsible for.

10. You've been passed by for a promotional opportunity. Should you stay or leave?

11. Your mentor has a number of political enemies. How will that affect you?

All these situations call for risk taking. Resolving them will involve your taking a risk—that is, exposing yourself to a situation whose outcome is uncertain and may involve danger or hazard but which offers the possibility of ultimate gain. If you handle these risky situations with skill and acumen, you will have a successful climb to the top. If you don't, despite your competence and experience, you may find yourself frustrated and out of a job. Career momentum versus career stagnation: Which will it be? If you are willing to take the right risks and use the information and skills noted in this book, you can have an exciting and rewarding career, filled with many promotional opportunities.

A NEW WAY OF LOOKING AT RISK TAKING

Many of us look at taking risks in a very literal and traditional way. In a business sense, making an investment is risky. So is expanding your plant facility in anticipation of increased sales volume. We accept these as bona fide risks.

Ironically, we tend not to view our interactions with people in our organization as involving risks. This key mistake in perception is the root of why so many people in today's world of work—despite state-of-the-art information, advanced degrees, competence, and experience—seem to be frustrated in their attempts to advance in their careers.

Taking risks in managing people and conflicts is an even more important determinant to your success than any of the other factors that I have mentioned. So the first step in taking necessary risks is to be *aware* that such situations are risky and require you to act to resolve a problem or dilemma.

Let's take a closer look at some of the many areas where you must be prepared to take risks.

PLAYING POLITICS

We all accept that politics exist in most organizations. Yet most people are playing a game without knowing the rules. Their ignorance may result in risking job and career. For example, each organization has its own political hidden rules that you must observe if you expect to be successful and promotable. One hidden agenda (informally) states: "If you decline a relocation assignment, you can forget about a future promotion because you won't be asked again."

Risk: You face career stagnation because of your ignorance of the hidden rules in the organization.

DELEGATING TO OTHERS

If you have all the responsibility without the authority, you may find that you are doing all the work. So you must know how to get co-operation, especially with individuals over whom you have no direct authority. How are you going to get competent assistance and support to get the job done on time according to high quality standards? You must know the pitfalls of delegating to others.

Risk: You may look incompetent by failing to get the work done or having it done poorly by staff.

BEING A LEADER

You are looking forward to increased responsibilities and an opportunity to supervise more staff or a larger department. Yet you do not carry yourself in a charismatic manner that causes upper management to notice you and acknowledge your abilities.

Risk: You will remain in a low-level staff or managerial position because you are not perceived as being a leader.

PUBLICIZING YOURSELF

You have just won an award for superior achievement in your industry trade association. Yet despite the honors you receive outside of work, you don't seem to get any recognition from people in your organization. You would like to let the right people know about the awards you have received, but you are much too concerned that they will think you a showboat or a braggart.

Risk: If you don't promote yourself properly, you will be viewed as being a show-off or egomaniac—and you won't be fairly recognized for your achievements.

USING POWER

If you don't know how to use power, you will soon lose it. Worse yet, if you don't know how to deal with people who would undermine your power, you face certain exploitation. In addition, your influence and ability to get things done will be hampered.

Risk: You will be seen as being powerless and ineffectual in your position and not a candidate for a more powerful position.

CHOOSING A MENTOR

It may seem like a great idea to have someone take an interest in you and your career—someone who can give you advice and talk over strategy with you. However, if you are associated with someone with many political enemies in the organization, the relationship may be a liability. How can you tell the difference between a mentor who can help you and one who can hurt you? Not knowing can be dangerous.

Risk: Guilt by association may result in a dismal future and even potential firing if your mentor leaves or is fired.

PLANNING YOUR FUTURE

If you are interested in climbing the ladder in your organization, you will need a plan to map out how you are going to get to the position you ultimately want. This means looking at the typical background and experience that are requisite to obtaining the position you want in your company. However, some of the necessary experience may be in an area that you have no interest in, such as having to spend two years in the field sales force. You should know what experience will be expected of you in order to be competitive with others vying for the same position as you.

Risk: Ignorance and insufficient planning can result in limited upward mobility.

Your new way of viewing risk taking should include an awareness that both the people you interact with and the activities you engage in require you to take risks in order to win promotions.

WHY ARE PEOPLE AFRAID TO TAKE RISKS?

Most of us are not socialized or encouraged to take risks, especially in our relationships with people. We have not been taught very much in our schools or colleges about interpersonal communication skills or the people skills that will build our confidence in working effectively with others—and in the process assist us in taking necessary risks. To the contrary, most of us are taught to be cautious, placating, and nonconfrontational in our dealings with people. Thus many people become more adept at avoiding or sidestepping risky situations. Others rely on manipulation tactics or end up playing politics rather than take the risk to stand up to a person or situation. We have not been educated to the fact that we risk our job success by not knowing how to deal effectively with people, just as surely as we risk our money when we invest in a new plant or stock offering without the proper knowledge.

HOW CAN YOU BECOME A RISK TAKER?

The secret to becoming a risk taker is to take risks. This may sound like a catch-22, but it's true. Only by practicing risk taking can you experience the tremendous sense of achievement and rewards that will come to you for your efforts. All the skills and information that you can get from books or from the advice of others will not substitute for your applying what you learn by going out there and taking risks.

It has taken you many months and years to become the way you are. It will take time for you to change some of these patterns. Be patient. And remember that being a confident risk taker is a process. It begins and continues each time you are willing to engage in an uncertain situation.

Repeated practice in engaging in risky situations will give you an opportunity to refine your ability to apply different skills to different situations. This will help you feel more confident and in control. Soon you will have the confidence to tackle any risk and begin working toward the highest level of risk-taking, mastery.

In the risk-taking state of mastery, your confidence is so high that you are positively challenged by opportunities to take risks. You shift your point of view about risk taking from a fearful experience to avoid or dread to an opportunity to grow, develop, and advance your career.

Let's now address the important question of how you can be a confident risk taker.

BE AWARE

The first step in becoming a risk taker or taking even more risks is to be fully aware that *any time you expose yourself to a situation whose outcome is uncertain, you are taking a risk.* The risk you take may be in (1) dealing directly with an individual at work, (2) an activity that you engage in, or (3) an action you take.

This new awareness will help you reframe, that is, view the notion and importance of risk taking in a new light. This is the first step in preparing yourself psychologically to face the realities of the real world of work.

CREATE THE RIGHT MINDSET

The right mindset is knowing that your willingness to take risks is the key to succeeding on the job and winning future promotions. In other words, you are "risking to succeed." It is vital that you develop (or improve) your ability to willingly confront situations that are risky. Notice I said "willingly." Many people avoid risks until they have little choice. By that time, they are reacting defensively or from a far less advantageous position than if they had anticipated the inherent risks in a situation. Taking risks can be fun, challenging, and very exciting. As you learn more from yourself and others about the true nature of taking risks, you will find yourself more willing to pursue the many opportunities that are available to you.

Remember that fear and failure are all part of the risk-taking process. Don't apply the acid test of being comfortable in order to take a risk. It is absolutely unnecessary to be comfortable or even very confident in order to take risks. If this is your criterion, you will not take some very important risks that, by their nature, will make you uncomfortable and even out of control. If you feel too comfortable taking a risk—if you are dead sure of the outcome—you are probably not taking a risk.

People who do weight lifting expect their muscles to be sore after an intense workout of pumping iron. Weight lifters say, "No pain, no gain." In the same way, entertainers will tell you that it is natural to feel butterflies in the stomach and very nervous before a show. They, too, recognize that there are many predictable and often uncomfortable feelings associated with their work.

Risk taking requires courage. One definition of courage that I like is "being afraid of something and doing it anyway." In taking risks, expect that at times you, too, will feel nervous, unsure and scared. In time, those same risks will feel much more comfortable because you have had experience and success in taking them. Each experience of risking and succeeding—often in small increments— will give you further confidence to take even greater risks.

DEVELOP YOUR CONFIDENCE

One of the biggest reasons why people don't develop their risk-taking potential is that they imagine only the worst possible outcome to the risk they would like to take, instead of remembering that there are always three possible outcomes in any situation: (1) positive, (2) neutral, and (3) negative. The result is that many people focus on the negative outcome and psych themselves out of taking the risk.

You can develop your confidence level and thus your risk-taking ability by taking small risks and then graduating to more difficult risks. Don't compare yourself to other people. Risk taking is relative. Remember, *anything you think of as a risk* is *a risk for you.* Comparing yourself to others is irrelevant and only serves to undermine your confidence level. When you face a risk, go over in your mind the three possible outcomes of taking that risk: positive, neutral, and negative.

Since we'll be discussing throughout this book specific business risks that affect your promotability, let's begin with a simple, everyday risk. You are in an elevator and a man lights a cigarette. You want to ask him to put it out. What could possibly happen?

POSITIVE: The man says, "Sorry, I wasn't thinking; thanks for reminding me," and puts out the cigarette.

NEUTRAL: The man says nothing and puts out the cigarette.

NEGATIVE: The man tells you to hold your breath until the elevator gets to your floor. He continues to smoke.

This is a good risk to take because no matter what the outcome, you will not be seriously damaged. You will probably never see this man again. This is also a low-risk situation in that you aren't really concerned about this man's opinion of you, anyway. By voicing your feelings and taking the risk, you have an excellent chance of discovering that this man is basically considerate. And you will get to enjoy a smoke-free elevator ride. Most important of all, you will gain an inner satisfaction of taking a risk in an assertive fashion and, in the process, building up your confidence level.

By contrast, nonassertive people (about whom we will talk later) would never take the risk of asking the smoker not to smoke. Instead they would complain to others about "this rude man on the elevator who was smoking." Unlike risk takers, nonassertive people are victims because they are afraid to take life's necessary risks.

BEWARE OF GUARANTEES

Part of the process of risk taking includes your awareness that you are not looking for a guaranteed outcome. If you were, it would probably not be a risk. Obviously, this is not to suggest that you engage only in situations where the outcome is uncertain. We all love to enter a situation knowing that we can be sure of a positive result. Remember that many of the work situations you have to confront will not come with a guaranteed outcome, although you may have a strong hunch, intuition, or belief. That's fine, as long as you do not require a guarantee to take a risk.

Many people don't take a risk only because this is their strategy for avoiding failure. In the same process, they also avoid promotions, big salary increases, and on-the-job happiness and fulfillment.

Kevin was a relatively new employee who wanted to be considered for a promotion before Amy, another employee who had more seniority. However, Kevin believed he was more qualified for the promotion than Amy. Although Kevin was nervous about approaching his manager, he realized that it was a risk worth taking. Because of his skills and assertiveness, Kevin won the position.

DO SOMETHING DIFFERENT

What kind of book would this be if I didn't take one of my cherished dicta and turn it into a law with my name in front of it? Schwimmer's Law states: "If at first you don't succeed, don't try harder—do something different!"

Often we don't take a risk because we believe that our chances—based on doing it the way we have always done things—will probably not yield the outcome we are looking for. By applying Schwimmer's Law, you will instead take a fresh look at any risky situation and revise your perception. *Do something different!* The results can be unpredictable. By doing this, you create the possibility of a new, more positive outcome. When something doesn't work, be willing to try anything else.

BEGIN WITH THIS RISK-TAKING EXERCISE

Resolve to take one risk each day for five days. Tell a friend, colleague, or loved one of the risk you are going to take before you take it. Choose someone who will support and encourage you. There are many kinds of risks you can take, even outside of work. Each risk you take will build your confidence level and willingness to move on to even riskier situations—with the potential of greater rewards. Be patient with yourself. Becoming a confident risk taker is the product of taking thousands of risks and learning, growing, and experiencing, thus building confidence.

In addition to any risks you may choose to take, consider some of the following:

- Ask someone out for a date or social event whom you are afraid will refuse you.

- Ask to join a group of people for lunch who have never invited you before.

- If food comes to your table lukewarm and you like it hot, send it back and tell the waiter to have it prepared the way you like it.

• Ask someone who is smoking in a nonsmoking area to stop smoking.

If these sound like mundane risks, they are. Every day of our lives, there are countless situations where we are at risk. Because we are afraid of a negative outcome, we do not take the risk. All this does is undermine our confidence level. Remember, the greater the likelihood of a personal confrontation with someone, the more uncomfortable you may feel about taking the risk. Take it anyway. This is an exercise for you to learn from. Give yourself permission to do this as if you were a scientist gathering information from firsthand research. Keep in mind that you will be using your new risk-taking mindset in the many work situations discussed in this book.

Exercise: RISKS I WILL TAKE THIS WEEK

Directions: Write down at least five risks you will take this week, one risk a day. They can be small, medium, or large risks. Anything that you think is a risk is a risk.

1. _____

2. _____

3. _____

4. _____

5. _____

Choose a "support partner" (friend, colleague, loved one), and agree to call this person on a specific day and time to report the progress of your risk taking.

My partner's name: _____

Phone number: _____

Date I will call to report: _____

GET TO KNOW OTHER RISK TAKERS

To become more of a risk taker, it is absolutely essential that you experience taking risks. This will build your confidence in your ability to produce results through risk taking—as opposed to risk avoidance. It can also be very helpful to talk directly to others inside and outside your organization whom you consider to be bona fide risk takers. Find out how risk taking helped them win promotions and advance in their careers.

This is a wonderful way to learn the personal insights of others and their attitudes, frustrations, and successes in taking risks. You will quickly learn that you may have ascribed some unrealistic mystique to people who take risks. In reality, such people are more like you and me than you may have ever stopped to consider.

In choosing people to interview, select the rising stars—the fast trackers—in your company, people who had to take risks to get where they are. If you feel intimidated about asking them for 10 or 15 minutes of their valuable time, good! That's an excellent risk for you to take.

Most people are very flattered that someone wants to hear about their experiences in risk taking and how it relates to their obvious success in their organization. Another benefit of this exercise is that it allows you to talk to someone whom you might not otherwise have an excuse to talk with, someone who is several levels higher than you in your company. This person could become a valuable ally at a later time.

When you make your appointments to talk with your risk takers, be sure you set limits (10-to-15-minute interview) so that they know it won't be a lengthy session. Most people being interviewed end up talking much longer than that, but that's their choice once the interview gets started.

Have all your questions written out beforehand, and *listen* to the answers. Take notes. Don't get involved in discussing your opinions; remember, you're the interviewer.

One of my students, Beth, who did this exercise, approached a very gruff, scowling senior vice president of the organization where she worked. Beth knew nothing about this man except that he *must* have taken risks to have arrived at his position. He was an extremely busy person, and even his staff had a hard time getting together with him to discuss their work. However, Beth was undaunted and took the risk of calling him for a 10-to-15-minute appointment to talk about risk taking and how it related to his work.

In the interview, Beth was astonished to find out that this man was really a kind and friendly individual; his outward appearances were just his defenses, not the way he really was inside. He not only warmed to the subject of risk taking, but he was very candid and offered a lot of information Beth didn't expect to hear. He talked with her for over an hour, and she totally changed her opinion about the man. She had prejudged him on appearances, and she now discovered him to be a real human being and a genuine ally.

Like Beth, you will learn a great deal and find that your association and the knowledge you gain from interviewing these risk takers will be valuable to you as you progress in your career. It will also give you even more confidence as you continue to take risks on the job.

Exercise: INTERVIEWING RISK TAKERS

Directions: Interview three people whom you consider to be risk takers. Write their names below.

1. _____

2. _____

3. _____

Here are some suggested questions you can ask them. Add your own questions to the list, too.

1. Do you perceive yourself as a risk taker?

2. How important is risk taking to your career advancement?

3. What are the attributes you think a person needs in order to be a risk taker?

4. How do you evaluate risks?

5. How do you feel before taking a risk?

6. Do you enjoy taking risks?

7. What risks have you taken that were the most difficult?

8. What risks have been the easiest?

9. What's the worst thing that's resulted from a risk you took?

10. What's the best thing that's resulted from a risk you took?

11. What did you learn from taking the risk?

12. Does risk taking get easier with practice?

13. Does risk taking at work transfer over to your personal life? Do you take risks in your personal relationships?

14. What part has risk taking played in winning you promotions?

VISUALIZE YOUR SUCCESS
AT TAKING RISKS

It is very easy to imagine some negative outcome to your risk taking. So you may find that just about every time you take a risk, you will have to visualize or imagine that you are successful in taking that risk. In doing this, you will begin to focus on how and in what ways you can maximize your success instead of fixating on the same negative thinking that inhibits you from taking a risk.

By imagining an optimistic outcome, you will begin to look at all the possibilities and resources that will make you successful. In the process of visualizing, remember that you are the playwright and all the people in your drama are actors following your script. Thus someone in real life—whom you are sure will act or respond in a certain way—can act totally differently in your visualization. Remember Beth's surprise in interviewing her risk taker when she discovered he was not at all like what she had thought.

Also note that doing this exercise will reveal the blocks and barriers that get in the way of your taking certain risks. If, for example, you imagine someone getting very angry at you, you may have to consider dealing with your concern about being yelled at or scolded.

Exercise: VISUALIZING YOUR RISK-TAKING SUCCESS

Directions: Pick any risk (large or small) involving another person. Imagine yourself talking with this person and having a successful outcome. You are creating the script and can have your actors say anything you want them to—all to your advantage.

1. Imagine very clearly the risk you want to take. Visualize the person you will talk to, the room you are in, the chair you are sitting in—everything to make the scene as real as possible in your mind's eye.

2. How are you really feeling about taking this risk (confident, scared, discouraged, pessimistic, etc.)? Notice what barriers or blocks come up for you as you do this (such as rejection, insecurity, fear, anger, anxiety, embarrassment).

3. You are now going to reexperience this risk as a successful and confident risk taker. You know you can handle whatever comes up for you in this situation. Tell the other person what you wanted to say. Feel yourself smiling with a new surge of confidence. See the other person agreeing with you and cooperating with your request. What you previously thought was difficult has become easy and natural. You will remember this feeling of confidence and ease whenever you encounter this person.

KNOWLEDGE, SKILLS, AND CONCEPTS

You are now on the road to being more aware of the whole gamut of what risk taking involves. We have discussed some of the ways in which you can build your confidence and willingness to take necessary risks to enhance your career success. Knowledge is very important, but it is more important that you begin to think in terms of how you can *apply* the knowledge and skills you learn.

By taking risks, you can further develop your risk-taking confidence level and discover not only the "right" risks to take but also how to take risks in a way that maximizes (but does not guarantee) your prospects for producing the results you desire. Best of all, you will find out that the real secret to winning promotions is to be a risk taker.

chapter 2

Hidden Rules for Getting Promoted

SITUATION

You've just joined the XYZ Company as controller, and while familiarizing yourself with the books, you note that the company has inordinately high expense account bills. Since cutting costs is one of your functions, you circulate a memo announcing that from now on you'll be checking expense accounts very carefully and you expect all managers and sales representatives to justify all expenses. You feel confident that you have taken the right stand.

However, three days later you are called into the president's office for a reprimand. The top sales people have complained about your policy and have threatened to leave.

What went wrong? You took the *wrong risk!* You've shown that you've got no business savvy. You violated one of the prime political commandments of business by failing to evaluate not only whether your idea was correct or beneficial but whether it would be *acceptable* in terms of the company's method of operation. And in the process, you stumbled on one of XYZ Company's hidden rules: The sky's the limit on expense accounts for successful executives and sales reps. No one, from the president on down, will support or appreciate your efforts, well meaning though they may be, to save the company money in this particular way.

Thus it is not enough to be willing to take a stand. It is just as important to understand the politics and hidden agendas of your corporate environment so that you don't take the *wrong* stand and unnecessarily jeopardize your career advancement.

HIDDEN RULES FOR SUCCESS AND UPWARD MOBILITY

One of the big problems for many of us is that we are not sensitive to the fact that in business and industry, many factors beyond skill, competence, and experience determine upward mobility and success. There are hidden agendas or rules that no one will tell you directly that you must know to be able to climb the ladder and be successful.

HIDDEN RULES OR AGENDAS: the informal policies, attitudes, and preferences of the hierarchy in an organization that dictate or strongly influence who gets hired, fired, promoted, or left to stagnate.

Hidden rules or agendas are a part of every organization and a major factor that can affect upward mobility. These rules can relate, as in the example, to implicit policies, the violation of which can seriously undermine your promotability in management's eyes. Although a minor or single infraction may not have serious consequences, you cannot rely on the excuse that you "just didn't know." That would only compound the problem, since it clearly signals to management that you are inexperienced or naive and that you don't know the rules of the game.

More important, you must understand which hidden agendas will affect your future promotability. For example, in some companies, you'd better be a jock if you want to get along with the "boys" in the boardroom. In other companies, you may be expected to take an active role in community affairs or join a particular club. Perhaps there's an unwritten rule about lunching with the "office leper" or being seen taking one drink too many. Perhaps you've joined a company that prefers to fill its executive ranks with yes men, or perhaps the president appreciates corporate mavericks who are tough, tenacious, and willing to speak their minds.

Unless you're sensitive to these many informal rules, you're likely to run smack up against obstacles that will impede your progress. If you're an action-oriented, innovative type, you may be wasting your time in a company that's filled with conservative, stodgy executives who resist change. If you've come up through the ranks the hard way, with limited education, you may never progress past a certain point in an organization that prides itself on the number of advanced degrees its executives hold.

COMMON HIDDEN RULES AND AGENDAS

1. You must go out drinking with the "boys."
2. You must have the right mentor or godfather sponsor.
3. You must be willing to take on a pet project of the president, for example, the Community Fund drive.
4. You must have a degree from a prestigious school, for example, a Harvard MBA.
5. You must have a strong sales or marketing background.
6. You must not be seen hanging around with the wrong crowd (the company "turkeys").
7. You must be willing to relocate.
8. You must take opportunity when it knocks (accept any promotion offered).
9. You must not be seen as a "boat rocker."
10. You must have visibility to other corporate departments, headquarters, top brass, the community, etc.
11. You must know how to use the office grapevine effectively.
12. You must dress the part.
13. You must be seen as supportive and a team player, not someone who hogs the ball all the time.
14. You must be seen as a diplomat.
15. You must be skilled in communicating with memos.
16. You must be seen with the right crowd of executives.
17. You must never be seen bringing a brown bag lunch or eating in the employee cafeteria (only in the executive dining room).
18. You must pretend to know, even if you don't.

19. Your name must be on the routing list for important reports and periodicals.

20. You must play a particular sport that influential executives play, such as golf or tennis.

21. You must be invited to informal meetings that go on after 6:00 P.M.

22. You must look good physically.

23. You must show your loyalty to the boss by standing up for him.

24. You must be willing to work long hours.

25. You must be known as having a very positive attitude.

HOW TO FIND OUT HIDDEN RULES AND AGENDAS

There are many ways of unearthing your organization's hidden rules. However, since such rules are not neatly printed up in a personnel manual, you will have to use both conventional and unconventional means to find them out. Most people learn their organization's hidden rules through observation, intuition, gossip, and innuendo.

Actually, it is not very hard to find out your company's hidden rules. Begin your own discovery process by observing the people in positions of power in your organization. Their background, education, and values will give you insight into possible hidden rules that are operative in your organization.

Remember one basic principle behind the hidden rule structure in every organization: *People in power want to work with people who are like themselves.* For all the lip service you may hear about how companies like mavericks, free thinkers, and people "with their own minds," don't believe it! Some organizations may be a bit more tolerant of independent and unconventional types than others, but make no mistake: The glue that keeps an organization bound together is shared beliefs, attitudes, values, and lifestyles prevalent among those in upper-echelon positions. Those in power will strive to perpetuate their beliefs, attitudes, and values by hiring and promoting others who profess similar and compatible beliefs. By observing and asking the right questions of those influentials, you will be able to uncover the hidden rules where you work.

ORGANIZATIONAL PERSONALITY PROFILE

Every organization has its own distinct personality based on the kinds of people that it chooses at each hierarchical level. The object in establishing an organizational personality profile (OPP) is to single out the influentials, rising stars, and fast-track executives and through a series of key questions discover the traits and qualities they share.

For example, what is the educational background of these fast-track stars? Are they East Coast preppy types? What are their political inclinations? Are they conservatives or liberals? What sports are they interested in? Are they football fans or tennis buffs?

By profiling these rising stars and the traits they have in common, a picture will emerge that will tell you what qualities fast trackers have in common. In this process you will discover a number of the organization's hidden agendas, which you must know if you expect to have your own upwardly mobile career. As you establish this profile, you will want to compare yourself and where you stand relative to other fast-track types.

At the end of this chapter is an exercise on making an OPP. Since it is important to identify the fast-track types in your organization in order to complete the OPP, let's take a moment to determine how you can find out who they are.

IDENTIFYING THE FAST-TRACK TYPES IN YOUR ORGANIZATION

A person on a fast track is someone who is recognized in management as having the right talents and abilities to move up rapidly in the organization. Often such individuals seem to be cast in the exact image as other management stars. Just like a promising baseball rookie who has the talent and ability to be a serious prospect for success in the major leagues, a fast-track star is seen as a promising candidate for an upper management position.

While there are many qualities to look for in evaluating whether someone is a fast-track candidate, most typical rising stars

- Have a high degree of self-confidence.
- Project a very positive "can do" attitude.
- Hold the organization's goals above personal goals.
- Project maturity well beyond their age.
- Dress and groom themselves immaculately.
- Set goals and follow through.
- Are seen as risk takers.
- Show natural leadership abilities.
- Are intelligent and educated.
- Communicate confidently with people at all levels.
- Are ambitious and seize opportunities.
- Enjoy working, even long hours.

Despite our assessment of who the fast-track stars are, sometimes we are very surprised when we discover that a certain rising star in the organization doesn't get the promotion that we were so sure was his or hers. Or we are astounded when he or she gets unexpectedly fired. So you must double-check your choices of fast-track stars in your company by informally interviewing upper-echelon executives, your own manager, and secretaries to high-level executives and get them to validate by consensus your list of rising stars.

I have been able to do that by literally making a favorable comment about the star's future with the organization and then asking for a reaction from the individual I am talking with. For example, I just stopped by the director's office to see if he saw the big football game on Sunday. After we chitchatted for a while, I said to him, "Vern, you know who I've heard is destined for the top in this organization? Forrest Barrington. He's supposed to be pretty sharp! What do you think?"

By asking key influentials their opinion in a nonthreatening way, you will begin to get an idea of how others see your choice for who are the superstars and heirs apparent in your organization. You'll also see which individuals look popular but in reality are not considered upwardly mobile. The consensus of these influentials will assure you that you are using the right people in developing your organizational profile.

Keep in mind that your savvy to the existence of hidden rules and your willingness to discuss them openly with others will play an important part in determining how revealing the people you talk with will be with you. If you are angry and self-righteous because the higher-ups evaluate you by how well you observe hidden rules ("I can't believe this company promotes people on the basis of their dress!"), count on the fact that people will hide hidden rules from you.

If you have a distaste for organizations that insist on dress as a greater indicator of promotability than true executive skills, I suggest that you work to get into a high-level position where you will have the power to eliminate this hidden rule. Meanwhile, your upward mobility rests on your awareness that you are much more likely to be promoted by observing these hidden rules than by rebelling against them.

To observe these rules, you must pick the people and the places where you are most likely to find out what these hidden rules are.

BREAKFASTS

Breakfast meetings are a great time to ferret out information. I like breakfasts because I can meet with people (even those I don't like) for a short period of time and get their opinion as to the most important hidden rules to observe in order to advance in the organization.

"Hello, Hank. I wanted to phone you to see if we could arrange to meet over breakfast. I have some questions I would like to ask you about how to get ahead in this organization. I know that besides skill and experience there are other factors that are considered in winning a promotion. With your eight years of experience here, you would be an excellent person to speak with. Would you be able to meet me Thursday morning at 7:30?"

Breakfast as a meeting time helps to assure that my meeting will be more confidential than at more public times such as lunch. Also by meeting in the morning, notice that I have set a defined limit for a focused period of time, since we both know we have to be at the office at a certain hour. In contrast, meeting someone for drinks after work can be awkward and time-consuming because it could go on and on with no specific limit.

SECRETARIES

Another way to find out hidden rules and agendas is by asking secretaries. This is one of the many reasons you should cultivate positive relationships with them. They are a tremendous source of informal information in the organization. If you alienate them, you will cut yourself off from much valuable knowledge of the organization. Secretaries have a special grapevine based on information they exchange with the secretaries of other managers. Their informal information stems from being privy to meetings, correspondence, and personal contacts with influential managers. Consequently, secretaries know what factors beyond skill and experience the current management values.

Again, breakfast is a good time for an informal get-together. In one company I worked for, I used to meet with the secretary to the executive vice president. If I had taken her to lunch, key people would have looked on me with disdain because of the hidden rule that middle-level managers should not fraternize or lunch with secretaries. Also, if people saw me with this secretary, they might have been concerned that she was telling me all the secrets of the department—which she was! So it was much better for her sake and mine that I get together with her in a more private setting.

COMPANY HISTORIANS

In every organization there are influentials or "old-timers" who have been through many administrations, reorganizations, and changes. They are an excellent source for finding out the informal factors that upper management values in meting out promotions. Such people can give you sage advice and point to examples of those who have the credentials, demeanor, and makings for a fast track to the top.

These historian types can tell you which hidden rules to be aware of as pitfalls to your upward mobility. Best of all, their experience with a diverse group of the organization's management can result in their giving you an excellent evaluation of your prospects of being promotable and successful in the organization.

YOUR MANAGER

If your manager has been around your organization for a while, he may be able to make you aware of the hidden rules you will want to abide by. However, getting your manager to be honest about hidden rules will have a lot to do with your personal rapport with each other. And before you put much stock in what your manager says, consider whether he is on a fast track or not. Most fast-track people are very savvy to how the organization works formally and especially informally.

SOCIAL EVENTS

Social functions are a great way to find out what the hidden rules or agendas are by meeting and chatting with executives' spouses. For example, at a cocktail party an executive's wife said to me, "My Jason, he's a tiger at work, but on weekends he's a pussycat. He loves to sail, says it really helps him unwind. Myself, I get seasick, so he's always looking for sailing buddies. I think he'd promote anybody if they only knew how to sail."

"Really?" I replied. "I was just thinking of taking a course on sailing at a local community college."

By the way, keep in mind that many male executives have traditionally minded wives who have a very valid career: being a homemaker. Many of them are threatened by a woman who chooses business as her career. They don't understand her; they don't want her traveling with their husband. Hidden rule: You won't get important (long-distance) opportunities if the wife of your manager considers you a threat.

One of the simplest ways to alleviate this concern is to anticipate it. If you are a woman, when you meet the wife of an executive, let her know how madly in love and committed you are in your current relationship. If you have to, make one up. But be involved in a relationship.

At one social event I attended, I talked with a president of a company I'd just joined. I found out he was from Norway, and I told him that I'd spent an entire summer working on a marketing research project in Oslo. He was pleased and suggested that we get together for lunch. This was a great opportunity for a special interface because of our common interest.

However, the next day I immediately talked with my boss to get approval on the lunch date. I mentioned it in a casual way because I didn't want him to perceive me as being overly ambitious or doing something behind his back. By asking for permission and catering to his self-interest, I allowed my boss to be part of the plan and to feel in control.

So I said to him, "You know, the president's very interested in talking with me because I once lived in Norway and he comes from there. I would like to ask you if you have any problems with my having lunch with him? I think it would be great exposure for me and the department to get some visibility with him. I think he would be more likely to approve our ideas if he felt comfortable and knew executives who work for you."

Naturally, my boss said, "Sure, that sounds like a great idea."

At social events, it's also a good idea to ask questions of anyone who is drinking heavily. They'll usually be very uninhibited and more likely to share candid information about hidden rules and agendas.

But make sure you are never in the company of anyone who is drunk. Drunks may make fools of themselves and then may never forgive you or forget you were there. They may figure that eventually you will tell somebody about their drunkenness. You're a potential threat. The simplest thing to do is excuse yourself and make sure that the next morning you call and mention casually, "Things were going pretty well when I left. What happened? Everybody seemed to be having a good time."

Another alternative, if you have to be around somebody who is drunk, rude, and vulgar, is to make sure that the next morning you let the other person know that you were so drunk yourself that you don't remember what happened. Then apologize. This way, the other person believes you don't know anything embarrassing.

You can see how necessary it is for you to uncover your organization's hidden rules in order to be upwardly mobile.

The following exercises will help you uncover the hidden rules necessary to win promotions. The exercises will also give you insight into your own organization's personality. It is important for you to be aware of the characteristics that are valued by upper management in deciding who gets promoted in the organization. Once you are in the know, you can plan both short- and long-term strategies to advance your career within that organization.

Exercise: IDENTIFYING THE HIDDEN RULES

Directions: List five informal rules you must observe if you expect to be successful and promotable in your organization.

1. _____

2. _____

3. _____

4. _____

5. _____

Exercise: DEVELOPING AN ORGANIZATIONAL PERSONALITY PROFILE

Directions: Select two comers in your organization—individuals who are *one level above you* and who are clearly influential, upwardly mobile, fast-track types. Then choose two people *at your own level* who fit those criteria. Finally, add two people *at a lower level* who appear to be rising stars. Use the following table to record, for yourself and the six colleagues you selected, answers to the following questions.

1. How do they look physically? Are they attractive? Are they mostly in their thirties, white, and male? Or are many age and racial groups represented?

2. How do they dress? Conventional business suits? Sports jackets and open-necked shirts?

3. Are they interested in sports? If so, what kinds? Are they football

fanatics who can't wait to get in on Monday morning to discuss Sunday's game? Devotees of Wimbledon and the U.S. Open? Or do they spend their weekends traveling to local chess tournaments?

4. What is their educational background? Are they East Coast Ivy League types? West Coast sun and surf worshipers? Or did they graduate from the University of Hard Knocks and work their way up from the mailroom? If so, they may not be impressed by, or appreciate, your efforts to complete your MBA at night.

5. Are they drinkers and party goers? Does the in crowd always stop at Harvey's Lounge for a quick one after work? Do they frown on employees who have a glass of wine with lunch? Do they socialize with one another and give frequent parties? Are nonattenders considered spoilsports?

6. Do they "play around"? Is infidelity accepted behavior, or are monogamous relationships the only acceptable ones?

7. Are they smokers or nonsmokers?

8. Are they involved with health and physical fitness?

9. Do they swear much? (Women, watch out! There's often a double standard here.)

10. What working hours do they keep? Is it in by 9:00, out by 5:00? Or are fast trackers expected to arrive by 8:00 A.M. and not leave until after 6:00 P.M.?

11. What are their attitudes toward social issues? How do they feel about abortion and capital punishment?

12. What are their political attitudes? Do they feel strongly that the nation should be in the hands of a conservative political party, or are they liberals who mourn the good old days of marches, dissent, and flower power?

13. Do they get involved with community activities? Does the company support charitable causes and expect anyone who wants to get ahead to volunteer some time to community projects?

14. Are they religious? If so, what beliefs predominate? Do people of that religion seem to be in the top positions in the company?

Add some of your own questions in the remaining spaces in the table.

ORGANIZATIONAL PERSONALITY PROFILE

	YOU	SUPERIOR	PEER	SUBORDINATE
1. Appearance				
2. Grooming, dress				
3. Sports				
4. Education				
5. Drinking, partying				
6. Fidelity				
7. Smoking				
8. Physical fitness				
9. Swearing				
10. Working hours				
11. Social issues				
12. Political inclinations				
13. Community activities				
14. Religion				

chapter 3

The Right Communication Style: Getting Heard and Getting Results

SITUATION

Steve, one of John's staffers, has turned in an important report that is riddled with errors—sloppy work that is clearly the result of his lack of interest. John calls him in to let him know he won't tolerate this kind of work, but within minutes the discussion escalates into a screaming match, with each of them flinging angry accusations at the other. What went wrong? How should John have handled the problem?

SITUATION

Chuck has just been promoted to department manager, and he's called in his "troops" for his first general staff meeting. Not more than five minutes into the session, Chuck is wishing he could sneak out the door. Everyone is talking at once, no one is paying any attention to his ineffectual pleas for silence, and it's obvious to all that he's lost control of the situation. What should he do?

SITUATION

Ray, one of Barbara's most important clients, persists in calling her "honey." Barbara has requested that he refrain, but he merely smiles and tells her that he doesn't really mean anything by it, it's just his way and he does it because he likes her. Must Barbara put up with this behavior, or is there an effective way she can solve this problem without alienating Ray?

All of these situations call for the most crucial skill any promotion-minded professional can develop: the ability to manage conflicts with people assertively. This is also the key to developing a reputation as a charismatic leader who can take charge when working with others. Yet handling conflicts such as these will provide you with some of the riskiest situations you will have to confront. Here's where you really need to be a confident communicator in order to advance in your organization.

Your skill and poise in handling such dilemmas will determine whether others see you as charismatic and upper management material or whether you're in over your head. Keep in mind that winning an executive title will mean little if you can't command the respect of your staff and let them know that you're in charge.

Business is played for high stakes. At every level, there are men and women who will be eager to undermine you, whether in a deliberate attempt to wrest power from you or simply because they honestly believe that their methods or ideas are superior.

Your position in the hierarchy alone won't give you enough authority and power. It will certainly give you an edge, but if you can't parlay that edge into a strong personal leadership style, you're going to have trouble staying in the game. The moment others perceive you as ineffectual, weak, indecisive, or powerless, the authority conveyed by your title will be meaningless. And it won't take long for upper management to recognize your inability to take charge and consign you to the ranks of the unpromotable.

If you want to survive and thrive, it's up to you to develop productive and cooperative relationships with your staff and your superiors. To do that, you have to earn their respect by carrying yourself as a leader, one who shows the ability to handle people in all kinds of situations. This is one of the primary reasons for developing an assertive communication style.

THE RIGHT COMMUNICATION SKILLS

In analyzing leadership ability, it is impossible to minimize the importance of developing strong communication skills. After all, leadership is the art of managing people, some of whom will be defensive, aggressive, hostile, indecisive, or passive. To a great degree, your success or failure will depend on your ability to convey your wishes and needs appropriately and decisively. And your ability to communicate effectively will give you the confidence you need to face these situations.

There are three main styles of communication: nonassertive, aggressive, and assertive.

NONASSERTIVE

The nonassertive, passive style characterizes organization types who like to cover their posteriors at all times. These people tend to practice a self-denying, inhibiting kind of leadership. They deny and rationalize away their own rights, needs, and feelings. These people are afraid of conflict, confrontation, and risky situations. They end up subordinating themselves to others in the hopes of avoiding conflict. This is an emotionally dishonest kind of behavior because what they tell you on the outside is not what they really feel on the inside. Thus you get a double message.

These individuals can be found at all levels of the corporate hierarchy, ranging in type from the classic yes men to those who hang onto their power only through guile or subtle manipulation. But in general, passive individuals don't tend to develop or sustain a genuine power base in their companies. They are so terrified of conflict that they will almost always back down in a confrontation, which, of course, leaves the field wide open for someone else to move in and grab power. They communicate in a very indirect fashion, almost always afraid to take responsibility for a project or idea. Therefore, this is an extremely ineffectual leadership style. Upper management views these personality types as not being promotable or effective in managing people. If these individuals are promoted, it is usually to lower levels in the organization, where they end up stagnating.

AGGRESSIVE

The aggressive style is favored by those who rely on hostility and intimidation to get things done. Generally, such people operate out of a need to dominate everyone else around them, and they tend to discount the feelings and needs of their staff. Although intimidation can be very effective in the short run, in the long run it's a costly strategy.

Very few people enjoy working for someone who relies heavily on put-downs and hostility to maintain control, and eventually such managers lose talented employees or find themselves sabotaged in subtle ways. Once upper management learns, via the grapevine, that these people can't hang on to good employees, they're not likely to be targeted for promotion. Also, upper management often views these personality types as reckless risk takers, unable to distinguish between situations to go for and situations to back off from.

ASSERTIVE

The assertive style consists of *communicating directly and honestly in an appropriate manner.* It is an emotionally honest kind of behavior because what assertive people feel on the inside they express on the outside. Their ideas are clear, direct, and focused. Assertive people are not afraid of conflict, and they're willing to stand up for their rights, but not in ways that violate the rights of others. They have the self-confidence to take risks. Assertive leaders command the respect of their staff because they know how and when to criticize, how and when to compliment, when to give credit, and how to give orders without making them seem like arbitrary demands. Upper management sees these personality types as managers who prudently take risks in managing people and in making strategic decisions.

Most of us use a combination of all three styles, although we tend to rely more heavily on one. Certainly, there are times when it may seem appropriate to be passive or aggressive, but by and large, the assertive style is the one that will maximize your chances for success in dealing with people and obtaining positive results.

However, there's another wrinkle in this equation. An assertive person is sometimes mistakenly labeled "aggressive" simply because many people are unused to working with an assertive person. These business people are therefore understandably confused about the differences between assertiveness and aggressiveness.

The next time a colleague intimates that you're coming on too strong or aggressively, check out your behavior with this simple question: Was your intent to humiliate or vent anger? If so, you were operating aggressively. So don't be surprised if your outburst provokes hostility or defensiveness. On the other hand, was your intent to instruct, inform, or help that person change a specific behavior or performance? If so, congratulations! You've mastered the assertive style and should ignore all hints to the contrary.

SKILLS FOR TAKING INTERPERSONAL RISKS

Let's go back for a moment to one of the opening scenarios and take a look at the communication process in action. When Steve entered John's office, John was hopping mad about the quality of Steve's work, and John launched an attack without considering its likely outcome. Not surprisingly, Steve, like most of us, immediately became defensive, and counterattacked. In minutes, what should have been a calm discussion to clear the air and solve a problem had degenerated into a full-fledged battle. Why? Because John was relying on the aggressive style. The result—increased tension between him and Steve, and a still unsolved problem—shows just how ineffective aggressive communication can be.

What should have happened? Let's replay the scene, assuming that John has learned some of the techniques of assertive leadership. John is still angry, but he concentrates on explaining his reaction to Steve's work: "Steve, I'm upset by the quality of this report. I know what good work you can do, and I don't think this represents your best efforts. I know you were unhappy about getting this assignment, but it's quite important, and I'd certainly like to be able to tell the president that you turned in a top-notch report. Please rework it and correct the errors that I've noted. I'd like the report back in my office by tomorrow afternoon."

Notice that John hasn't been aggressive by humiliating or attacking Steve. John merely pointed out that Steve's work wasn't up to par, and in the process John also let Steve know that he was a valued employee and that it would be in his best interest to improve his performance.

Steve's reaction: "You're right, John. I wasn't really happy about getting this assignment, and I guess I rushed through it. Now that I know how important it is, I won't make those mistakes again. Thanks for letting me know. I'll have the report back on your desk by three P.M. tomorrow."

Not only has John solved the problem quickly and without any recriminations on either side, but John has also gained a loyal ally and supporter.

In the revised exchange, John used five specific techniques designed to elicit cooperation and solve a wide range of common office problems and conflicts. Learning these skills will make it much easier to take risks in your interactions with people. Let's take a closer look at them.

1. "I" VERSUS "YOU" LANGUAGE

Believe it or not, the pronoun you use when making statements to others can elicit cooperation or resistance from them. Dr. Thomas Gordon, in his book *Parent Effectiveness Training* (Wyden, 1970), points out the importance of using "I" messages to gain cooperation from children. However, this same concept can be applied as successfully at work when you want to gain the cooperation of adults.

Use the pronoun "I" when expressing your ideas, opinions, and criticisms to the people with whom you work. This helps you to avoid the resistant or defensive reaction that can occur from using "you" statements.

For example, when John told Steve, *"I'm* upset by the quality of this report," John was taking complete responsibility for his comment by prefacing it with an "I" statement, rather than opting out of any responsibility and sounding accusatory by saying, *"You* turned in a really sloppy report, Steve!"

Your statement criticizes only someone's behavior or performance, *not* the individual. Further, by saying "I," you acknowledge that your viewpoint is your own perception of the situation.

When you preface your statement with *you,* however, the statement tends to sound accusatory, judgmental, and threatening: *"You* are wrong," *"You* made a mistake," *"You* are making me feel uncomfortable." The outcome? People respond defensively. They feel personally attacked and are therefore more likely to justify their position instead of considering your comment or criticism. This is because the style in which you criticized was humiliating.

But when you use "I" language—"*I* believe you are wrong," "*I* think you made a mistake," "*I* feel uncomfortable about what you said"—the whole tone is changed. When you use "I" language, you are taking complete responsibility for what you're saying, and you're far more likely to promote cooperation and understanding and avoid a defensive reaction from the other person. The "I" versus "you" technique will go a long way toward fostering mutual cooperation when giving advice or criticism. Remember: your ability to work effectively with people is vital to your being promotable.

2. ANTICIPATION

When John told Steve that he was aware of Steve's feelings about not being happy about getting the assignment, John was employing another valuable communication technique called anticipation. This skill is based on your ability to predict the other person's response to your criticism or complaint. By doing so, you can avoid the other person's meaningless or irrelevant explanations that only muddle the issue at hand. Thus you have a greater likelihood of resolving the real problem.

For example, if John had not made the anticipatory comment ("I know you were unhappy about getting this assignment"), Steve might well have launched into a long justification of his lack of interest in the assignment, thereby confusing the real issue of his poor performance. But by anticipating Steve's reply, John left Steve with no excuse but to admit the real problem.

The skill of anticipation is a way of acknowledging the other person's reaction, so that he feels understood, and at the same time focusing on the main issue that you want to resolve. It can also be used to protect yourself from the manipulations of others.

For example, Janice, a colleague of yours, drops in to your office to ask you to take over one of her projects. You explain that you're extremely busy already, only to have her respond, "Well, just do the best you can." Janice often uses this meaningless and irrelevant phrase in situations like this.

If you've been left holding the bag before, learn from your mistake, and use her response before she has a chance to say it. Simply reply, "I really wish I had the time to help you out, but I'm already doing the best I can." Janice has little choice then but to leave your office in search of another patsy.

3. SELF-INTEREST

Self-interest is defined as "the reason why somebody will do or give you what you want." People are motivated to action and cooperation on the basis of how well you further their self-interest. Some people's self-interest is a raise, a promotion, security, status, or popularity. By keeping other people's self-interest in mind, you are much more likely to gain their cooperation and support. This is a way of being relevant, motivating, and compelling to those you work with.

John didn't neglect this technique, either. He was smart enough to point out to Steve that it would be well worth his while to do a first-rate job on the report. After all, John wanted to tell the president about it proudly. That would certainly be in Steve's self-interest, and this technique paid off. Because John took a few extra minutes to explain to Steve how he might benefit, John also benefited—by gaining an employee eager and positive about redoing the report. By using self-interest as a motivational tool, your request becomes relevant and compelling to the other person because he is going to profit, too.

4. METATALK

Derived from the Greek word *meta,* which means "above and beyond," this technique consists of active listening. You pay attention to other people's communication beyond the actual words they are using. This includes listening for underlying feelings, emotions, or innuendos that may not be directly expressed. Then you comment on those underlying feelings. By doing so, you can open up a dialogue to resolve the situation.

For example, let's assume there was more to the problem of Steve's sloppy work than meets the eye. In several past conversations with Steve, John has heard subtle innuendos of sarcasm in Steve's voice. Steve's body language—tone of voice, reactions, gestures—

have given John the impression that Steve is upset about something that he is not speaking about directly.

So, after commenting briefly about the immediate problem—the sloppy report—John says, "Steve, I've been getting the feeling lately that you're angry or upset about something. Your work is usually very good, so I'm guessing that something is interfering with your concentration. I'd really like to talk it out with you and try to resolve the problem." This gives Steve the perfect opportunity to discuss the problem that may be interfering with his work.

By being sensitive not only to what people are saying but, more important, to what they are not saying, the technique of metatalk helps you resolve many conflicts with people who are not assertive enough to tell you openly and directly what is bothering them. Paying attention to the metalevel of people's communication will lessen the likelihood of people doing substandard work because of an underlying attitude problem that should be resolved before they can be productive. Keep in mind that your ability to get the most out of people at work will win you recognition from upper management and thus make you more promotable.

Let's take a look at another example of metatalk. Blake goes over to Cathy's desk and says, "Cathy, can I ask you a question?" Cathy replies in a nasty, sarcastic tone of voice, "Sure, what's your problem?" Blake now knows he has a bigger problem than he had when he first approached Cathy.

This can be resolved on a metalevel, which Blake uses when he responds to the underlying attitude that Cathy projected. He says, "Cathy, before I ask my question, from the sound of your voice I get the feeling that you're angry about something. Is something wrong?"

Cathy responds, "Well, now that you've mentioned it, I can't get any work done because everybody around here stops and asks me questions. What do I look like, a halfway house for people who need help?"

Blake replies, "Of course not. I can understand why you are frustrated. When would be a good time for me to stop by later and talk with you about my question?"

Cathy says, "Thanks for understanding. Why don't you come back after lunch?"

By being sensitive to Cathy's upset feelings and acknowledging them openly for discussion, Blake has an excellent chance to come to some kind of understanding with Cathy and gain her cooperation in the process.

5. LIMIT SETTING

This technique uses the concept of defining the limits of a relationship or task in advance so that both parties know what they can expect from each other. It is an excellent way to clarify individual expectations and avoid misunderstandings that occur when details or responsibilities are left open, unsaid, or taken for granted. It is also a useful way of avoiding potential conflicts. By using limit setting you can maintain control of a situation and yet still appear flexible regarding the other person's wishes.*

For example, Karen is a saleswoman who has traveled out of town to "close" a large order with a client, Chris. Chris subtly insinuates that Karen will get the order if she socializes and has dinner with him. However, Karen's intuition tells her that Chris wants a little more than just dinner. How can she deal tactfully with the situation without alienating Chris or losing the order?

Karen says, "Chris, that's very kind of you to invite me to dinner. I'll accept, providing that you understand that I must leave at nine o'clock." Setting a limit in advance will make Karen feel comfortable and in control of her evening with Chris.

When Chris meets Karen for dinner, she reminds him again of her time schedule, and promptly at 9:00 she thanks him for a lovely dinner and leaves.

Another example of limit setting is in dealing with a coworker who doesn't keep his agreements. Stan needs Jack to give him information about a report he is writing. Jack, however, is notorious for promising and not delivering. Here's how Stan sets limits:

Stan: "Jack, I really need that financial information for my report."

Jack: "Yeah, sure, I'll get it to you."

Stan: "Can I expect it by this Thursday?"

---

* This discussion of limit setting was inspired by Pamela Butler, *Self-assertion for Women* (New York: Harper & Row, 1976), p. 138.

Jack: "No . . . I can't get it to you by Thursday."

Stan: "How about Friday?"

Jack: "Yes, I think I can have it ready by then."

Stan: "Good. Can I expect it in the morning, say, by eleven?"

Jack: "No, that's too early."

Stan: "How about in the afternoon, by four?"

Jack: "Yes, I can have it ready by four."

Stan: "Thanks, Jack. I'll just make a note on my calendar here that you will have the financial information ready for me by four o'clock this Friday, and I'll be expecting it."

Stan has refused to accept Jack's evasions and has repeatedly set limits through establishing agreed-upon completion dates. Jack must commit to having the information by a specific time. Stan further formalizes the conversation by writing it in his calendar and making Jack clearly aware of his expectations.

These five techniques, "I" versus "you" language, anticipation, self-interest, metatalk, and limit setting, used singly and in combination, will enable you to handle difficult people and sticky situations and withstand almost any kind of threat to your authority and influence. Therefore, if you want to defend your position and hold your ground, you must know the kinds of threats and conflicts you are likely to face and how to apply these techniques to emerge victorious. This is what will ultimately give you the confidence to communicate effectively with others, thus paving the way for your future promotions.

MATCHING THE SKILL TO THE SITUATION

Effective leaders have the ability to match the appropriate skills to the particular situation or problem. To help you develop that ability, we're going to examine common office problems that are characteristic of how power is undermined and look at the techniques that can be used to thwart these threats. As you read through these scenarios, try to imagine how you would handle the problem. That will help you pinpoint the degree to which you've mastered these techniques.

INTERRUPTIONS

Interrupting someone is a classic example of how disrespect is exhibited. When it's directed at you and you permit it, you are telling everyone, "I can't assert myself. I have no confidence in my viewpoint. What I had to say wasn't that important, anyway." If it happens once or twice, it may have little or no effect, but in the long run, you will begin to notice that you've lost the respect of your staff or colleagues and that more and more people will feel free to interrupt you. You, in turn, will find that some of your best ideas will not be heard. Furthermore, when you need to express your point of view, you may be stymied.

Being interrupted is a particularly difficult problem for nonassertive people who are perceived as being powerless. Others know intuitively that nonassertive people will not stand up for their ideas and are easily dominated. Nonassertive people are fair game for more aggressive types to interrupt at will.

SITUATION: A STAFF MEETING

There is perhaps no other business situation in which it is more vital to maintain control and establish authority. Meetings are a showcase for your charismatic leadership style—a chance for others to observe your poise and confidence. With that in mind, imagine that you are chairing your first staff meeting. In the middle of your presentation, George suddenly cuts you off and begins talking to the group without any apology or acknowledgment from you. What should you do?

SOLUTION: "I" VERSUS "YOU" LANGUAGE

Turn to George immediately and say, calmly and firmly, "Excuse me, George, *I* would like to finish what *I* was saying before we move on." That simple sentence serves to reestablish your authority, and it leaves George with no option but to return the floor to you.

Suppose you had reacted angrily and said, "George, *you're* interrupting me! The least *you* could do is let me finish and not be so rude!" You would have come across sounding accusatory, hostile, and very aggressive, and George might easily have responded in kind. And you would also be letting the rest of your staff know that you're easily flustered and shaken. By humiliating George, you can count on the fact that he probably won't support your idea.

Occasionally, a staff meeting can turn into a free-for-all, with everyone trying to speak at once. When this happens, as it did with Chuck at the beginning of the chapter, you must assert your authority at once. Here's a very simple trick to help you do so. Pick out the most influential person in the room and shout out that person's name: "Connie, Connie, I'd like to have your attention, please!" In a matter of seconds, everyone will stop talking and look at Connie, wondering why you're focusing on her. The outcome: complete silence.

In this or similar situations, the one thing you must never do is to keep yelling, "Guys, guys, please be quiet!" That simply lets everyone know that you've lost all control of the meeting. Remember, a meeting is more than just an opportunity for you to make a presentation or a speech; it is an opportunity to demonstrate your leadership abilities and show others that you have presence of mind under fire and are capable of maintaining control in group situations.

SEXIST REMARKS

Allowing yourself to be called "honey," "sweetie," or "babe," puts you in a perpetual one-down position. It is demeaning, and it results in your not being taken very seriously. How effective do you think you're likely to be in a tough negotiation with a client who calls you "honey"?

SITUATION: IMPORTANT CLIENT WHO USES PERSONAL ENDEARMENTS

Remember Barbara, the woman who had to deal with this problem in one of the chapter's opening scenarios? She's asked her client, Ray, to refrain from calling her "honey," but her appeals have fallen on deaf ears. And she's afraid to come on too strong because he's a very important client.

SOLUTION: ANTICIPATION AND "I" VERSUS "YOU" LANGUAGE

What's the first thing someone is likely to say to you when you complain about a derogatory remark? "I really didn't mean anything by it." So Barbara anticipated Ray's answer and beat him to the punch.

"Ray, I know you don't mean anything by it, but I really feel uncomfortable when you call me 'honey.' From now on, would you just call me Barbara? I would appreciate it."

Unless Ray is a complete boor, he will get the message, and he may even think twice before he calls any woman "honey" again. And Barbara has managed to make the point without accusing Ray of sexism or putting him down in any way. She gave Ray a graceful way out of a potentially difficult situation.

Of course, there's always the possibility that Ray really *did* mean something by his remarks. But it doesn't matter. The issue is not whether Ray did or did not mean anything by his remarks. The issue is simply getting Ray to stop this unwanted behavior.

Since old behaviors die hard, be prepared to make such assertive statements over and over again to the same person. This will reinforce how serious you are about your request.

AGGRESSIVE BEHAVIOR

With malice aforethought, many individuals will attempt to ridicule or intimidate you with hostile and sarcastic remarks. This is the tactic of bullies, and your caving in will only whet their appetite for more. So you must respond assertively, but never at their aggressive level. By dealing with such behavior coolly and professionally, you'll not only diffuse such bullies, but you may succeed in making them look slightly ridiculous, if only because of the contrast between your demeanor and theirs.

SITUATION: A STAFF MEETING

You've just joined the company a month ago, and so far you've made no contribution to any of the weekly staff meetings. Today, you raise your hand to contribute a useful suggestion, and no sooner is the last word out of your mouth than the intimidating vice president states flatly: "That's totally ridiculous. It will never work!" All eyes are on you; they're waiting to see what the "new kid on the block" is going to say.

PUBLIC SOLUTION: DEFUSE AND DEFENSE

A meeting is not the appropriate place for a direct confrontation with the VP. So use a strategy called "defuse and defense." First, *defuse* the aggressive remark by saying politely, "I'm sorry, but I don't think it's a ridiculous idea." Then put the VP on the *defense* (i.e., make him accountable for his aggressive remark) by saying, "Why do you believe it won't work?"

This tactic is designed specifically for public situations. It shows that you can handle yourself under the gun, that you're not easily flustered, and that you have poise and presence.

PRIVATE SOLUTION: "I" VERSUS "YOU" LANGUAGE AND METATALK

When you can schedule a few minutes alone with the vice president, let him know that you won't fold under pressure. "Mr. Jefferson, I wanted to tell you that I felt very humiliated this morning ["I" versus "you" language]. Even though you and I might not agree on certain issues, I believe it is my responsibility to contribute my ideas and input. And I want you to know that I will continue to do so. Also, I was a little puzzled by the anger and resentment that I heard in your voice, and I wonder if I've offended you in any way [metatalk]. If so, please tell me because I'd like to clear the air. We don't have to agree on every question, but I do think it's important that we respect each other as professional colleagues."

Mr. Jefferson responds, "Well, now that you mention it, I think it's a little unusual for a newcomer—and someone who's as young as you—to think you know all the answers."

"That's not true, Mr. Jefferson. I certainly don't think I know all the answers. I may have a fresh perspective, but I know I could learn a lot from you, with all your experience. And I'd be happy to bounce some of my ideas off you in advance and hear your comments."

The final result? The vice president is completely disarmed. You may have even found yourself a powerful ally and supporter. Bullies usually respect those who stand up for themselves.

ROLE CONFUSION

Role confusion refers to the tendency of others to view your role as unacceptable or inappropriate for you. This confusion may be based on the others' prejudices or stereotypes or just rigid beliefs based on limited experiences. For example, a young manager fresh out of graduate school may find that the "old-timer" who is now reporting to him seems resistant and uncooperative in taking the young manager's directions. In this case, the old-timer can't imagine how a "young kid" could tell someone like him, who's been on the job for 20 years, what to do. The old-timer views the young manager's role as unacceptable and inappropriate. He is confused because he associates authority with age—and now he thinks a youngster is trying to tell him what to do.

Role confusion affects each of us differently. For example, many men have a tendency to treat professional women as social beings instead of business professionals. The sad fact is that they simply don't know how to relate to women in any setting other than a social one. Thus they tend to make remarks that would be perfectly appropriate on the dance floor or at a cocktail party but are definitely not appropriate for a business setting. Other men put women in a social role because it makes the men feel that they are in a more dominant position.

Keep in mind that whether it's a defensive reaction from the old-timer to the young manager or an inappropriate social remark to a professional woman, the confusion and conflict that result must be dealt with assertively. Often no malicious intent is involved, but that is irrelevant. It is important to recognize that standing up to these kinds of situations is a communication risk that you must take. It becomes a way to earn the respect of your colleagues, and it demonstrates your ability to resolve conflicts and enhances your charismatic leadership image. This ability contributes to the perception that you are promotable because you know how to handle people.

Inappropriate remarks that are a by-product of role confusion undermine your authority. Such remarks must not go unchallenged, however well intentioned they may be. The key is to respond assertively, not aggressively, and never to overreact. Let's examine another role-confusion situation.

SITUATION: FIRST MEETING WITH MALE COLLEAGUES

You've just joined the LMN Company as its first female product manager, and you've been invited to a high-level staff meeting to meet your colleagues. The vice president introduces you: "Gentlemen, I'd like you all to meet Vicki Smith, our first woman product manager, and, I might add, a very good-looking woman, too. Stand up please, Vicki. I'm sure we're all going to enjoy working with someone as pretty as you."

PUBLIC SOLUTION: ACKNOWLEDGE AND REFOCUS

In group situations, it is especially important to handle such social remarks adeptly because your image is on the line. Everyone will be watching your response. For this reason, use the technique of acknowledge and refocus to show off your presence of mind. First *acknowledge* the vice president's remarks: "Thank you very much, Gary, for those flattering remarks." Then *refocus* to the professional image you want to convey: "I appreciate the compliment, and I hope you'll be just as complimentary when I help bring in the third quarter sales budget."

PRIVATE SOLUTION: "I" VERSUS "YOU" LANGUAGE AND SELF-INTEREST

When the meeting has broken up, deal with the basic problem itself, in private, with the vice president. "Gary, I'd like to talk to you for a moment about this morning's meeting. Although your compliment about my appearance was very flattering, I want you to know that I felt very uncomfortable ["I" versus "you" language]. You see, when I'm complimented about my looks at work, men tend to view me in a typical female role. As a result, I'm taken less seriously, and I believe it undermines my productivity and my ability to get their cooperation. I know you expect me to perform and deliver results like everyone else [self-interest]. And I really believe I can be more effective if I'm looked upon as a professional, not a typical 'pretty female.' I would appreciate getting your support in this area."

In both cases, you've made your point: Your public dual message let every man in the room know that you are a professional who expects to be treated accordingly, and your private chat made the vice president realize that it was not in his best interest to treat you any differently from his male managers.

STEREOTYPING

Most people at work are confronted with the stereotypical attitudes of others. For example, someone—perhaps your manager—decides that you have a limitation that makes you unqualified to do something that he or she would otherwise believe you could do. If you work with someone who makes decisions based on stereotypes, it will affect the kind of responsibilities you are given, the promotions you get, and the salary you make. So it becomes extremely important to take the risk of confronting people about a stereotype they may have about you. If not properly handled, such stereotypes can be tremendous blocks to your upward mobility. Here are some of the most irritating stereotypes:

- "You're young. What do you know?"
- "You're old and out of step with the times."
- "You're in management; you'll never understand us working stiffs."
- "You're nontechnical; we're technical."
- "You're an accountant—you work with numbers. What could you know about working with people?"
- "You've been living in an ivory tower. What would you know about the real world?"
- "You're too easygoing. You wouldn't be tough enough to handle this account."

What compounds this problem is that you can rarely get anyone to admit to such beliefs, which means that you are fighting in the dark; you may not even be sure what the real problem is. Let's take a look at a typical problem caused by stereotyping.

SITUATION: A BUSINESS TRIP

Jayne is a sales rep for a major manufacturing firm. She's noted that in the last two years her travel itinerary has never included any of the major metropolitan markets. Instead, her travel assignments are to smaller local markets. And to get ahead in her company, she's got to prove that she can handle the major clients in larger markets. She suspects that her boss simply isn't comfortable with the idea of sending out a woman on the road.

SOLUTION: ANTICIPATION AND SELF-INTEREST

Jayne makes an appointment to talk with her boss. She anticipates his considerations in advance, based on what she perceives as his stereotypes toward women.

"Melvin, I'd like to talk to you about my travel schedule. I've noticed that I haven't had the opportunity to travel to any of the company's major markets, and I wanted to let you know that I'd really like the chance to go to New York, Chicago, and Los Angeles and prove myself. I love to travel, and I can leave at the drop of a hat. In fact [anticipation], I've got my children in a full-time day-care center, and my husband is there at night, so there's no problem on the home front.

"And my husband is really supportive of my traveling. Why, just the other day he said, 'Jayne, if you ever have the chance to travel, please go!' I also believe I could really help the company develop the new widget line if I had the necessary input from some of the major clients in the larger metropolitan areas [self-interest], and that would go a long way toward helping this department bring in the fourth quarter sales budget."

With this well-thought-out speech, Jayne has applied the concept of anticipation and has confronted Melvin in a nonthreatening way to allay his possible fears and concerns. Notice that she never actually accuses him of holding her back because of his stereotypical attitudes toward women. Had she done that, he probably would have responded defensively, and they would have been locked in a circular battle, she accusing, he defending, during which nothing constructive could occur.

NO COOPERATION

Many times at work you are given the responsibility to complete a project or task. Yet in order to do so, you may need the help and cooperation of other people. Since you may have no actual authority over them, you must depend on their goodwill and desire to assist you. However, what if they aren't cooperative and willing to help you, despite your many polite requests?

SITUATION: YOUR PHONE CALLS ARE NOT BEING RETURNED

Phil is a marketing manager and works at headquarters with the vice president of sales. There is no reporting relationship between Phil and the VP. However, from time to time, Phil needs special data from one of the VP's sales people: Joe, the West Coast sales manager. The problem is that Phil has to call Joe three or four times and leave messages in order to get one phone call returned by Joe.

Phil has already explained to Joe how important it is to get his phone calls returned promptly because this data is vital to Phil's marketing report. However, Joe yesses Phil to death and says he's sorry and will try to do better. Joe seems always to have an excuse: "Gee, I'm sorry, but I have lots of customers to call on."

Phil has used both anticipation and "I" versus "you" language: "Joe, I know you have a lot of calls to make, but I am upset at not getting my phone calls returned more promptly. I really need your cooperation and help." But Joe continues to ignore Phil's phone calls. What should Phil do?

SOLUTION: CONSEQUENCES VERSUS THREATS

This is a power concept that we haven't talked about yet, because it's designed to be used when all else fails, when you need to bring out the big guns to protect yourself. In fact, "protect" is the operative concept here.

A consequence is protective.* It is an action or sanction you will use to protect yourself from someone's unprofessional or irresponsible behavior. A threat is aggressive. No one likes to be threatened, and the use of a threat may protect you, but it isn't likely to allow you to extricate yourself from an unpleasant situation without creating more unpleasantness. A consequence, on the other hand, lets people know that you're ready to take action but permits them a graceful way out.

There's one important stipulation, though: You must have the legitimate power to back up a consequence. An empty consequence is completely meaningless. Bear in mind, too, that this is a powerful tactic, to be used only when all other methods have failed.

Now, let's return to Phil and Joe. The next time Phil's phone calls are ignored, he keeps on calling until he finally reaches Joe. When he does, he states very assertively (without anger or hostility): "Joe, I have talked with you on a number of occasions about returning my phone calls. I need to rely on your data for my marketing reports. And I believe this data will also help you increase sales in your territory [self-interest]. Yet I continue to have this problem of not having you return my calls. I want you to know that if I have this problem again, I will take up this matter with your manager, the VP of Sales, and

---

* Butler, *Self-assertion for Women,* pp. 140–141.

tell him that I don't believe I am getting your full cooperation and help [consequence]. And I'll ask him to set up a meeting among the three of us so we can get this problem ironed out once and for all."

What would be Joe's response to Phil's consequence? Suppose Joe said, "Phil, that sounds like a threat!" Phil would answer, very assertively, "Joe, my intent is not to threaten you—I am just telling you that I must have your help and cooperation. And if what it takes to get it is for me to go to your manager and have him impress upon you the importance of your cooperating with me, I will!"

However, it is much more likely that once Joe hears how seriously Phil regards this matter, he will realize that it is in his own best interest to resolve this problem. "Look, Phil, I know you're upset about this whole thing. But there's no need to bother the VP about it. Now that I know how important this information is to you, I promise that I will return your phone calls much more promptly. Let's work this out ourselves."

One of the big problems for people in using consequences is that the art of issuing a consequence to another person involves being sensitive to what is appropriate and what is not.

For example, suppose you told one of your staff who makes mistakes, "Leonard, if you make one more mistake, you're fired!" That would probably be inappropriate and much too severe. Many people use consequences only at the extremes of a nuclear bomb or a fly-swatter. Yet, there are in-between levels of consequences; for example, "If you make any more mistakes,

- "I'll expect you to get some special tutoring to correct your errors."
- "I'll require that you spend additional time correcting your work after Lanie proofreads it."
- "I'll have to relieve you of this responsibility and give it to someone else."
- "I will not be able to recommend you for a merit raise."

It is important to realize that you have many consequences available to you between threatening to fire someone or saying nothing. In fact, people typically issue the most aggressive consequence out of pent-up frustration over not having previously issued lower-level consequences. In effect, what they are doing is saving up their anger and irritation toward the other person and then one day exploding and issuing a very severe and often inappropriate consequence.

So, when using consequences, make sure that the punishment fits the crime. And keep in mind that consequences are not really used for punishing. They are used to compel people toward responsible behavior and to let them know what action or sanction will occur if they are not professionally responsible.

In using a consequence, make sure you are using your legitimate power. Every situation has legitimate power; it's up to you to be aware of it. Suppose, for example, you have a position with the federal government and you habitually threaten your staff with the consequence "If you do that again, you're fired!" Your employees know that the procedure for firing governmental employees is cumbersome and difficult. Your staff will soon lose respect for you because they know you don't have the legitimate authority to fire people so frivolously.

Also, when using a consequence, make sure that you are willing to follow through on it. Quite often, people are not willing to do this, and the result is that the consequence lacks credibility. Let me illustrate this point with a nonbusiness example. Suppose that you are a single parent on a tight budget. In a fit of temper, you tell your 7-year-old son, "If you do that again, you'll be grounded for three months." If your 7-year-old knows that you are the only one who can babysit, he will know that you probably won't follow through, because that would mean you wouldn't be able to go out for three months, either.

Remember, when using consequences, you are not bullying people; you are merely letting them know what the consequences of their behavior will be. If someone works for you and is chronically late, you can't make them be on time. But you can tell them the consequence of their continuing to be late. Thus you are giving them a chance to make a responsible choice.

These techniques represent your business trump cards. Play them carefully and strategically, and you'll find yourself maximizing the chances of success when you engage in risky personal interactions. And keep in mind that these are the very skills that are necessary to win promotions.

Exercise: AGGRESSIVE, NONASSERTIVE & ASSERTIVE COMMUNICATION STYLES

Often it's not the words you use but the way you say them that communicates your feelings. Suppose you are asked, "What's your opinion of the new vice president?" Your response, "He seems friendly enough," could be spoken aggressively, with a nasty, sarcastic tone of voice and a scowl on your face. You would project your negative opinion beyond what your actual words are saying.

Or you could use the same words, but in a nonassertive way, as if you weren't sure, by acting ill at ease, avoiding eye contact, shrugging your shoulders, and expressing hesitancy in your voice: "He . . . uh . . . *seems* friendly enough."

Or you could respond assertively to the question by looking the other person in the eye and speaking directly and honestly, with no hidden messages: "He seems friendly enough."

Directions: Read each of the following statements aloud three times. The first time, use an aggressive communication style; the second time, use a nonassertive style; and the third time, use an assertive style of communicating.

1. "Would you mind helping me?"
2. "I think there's a mistake on my bill."
3. "Why haven't you returned my phone calls?"
4. "I'd like some cooperation."
5. "I am very displeased with the work you've done."

Exercise: USING ASSERTIVE COMMUNICATION TO HANDLE INTERRUPTIONS

Directions: Imagine that you are at a staff meeting. The chairperson has just recognized you to speak, and you begin talking to the group about an idea you have that will really help your organization. Think of an idea or suggestion that actually relates to your present company.

Now imagine that the members of the meeting are interrupting your presentation. Answer aloud each of the interruptions listed below so that you can practice hearing yourself "thinking on your feet," just as you would in a real meeting. Respond to each interruption immediately in an assertive and tactful manner. Do not become aggressive or timid. Take back the control you lost as a result of the interruption. Try to apply the techniques discussed in this chapter:

Acknowledge and refocus   "I" versus "you" language
Anticipation   Limit setting
Consequences versus threats   Metatalk
Defuse and defense   Self-interest

INTERRUPTIONS

1. "We've tried that before. It'll never work."

2. "That's totally ridiculous."

3. "Look, can we cut this short? I've got a big luncheon appointment."

4. (One person commenting to another) "Did you see that tennis match last Sunday? I couldn't believe it—what a match!"

5. (One person tapping a pencil and yawning) "Gee, it's getting late."

6. "I don't know about that idea, but your jacket looks fantastic on you! Hey, what do you all think?"

7. "Hey, let's 'can' this discussion. I'm starved!"

8. (Several people are having side conversations.)

9. "Now, that reminds me of an even better idea that I would like to bring up to the group."

10. "The president will never approve of your idea; it just costs too much money."

chapter 4

Thinking on Your Feet: Handling Yourself Under Pressure

Several years ago, I presented a seminar before a large group, and one woman raised her hand and said in a very sarcastic voice, "Mr. Schwimmer, it's awfully cold in this room. Of course, you probably don't care—you're wearing a three-piece suit."

My immediate reply was to go into my Steve Martin impression and respond in a similar sarcastic and humiliating fashion. "Well, ex-cuuuuuuuuuse me! Would you feel better if I was naked?" Of course, I got a big laugh out of the audience.

Although this woman was obviously being aggressive with her sarcastic statement to me, I later realized that I reacted to her aggression by responding with equal hostility (sarcasm is very aggressive). It taught me a valuable lesson in communicating: In order to think on your feet and manage people effectively, it is important to learn how to respond—not react—to the inevitable and often aggressive statements of others.

My sarcastic reply to this woman was that of a "stimulus-response" machine. In other words, her angry statement to me produced an aggressive reply from me. Another way of looking at it was that she "pressed my button," and just like a vending machine, out came my reaction. The result is almost always poor communication and sometimes severe arguments that end in long-term ill will.

Had I answered her in a nonreactive, assertive way, I might have said, "I'm sorry you're feeling cold. I'll see if we can get the heat turned up. By the way, I hear anger in your voice [metatalk]. Is anything else upsetting you?"

To think on your feet, you must not allow yourself to be manipulated into a predictably aggressive reply to other people. Otherwise, you are under their control. Remember, whoever angers you defeats you! The secret to thinking on your feet assertively is to respond to the communication of others and not react in the same aggressive manner. This is a key point in being able to communicate effectively in situations of imminent conflict.

A good illustration of this was the situation in Chapter 3 where the new employee was ridiculed aggressively by a vice president for making a suggestion. It would have been very risky for the junior employee to react aggressively to the vice president.

You can also put yourself at risk unnecessarily if you have the tendency to be aggressive as a knee-jerk reaction to the other person's aggressive statement. Many aspects of your promotability relate to your interpersonal communication with others at work, and we will see how much of your successful or unsuccessful communication with others is based on your ability to think on your feet.

Read the following statements and imagine that someone at work is saying them to you:

- "How could you make such a ridiculous mistake? I guess I gave you too much credit!"

- "I'd like to have you work on this new project, but I'm just not sure you could handle it."

- "The truth is, our new client just doesn't like you."

- "Listen, if you can't help me, I'll just have to find someone I know I can depend on!"

- "Ever since you got promoted, you've been acting power-crazy!"

- "Don't tell me I did this wrong, after all the mistakes I've seen you make!"

If you are like most people, these statements probably elicit certain emotions or feelings in you. Yet these kinds of statements are made constantly during a typical business day in many organizations.

These statements tend to produce conflict in people's minds. What *is* the best way to respond? Any response may be risky and may create more conflict and dissension.

When a statement elicits a strong emotion, people are especially uncomfortable. For example, a person whose feelings have just been hurt will probably find it difficult to think cleverly and clearly on their feet. In other words, they become "at the effect" of a statement that elicits a particular feeling or emotion from them. *The process by which you can confidently think on your feet is based on your awareness of those statements and resulting emotions that inhibit you or prevent you from responding assertively to the other person's communication.*

When you are feeling out of control and uncomfortable, you are less likely to take the risk of standing up for yourself, whatever the situation. So many people in business are totally out of touch with their feelings. They have had little training or practice in taking stock of their emotions. They don't know what about someone else's statement is bothering them, and they are often insensitive to others. If you want to manage people effectively and gain their cooperation, it is important to develop interpersonal awareness. It is another skill that will enhance your promotability within your organization.

You can begin the process of thinking on your feet more confidently by improving your awareness of the emotions and feelings that certain statements elicit from you. Someone who is defensive may have a predisposition to become angry over another person's statement, such as "Just what have you been doing all day?" Another person who is prone to having hurt feelings may be especially upset over a statement such as "The truth is, our client just doesn't like you."

The point is not to suggest that you become an unfeeling or unemotional person. But you must realize that to stand up for yourself effectively, you must *experience* your emotions and feelings but not let them control you or pretend that they don't exist. You do not have control over your feelings; all you can do is feel them. However, you *do* have control over your words and actions—providing you perceive options and alternatives to merely *reacting* to a situation.

Also be aware of the fact that you do not need to take other people's statements personally. After all, though there may be some validity to the content of other people's statements, the tone of the statement (such as sarcasm) may be a projection of their feelings about themselves or their own point of view.

To think on your feet, you must have knowledge in terms of specific skills and techniques. These will give you the confidence to respond in a constructive way to the statements people make in work situations. Above all, it is important to respond assertively and never lower yourself to the level of those around you who may be aggressive or nonassertive. Pay special attention to your communication skills. They will give you more choices of responses, so you will no longer have to react in old and ineffective ways. Once you become more aware of the kinds of statements that paralyze your ability to reply or evoke aggressive reactions from you, you will be more likely to respond in a positive and appropriate manner instead. Here are some additional suggestions that will help you think on your feet.

BE ASSERTIVE

Communicate honestly and directly in an appropriate manner. This is hardest to do when someone makes an aggressive statement that hurts your feelings or makes you angry. Many of us have a "machine" reaction to strike back. You are best able to remain assertive by remembering that the other person's statement is nothing personal. After all, that person did not spend all day thinking of the exact statement that would be most likely to hurt your feelings. He just expressed spontaneous feelings. Don't let yourself be hooked into the other person's anger or be upset by reacting to it. You can choose to react differently.

Instead, take a deep breath before you say anything. And before you respond or defend yourself, always acknowledge what the other person has said to make it clear that it was heard (for example, "I can really hear how angry you are").

An important part of being assertive is communicating to the other person how you feel about his statement. This may mean that you make it clear that you found the statement upsetting in a particular way. The worst thing you can do is to keep your feelings blocked up inside yourself, where no resolution is possible.

ASK QUESTIONS

Rather than reacting, find out more information about why that person has said what he did. If the statement was general (for example, "Your work stinks!"), ask the person to be more specific. Ask why he is upset. Make it clear that you are sincerely interested in understanding his point of view and correcting any problem or misunderstanding.

Even if the person who makes a statement to you is not upset, it is important for you to understand the basis and reason for his statement, especially if you do not understand it fully.

ANTICIPATE OTHERS

Chapter 3 speaks of the concept of anticipation. You can use this concept to anticipate the very situations where you may be called upon to think on your feet. For example, Victor attended a regional sales meeting. He knew that he was one of the sales people who had not made his sales budget. By anticipating statements and questions that might be made to him by others (his sales manager, other sales people, the president), he would be much more likely to give an intelligent and poised response.

You can use the same anticipation concept by understanding and anticipating the kind of statements that people around you have tended to make in the past. For example, Victor knows that his sales manager, Rolf, tends to become aggressive when sales budgets are missed. Victor knows that it is possible that Rolf will lash out at him with a statement such as "Why the hell don't you work harder? Then you'd make your sales budget!"

Victor also knows that his performance is generally excellent and that Rolf, as the sales manager, is feeling a great deal of pressure for the entire sales force to perform well. So Victor knows in advance not to take Rolf's angry statement as a personal attack. Victor will be much more likely to think on his feet in such a situation.

If you want to think successfully on your feet clearly and respond effectively, anticipate what the other person might say as a result of your action (i.e., not making your sales budget). Also anticipate their own personality style and job circumstances (i.e., Rolf's tendency to become angry when he feels the pressure from his own job as sales manager).

DELAY YOUR RESPONSE

Sometimes the other person's statements or questions catch you by total surprise. You don't know how to respond. Thinking on your feet does not necessarily mean that you have to give a perfect reply on the spot. It may mean that you will answer by delaying your response. Therefore, you may be much better off not responding at all and letting the other person know "I'll get back to you right away" with a well-thought-out reply. This buys you time. When you are confronted by especially aggressive people, this can give them an opportunity to calm down.

For example, your manager is "foaming at the mouth" because you made an error in a report that he presented to a meeting of other senior executives. You realize that he is not only upset at your error but also at having embarrassed himself in front of others. Thus it might be best for you to postpone your response until your manager has calmed down and is more likely to discuss your mistake rationally. "Tom, I can see you're upset about this. Let me investigate it, and I'll get you a full explanation first thing tomorrow morning."

TAKE RESPONSIBILITY

Sometimes thinking on your feet means that you accept the content of the other person's statement as accurate, even if what you objected to was the aggressive or hurting style in which it was said to you. Many people immediately become defensive, which is one of the major blocks of effectively thinking on your feet. By taking responsibility for what may be true (perhaps if you had worked harder, you would have made your sales budget), you are more likely to disarm someone's assertive or aggressive statement to you. Then a more open and fruitful dialogue can occur to clear up the communication.

As you can imagine, getting along with people is one of the pre-requisites for winning promotions. To be perceived as being pro-motable, it is important that others see you as someone who is in control of his or her emotions, particularly when dealing with aggressive or difficult people. You must be able to think under pressure.

The following exercise will give you an opportunity to know better the feelings and emotions you experience when reactivating statements are made to you. In doing this exercise, be aware of the statements and the emotions that cause you to react or even lose control. Examine your reaction to the statement. Keep reminding yourself that hurtful or aggressive statements say nothing personal about you. They reflect other people's point of view and have everything to do with the other person.

By recognizing that you do not have to react emotionally and may instead respond objectively, you will be in greater control and thus be more likely to resolve a potential conflict with the other person. This exercise will also give you the opportunity to practice responding assertively in a constructive manner so that you can feel greater confidence in your communication with all kinds of people.

Exercise: RESPONDING TO REACTIVATING STATEMENTS

Directions: To help you discover what feelings or emotions leave you out of control or likely to react, take a look at the following list of reactivating statements.

1. In the blank beside each statement, write down the emotion you feel when you imagine someone making that statement to you. Here is a list of feelings for you to choose from; you may also write down any other emotion you experience. You'll probably have a tendency to feel certain emotions more than others.

anger	fear	jealousy
anxiety	guilt	rejection
defensiveness	inadequacy	stupidity
depression	irritation	superiority
embarrassment	intimidation	sympathy

_____ "You are always late!"

_____ "If you were more careful, you wouldn't make so many mistakes!"

_____   "The truth is, our new client just doesn't like you."

_____   "Don't talk to me about my mistakes, after all the mistakes I've seen you make."

_____   "You're doing a great job, but I'm afraid there's just no money in the budget for your raise."

_____   "Look, if you can't help me, I'll just have to find someone I know I can count on."

_____   "If this happens one more time, you're fired!"

_____   "I can't believe you're turning down my request after all the favors I've done for you."

_____   "The rumor in the grapevine is that you've been spending a lot of time with the new staff assistant. . . ."

_____   "You are the only one in the entire company who can help me with this. *Please!*"

_____   "Your problem is that you're oversensitive and just take your job too seriously."

_____   "I've selected the people I want for the presentation, and I must tell you, you aren't one of them."

_____   "Maybe you just weren't cut out to take the pressure of this position."

_____   "When your boss hears about this, you'd better have a pretty good explanation."

_____   "I know I promised to help you tomorrow, but something else came up."

_____   "Why can't you ever be on time?"

_____   "I've already told you once. How many times do I have to repeat myself?"

_____   "Ever since you got promoted, you've been acting power-crazy!"

_____   "Just what have you been doing all day?"

_____   "You always give Hal the good projects and me the grunt work."

_____   "If this isn't done on time, you'll have to skip your vacation."

2. Next, write down at least three statements that people have actually made to you that have caused you to feel a strong emotion or reaction. Choose from the statements in section 1 if they are similar to statements people have made to you, or make up your own statements. Then write down your immediate *inner reaction* to these statements. Here's an example:

STATEMENT: *"You're always late!"*

YOUR INNER REACTION: *"You creep! I do twice as much work around here as anyone else! What right do you have to judge my hours! What about all the nights I worked overtime?"*

a.
STATEMENT: _____

YOUR INNER REACTION: _____

_____

_____

b.
STATEMENT: _____

YOUR INNER REACTION: _____

_____

_____

c.

STATEMENT: _____

YOUR INNER REACTION: _____

_____

_____

3. Now write down the assertive response you could make to these statements if you were thinking on your feet; for example:

STATEMENT: *"You're always late!"*

ASSERTIVE RESPONSE: *"That's not true. I'm late only occasionally. However, when I'm late, I make sure to work longer to make up for any lost time."*

a. _____

_____

b. _____

_____

c. _____

_____

chapter 5

The Fine Art of Self-Protection: Standing Up to Manipulation

MANIPULATE: to manage or influence by artful means, fair or unfair, especially to one's advantage or purpose

SITUATION

Manager: "Ben, I need you to come in this weekend to work with me on this special project. You're the only one I can trust to do a great job."

Ben: "Thanks for the vote of confidence, but I've already made plans to go away for the weekend. Why don't you try a few of the other people in the department?"

Manager: "Now look, Ben, I need *your* help, and I don't want anyone else. If I can't count on you, then I'll get someone I *know* I can count on! And I can't promise you that this won't affect your next performance rating."

What can Ben say?

Few of us like to think of ourselves as being manipulative, employing devious means to get what we want. In fact, in our social life, labeling someone as manipulative is perhaps one of the worst insults we can give. However, we often retain a sneaking admiration for individuals who have really mastered the art. They seem to get what they want.

Yet in business, manipulation is a common way in which people accomplish goals and achieve results. Conversely, it is also one of the reasons why there are conflicts and distrust among people. Understanding how manipulation works and how to use it in a positive rather than negative manner is of utmost importance to your advancing in the organization and winning the promotions you deserve.

Facing those who use manipulation tactics is part of your everyday existence at work, at just about any level in the hierarchy. After all, there's always someone who wants something from you, whether it's assistance, time, information, a favor, or just feedback.

For example, one of the manipulation tactics most often used is intimidation, which the opening situation in this chapter illustrates. Ben will undoubtedly be taking a very big risk in standing up to his intimidating manager, who will stop at nothing to get what he wants. If you, by contrast, are using this tactic, you run the risk of covert retaliation by the person who feels intimidated by you.

POSITIVE VERSUS NEGATIVE
MANIPULATION

There is nothing intrinsically evil about manipulation. Most of us use it all the time in one way or another, although we rarely think about it in those terms. Usually when *we* manipulate, it is for a good reason. When the *other guy* manipulates, it's because he is being underhanded or deceptive. So manipulation, especially the negative variety, is in the eye of the beholder.

The distinction between negative versus positive manipulation is whether you have the other person's best interest at heart or only your own.

Consider this example: When you employ the concept of self-interest to convince a colleague to do something for you, you are engaging in a form of manipulation. However, both of you will be benefiting. This is *positive* manipulation. If, on the other hand, you blatantly lie about the potential benefits that the other person will gain, knowing full well that what you are saying is untrue, you have crossed the line and are engaging in *negative* manipulation. Although in the short run you may get what you want, in the long run this could lead to your demise. Negative manipulation is a very foolhardy behavior. It risks your credibility and undermines your image as a leader.

MANIPULATING: WIN-WIN OR WIN-LOSE

We all manipulate. It is up to you to accept responsibility for whether you manipulate in a negative or positive manner or for win-win or win-lose outcomes. So accept manipulation for what it is: a tactic we all employ to one degree or another, sometimes appropriately, sometimes not. What's really important is to be *aware* of when you are doing it so that you use it in the most constructive way. Thus you can take full responsibility for its short- and long-term ramifications.

When people manipulate unfairly, they are disliked and not readily given cooperation by others. This can hurt their chances for promotions. Win-lose manipulation can cause people who are being manipulated to refuse to keep an agreement, once they realize that dishonest means have been used to engage them. Or such people may sabotage the manipulator as a means of seeking revenge or retaliation. Or they may just do a substandard job because they are resentful.

So it is in the best interest of anyone who consciously motivates others to strive for win-win manipulations. Make sure that others will get some real value out of whatever task you are trying to involve them in. This ensures not only that you will get what you want but also that you will feel good about how you got it. You will find that people will be much more likely to keep their agreements and give you the 100 percent effort that is required for producing successful results.

A NEW WAY OF LOOKING AT MANIPULATION

It is extremely important to be aware of the ways you can stand up to the manipulative tactics of others—always remembering that you, as an assertive person, have choices and options. You never have to be a victim or martyr. Having this knowledge, you will be in a much better position to stand up to manipulation tactics that are used in the real world of business, industry, and government. This will win you the respect and cooperation essential to your successfully climbing the ladder in your organization.

At the workshops I conduct, I have the participants do an exercise in which they manipulate and are manipulated. The purpose is not to train them to manipulate; it is to give them a direct experience from both sides of the manipulation fence. A great deal of learning comes out of this experience. Participants get a chance to practice standing up to different pressure tactics and discover which are the best ways to counter the manipulations of others. They also learn how important it is to respect the rights of other people's choices—even if it means that they don't get what they originally wanted. The participants learn that such tactics do work, particularly with people who are not aware of the strategies and ways to stand up to manipulation. They also realize that they have choices and must take responsibility for their behavior, instead of playing the role of the victim who has no choice but to give in to the manipulator.

THE FOUR BASIC WAYS PEOPLE MANIPULATE

Manipulation takes four primary forms. Although there are variations and derivatives of these forms, you will realize that most manipulation falls into these categories. People may not always be fully aware of their use of these tactics; their manipulation may be habitual or even unconscious.

1. FLATTERY

"Gee, you're the only one who can help me with this. After all, you're the best!"

Sound familiar? Flattery is the safest form of manipulation. It is also the least risky of the four manipulation tactics. Few people are going to get angry at you for telling them how great they are or how well they do something. They may not believe you, but at least they will listen. And in many cases, they will not only believe you but will appreciate you for acknowledging their talents. You can see why this is most people's favorite form of manipulation.

There is nothing wrong with sincerely complimenting someone who deserves the recognition or acknowledgment. This is very positive. It becomes negative when the manipulator knows very well that he is being dishonest. What the person really wants is to engage you to do something that (in his mind) you will be far more likely to agree to do if your ego is appealed to.

Also keep in mind that most hard-core manipulators begin their effort to win you by flattery. If that tactic proves ineffective, they will rapidly move on to much more severe tactics. Be sensitive to those who compliment with obvious ulterior motives. Sometimes they are so obvious that their request comes almost immediately following their compliment or praise.

Again, there is nothing wrong with complimenting or praising when it is done in a sincere manner. And there is nothing wrong with having an ulterior motive. After all, I wouldn't want you to help me do something if you possessed no talent for doing it well. But flattering is a big mistake and very dishonest behavior when you don't believe that your compliments are true. You already know that your sole motive is to get someone to do something. Worse yet, you end up giving the other person the wrong message—that he excels at something when in fact he does not. The result is that the person may not take the time and effort to improve because he believes your flattery.

2. SYMPATHY

"My job is really on the line here. I could even lose it if you don't help me."

Quite often the next level of manipulation is sympathy, especially if flattery is unsuccessful. People who use sympathy want you to feel sorry for them. They believe that once you do, you will be willing to come to their rescue. They are willing to lie or exaggerate in order to elicit your assistance.

Again, you have to make a distinction between the negative and positive aspects of this tactic. In a negative fashion, this tactic is clearly born out of the intent to engage your sympathy for the manipulators' benefit, whether it is justified or not. The intent is to make you feel bad if you *don't* help. Manipulators have no interest in giving you a choice to help. Instead, there is a conscious attempt to make you responsible for what may happen to them as a consequence of your not helping.

This is in contrast to a more honest use of sympathy, whereby the basis for the appeal for help is not solely over the dilemma that will be created for a manipulator ("I could lose my job") if you don't help. Instead, it is part of a much more honest and direct appeal for assistance. In its positive form, the manipulator is not making you responsible for what may happen to him but is instead playing to your self-interest, which may be that you will feel good if you know that you are helping in such a crucial way that it may even result in the manipulator's keeping his job. This represents a major shift from the implication that you may have to shoulder the blame and responsibility for the loss of his job.

If I were going to use sympathy as part of my appeal to engage the other person, I would be assertive, honest, and direct in making my request and then appeal to the other person to sympathize with my situation. For example, "Michael, in addition to the other reasons I have mentioned for wanting your help on this project, I want you to know that my job may be on the line. I don't want to lose it. Although the success or failure is my responsibility, I do believe your help and assistance could make the crucial difference. Will you help me?"

When the main thrust of your rationale for help is based on gaining sympathy, you are on shaky ground. It is much stronger to use a manipulation tactic such as sympathy as a minor part of your overall appeal to the other person. Notice that in my assertive appeal to Michael, I let him know directly that I wanted his help for other reasons (previously discussed) and that my job was on the line. However, I took full responsibility for the outcome. Yet I acknowledged that he could make a crucial difference. And I asked him directly to help me.

In using the manipulation tactic of sympathy, I hoped to appeal to Michael's compassionate nature and what I know to be his self-interest, which is to enjoy helping someone out of a pinch. Keep in mind he can now make his own choice as to what he wants to do. Michael is not only helping me do a project but, more important, helping me keep my job. This may make the difference in obtaining his assistance.

3. GUILT

"You've got to help me! Look at all the favors I've done for you, like last month during budget time when I helped you night after night."

If flattery and sympathy have been unsuccessful, quite often the manipulator will use guilt as a means of getting you to say yes. Using guilt is a way of being a martyr ("after all I've done for you . . ."). If this tactic works, you may find yourself the willing victim of someone else not because you want to help but because you don't feel you can say no. The manipulator usually makes you feel you have done something wrong by not providing what he wants.

Like sympathy, guilt is the manipulation tactic of the powerless. Quite often, they rest their whole appeal for gaining someone's help on past favors they have done for that person. In a negative sense, their intention is to make the other person feel guilty about saying no, so the person will say yes. This is truly a case of manipulators relinquishing responsibility to the other person instead of accepting it as their own. It also clearly shows that there were strings or expectations attached to the help they gave others. Such manipulators often set themselves up for the anger or disappointment that occurs when others are not manipulated or swayed by their use of the guilt tactic.

It is important to rely on substantive reasons for why people should want to help you. However, a part of the rationale for expecting them to give your request high priority is that you have helped them and hope now that they will make a sincere effort to help you.

Keep in mind that I am not suggesting there is anything wrong with "calling in favors" or letting others know that here is an opportunity for them to show their appreciation for the help you have given them in the past. (In fact, Chapter 13 speaks about the "Godfather" approach, where you purposely do all that you can to assist others, letting them know up front that someday you will ask them to be of assistance to you.) I might elect to use the guilt tactic not in the traditional sense of laying a guilt trip on others but instead to remind them directly of how I would consider their assistance a showing of appreciation for my past help; for example: "Paula, in addition to the other reasons I have mentioned for wanting your help, I am hoping that in light of the past help I have given you, you will see your helping me now as a way of returning the favor. However, if you can't, I want you to know that I have no hard feelings and will respect your decision."

Notice that after giving Paula my substantive reasons for why I need her help, I made a part of my appeal the manipulation tactic of reciprocity. And in this case, "guilt" is almost a misnomer. I reminded her of my past assistance to her and asked that she now return the favor. You can see the fine line between negative manipulation (which the word *guilt* suggests) and the more positive manipulation of reciprocity where I let her know that I would like her to see her helping me as a way of returning my past favors to her.

My point: we are really talking semantics. Both sides of guilt manipulation are different sides of the same coin. I know and Paula knows that the intent of my saying "Here's your chance to return the favor I did you" is bound to evoke some feelings of obligation in Paula.

The real distinction in using the tactic of guilt is that in the reply I just gave her, I did not appeal to her as a victim or martyr. I did not try to make her feel bad. My approach had the effect of making her feel some added responsibility in considering my request in light of my past assistance to her. However, it is mitigated by my willingness to understand and respect her decision to say no.

In using such manipulation tactics, realize that there are many subtleties involved. Yet because giving assistance on the job is often very subjective, the weight of a yes or no from someone is often based on the scale tipping a little bit more toward the yes than the no. This is precisely where a manipulation tactic can tip the scales in your favor.

I think we have all had the experience of wanting to help someone. Yet to do so would have resulted in some inconvenience to us. As a result, we were leaning toward saying no (or finding some excuse to say no). However, it seems that we have a special motivation to go out of our way to be of assistance once someone lets us know (1) how valuable we are (flattery), (2) how crucial our assistance is to their job security (sympathy), or (3) that we should return a favor (guilt).

This is truly the value I see in using these manipulation tactics in a positive manner: *to tip the scales in your favor.* However, if there is no goodwill in the form of substantive reasons for someone to assist you, negative manipulation can occur when you try to persuade not on the merits of helping but solely by relying on the manipulation tactic itself. The result is that problems and hard feelings will inevitably result.

4. INTIMIDATION

"I need your help, and if I can't get it, I can't promise that this won't affect your next performance rating."

This is the severest of pressure tactics. It implies an obvious threat (as opposed to a consequence) that some sort of harm will occur if you don't do what the manipulator is asking. Issuing a consequence is a way of protecting yourself from someone's unprofessional behavior. A threat is used to bully someone to do what you want, strictly for your personal gain.

Intimidation is the riskiest tactic to use because how people will respond is extremely uncertain and often unpredictable. The aim of people who use intimidation is to fill your mind with fears of what might happen if you do not do what they want. The obvious danger is that even if you give in, you may not do a very good job or you may subvert the manipulator or become a covert enemy who one day will rise up and retaliate. So intimidation is an imprudent tactic, at best a short-run way to motivate others.

Also, manipulators who use intimidation must be willing to follow through with their implied threats. Once people see that such manipulators are paper tigers, the manipulators' future efforts to intimidate will become ineffectual (and usually well publicized). Manipulators who use this tactic are soon singled out in the organization and often find their careers abruptly terminated. They cause high turnover and loss of executive talent. Rising stars will eventually leave the team when the captain is a tyrant who runs the team by "winning through intimidation."

However, while intimidation is not an advisable tactic to use to get things done, you can motivate and compel someone by issuing a consequence. In Chapter 3 I defined a consequence as an action or sanction you will take to compel someone to responsible behavior. Here, of course, you are not making a threat, but you are letting people know what you will do as a consequence to their not behaving in a more responsible manner. This is much more direct and allows the others to make their own choices based on concrete actions that you have advised them that you will take—versus a threat where you are implying through innuendo what you will do.

Consider the following situation to distinguish the use of intimidation as a negative manipulation tactic versus using a consequence to compel someone to responsible behavior.

SITUATION

Sharon and Ed are coworkers who have been told to work together on a project. However, Sharon has done most of the work and is getting no cooperation from Ed in doing his share. When Sharon asks Ed once again, he tells her to stop bugging him; he's too busy with other things. Sharon knows that Ed really is busy studying for a test for a night course he is taking. But she also knows that she will never get the project done on time without some help from him.

Using the manipulation tactic of intimidation, Sharon might say, "Listen, Ed, if I don't get some help from you right away, I may have to speak to a few people about your studying on company time—if you know what I mean."

You'll note in Sharon's use of intimidation, all she will do is provoke a fight and aggravate the situation. Sharon's innuendos suggest that her intent is to threaten Ed and make him fearful, not gain his cooperation.

Issuing a consequence instead of intimidation, Sharon might say, "Ed, I need your immediate cooperation on this project in order to get it done on time. I have already done most of the work. I need your help now to do the rest. If I don't get your full cooperation right now, I will see our manager and tell him directly that I have not received your help and cooperation and ask that he resolve this problem. I would prefer that we work it out ourselves. Are you willing to help me?"

In this case, Sharon issues a specific consequence. She states the problem, asks for what she wants, and then issues a consequence, which, in effect, gives Ed a choice as to what he wants to do. Sharon is direct, honest, and assertive. This approach lets Ed know that she sincerely wants to motivate him to cooperate with her. When she used intimidation, her emphasis was "I'm going to get you if you don't help." Remember, even a cornered rat will fight!

Before you consider using intimidation, think of a consequence that might be more likely to compel the other person to responsible behavior. And if the person isn't motivated to act responsibly, be prepared to follow through on the consequence you have issued.

When I go over each of these four manipulation tactics at a workshop or seminar, people always ask me about bribery as a manipulation tactic. My reply is that while there are still some people who use bribery, it is unlawful, and we have seen plenty of instances of high-ranking executives and politicians going to prison because of it. So I don't think it is even worthy of consideration as a manipulation tactic. You do not want to blacken your name or botch your career by any association with an organization where a tactic such as bribery is used.

FACING A SITUATION WHERE YOU ARE BEING MANIPULATED

The following situation illustrates all four manipulation tactics. As you read the dialogue between Neil (the manipulator) and Sally (the manipulatee), you will see how manipulation begins in a harmless manner and gradually becomes very serious "hard ball." It finally ends in Neil getting Sally to change her "no" to a "yes."

SITUATION

Neil has persuaded the vice president to give him a special opportunity for high visibility and exposure: the honor of cochairing the company's annual corporate fund-raiser. However, the vice president has agreed to Neil's request under one nonnegotiable condition: that Neil get Sally to accept equal responsibility of sharing the work load. The vice president believes that they will make an ideal team whom he can trust to do a first-rate job. Neil knows that if he fails to get Sally to agree to take on this responsibility, he will lose out on this opportunity and will lose face in the process. With all this in mind, he meets with Sally to discuss the matter.

Neil: Hi, Sally, I wanted to talk with you about a real special opportunity you're going to love being part of. Listen to this: I talked the VP into having you and me cochair this year's annual corporate fund-raiser. This is a great opportunity for visibility before all the big brass! We're going to be stars in this company. So I thought I would come in and give you the good news and talk about how we plan on working out the details on who does what.

Sally: Neil, that sounds great. But I just can't accept that responsibility. I know it's a fabulous opportunity for exposure and visibility. But it will take a lot of time outside of work, and I need to spend more time with my kids and husband. I mean, I travel enough the way it is already. Thanks anyway.

Neil: [Using flattery] Sally, I can't believe you would pass up this chance! You are so perfect for this job. No one has got the kind of organizational talent that you do. Everyone likes you and will do everything to support you. When those big shots see the way you work, your future as a VP is assured!

Sally: Thanks for the vote of confidence. It feels great to be appreciated. However, I still have to say no.

Neil: [Using sympathy] Sally, this is awfully important to me. This is my big chance finally to get the recognition I need to make my big move up the ladder. The VP made it clear to me that we're the team he wants. If I don't deliver on my word to get you, I'll look like a real fool. They'll never consider me for that big promotion. It will be downhill for me. The next thing you know, they'll be questioning my competence in other areas. Who knows, this could even cost me my job. Please, I need you to work with me on this fund-raiser. It'll be the greatest thing that could happen to both our careers.

Sally: Neil, I do understand how important this is for you. I know this would be a great opportunity for me, but I just cannot make this commitment. I'm sure that your stock in this company won't go down. You've done a great job so far.

Neil: [Using guilt] Sally, after all I have done for you, I just can't believe you're saying no! Several months ago you were in real trouble putting together second quarter budgets and I worked with you and even gave you one of my best staff assistants to help bail you out. I was there for you. Now, when the chips are down, I can't count on you. You call that appreciation?

Sally: Neil, you're right, you did help me. And I appreciated that so much. I want to help you. But I really need to spend more time with my family. My kids hardly recognize me, and my husband is already upset with all the traveling I do. I just don't know whether I can commit to anything more.

Neil: [Using intimidation] I understand all that, Sally. But this is such a fantastic opportunity for both of us in our careers. There's too much at stake: both our reputations. Do you know what will happen if I go back to the VP and say that I would like to work on this fund-raiser but Sally doesn't because she needs to spend more time with her family? Do you know what he's going to think? He'll figure, "She's just a typical woman who can't be counted on." Sally, I want to level with you: I really think it will affect your promotability in this company. After all, the VP reviews all promotional recommendations.

Sally: You have a point there; that does concern me. I know he tends to be a very traditional man. I've heard through the grapevine that he's a real chauvinist. I guess I've worked too hard to get this far and have my future affected. Maybe I'll just have to try to make my family understand how important this is to my career. OK, let's meet this afternoon and begin planning the details.

Neil: Great! I know you won't be sorry. This is really going to benefit both our careers.

The intent of this entire chapter is *not* to tell you to manipulate. Rather, it is to make the point that manipulation tactics are used—and they work. They can be used in a positive or negative manner; the choice is up to you. What is most important is that you are aware of the use of these pressure tactics and that you do have options and alternatives in how you stand up to those who use these tactics. Above all, you will need to have confidence in facing those who use these tactics. And you will need to be assertive. Some of the toughest on-the-job risks you will confront will be in standing up to those in your organization who will use manipulation tactics to undermine you and get their way.

HOW TO STAND UP TO MANIPULATION TACTICS OF OTHERS

CONVICTION

When it looks, sounds, and feels like you mean no, people are likely to believe you. However, when your response to someone's request, for example, is wavering, perhaps through your body language or shaky voice, you look like a *no* waiting to become a *yes*. And manipulators, like sharks who can smell blood, sense this and move in for the kill. Be persistent when saying no. You don't need to add words or explanations each time you reply with *no*.

SELF-ESTEEM

Having high regard for yourself helps you realize that you have your rights, too. You view yourself as a deserving person whose self-worth is not based on the approval of others. Knowing this supports you when manipulative people use sympathy ploys, guilt trips, or intimidating methods to get their way. Your self-respect makes you less likely to give in or be vulnerable to manipulative attack by others. This self-esteem will become apparent to management, who will have confidence in your ability to get the job done and recognize you for higher leadership positions.

PRIORITIES

Nonassertive people only have priorities up until the point at which you manipulate them sufficiently. Then your priorities become their priorities. Nonassertive people have no backbone. As an assertive person, you feel comfortable and reassured knowing that you are in charge of and responsible for your own priorities. Having a sense of your priorities means that you take charge and decide what you can and cannot be responsible for. If you are easily manipulated, you'll find that your priorities will be constantly rearranged the moment you feel pressure from someone who is trying to manipulate you.

CONFIDENCE

When a tennis pro can win three sets out of five at Wimbledon or a great boxer can knock out his opponent in the ring, you can imagine how much confidence they must have in themselves. Similarly, you, as a talented professional, can also feel confident when you do a superior job. Knowing that you do your job well and that others respect you for that ability makes you feel even more secure, even in the face of a manipulative tactic such as intimidation. If your job hangs in the balance at the drop of an ego, you are in big trouble. Professionals are too highly valued to be dispensed with frivolously, even when they stand up assertively to the manipulating bully.

CONSEQUENCES

Naturally, there are consequences when you take a stand on anything. As a responsible professional, you expect that there are consequences for anything that you do, and you are willing to accept them. When people realize that you are not bluffing and that you are savvy to the consequences of your actions, they will be less likely to look at you as someone who can be manipulated. You may recall from your childhood that the neighborhood bully seemed to go away only when you finally stood up to him.

AWARENESS

If you are highly sensitive to the manipulation practices of others, whether the tactics are conscious or unconscious, you are in a position to prepare yourself for such encounters. Being aware acts as a deterrent to being caught off guard or naively being manipulated and then regretting it later. You are in charge, in control, and responsible at all times.

SUPPORT AND VALIDATION

Have you ever had second thoughts about whether something you agreed to do was in your best interest? At the time you weren't sure, and as you thought about it, you became less sure. You wanted a more impartial perception. So you stop off at a colleague's office to bounce your concern off him. He says, "I agree with you. It sounds like that project would be a lot of grunt work, which you don't need." That kind of special support and validation has the effect of assisting you to stand up and say no when you need to, even though it was the manipulation tactic itself that got you to consider the bad proposition in the first place.

BEING LIKED

Often we are very easily manipulated because we are striving for the personal approval of others. At work it is important that we have mutual respect and be highly regarded professionally, not necessarily personally. At work, when we relate to one another on a personal level rather than a professional level, we can have difficulty saying no because emotions and feelings get in the way. A perfect example of this problem is someone who helps you in a pinch. When she asks for a return favor, she takes your refusal as a personal rejection. This is another place where being assertive and having high self-esteem are important so that you can distinguish between rejecting the request and not the person.

NO EXCUSES

You can stand up to manipulative tactics by *not* giving excuses. Sales people love excuses. And once they overcome your objection (as they are trained to do), you are left vulnerable, exposed as a dishonest person. So stay away from excuses. People will respect you and take you more seriously. They will be less likely to have hard feelings when they know they have been dealt with honestly and directly.

STIMULUS-RESPONSE MACHINE

Because of our upbringing and our own psychological makeup, many of us have automatic, predictable responses toward the behavior of other people. People who work with us soon learn what buttons to press if they want to get a certain reaction. In effect, we teach them how to manipulate us.

For example, Warren can't stand the thought of any fighting or conflict. "Peace at any price" is his motto. Others know that they can get their way with Warren by using intimidation on him. Jill desperately wants the approval of others. Therefore, some of her coworkers manipulate her by letting her know that she will be liked and appreciated if she helps with their pet projects.

Become especially aware of the kind of pressure tactic (stimulus) that evokes a predictable behavior (response) from you (the machine). This way, you will be less like a machine that others control at their will. Once you become aware, you can begin to find ways to avoid being manipulated in the same predictable manner.

BEING RESPONSIBLE

Remember, you are not manipulated; in actuality, you *allow* others to manipulate you. By relinquishing responsibility for your behavior to other people, you give up your own personal power. This is why you will want to become aware of the specific manipulation tactics that tend to make you feel victimized by others. Once you know, it is up to you to stand up for yourself and be assertive. You will be in charge and in the best position to choose consciously what you will and won't do.

WHAT IF MANIPULATION TACTICS ARE USED IN YOUR ORGANIZATION?

Don't even worry about the "what if?" The answer is, they are. Manipulation is an integral part of the way the real world of work operates. This is why I differentiate between using manipulation in positive ways versus negative ways.

So, please spare yourself the naive search for an organization where "everyone is fair, there are no politics, and no one gets things done by manipulation." It is much easier to acknowledge the world you live in and seek constructive ways to change it than it is to practice denial and dream of a fantasy world you wished you lived in.

You may be in an organizational environment where you continually feel that others are trying to manipulate you or constantly trying to bend you to their will, for example, through intimidation. If this is the case, you may want to consider finding a new environment where there is an emphasis on sincere esprit de corps, where people want to empower others through cooperation and positive incentives rather than disempowering them through politics and pressure tactics.

Realize that a supportive and nurturing environment brings the most out of everyone. *Under no circumstances is it good for your mental health or professional development to stay in a work environment that seems more like a war zone than an organizational setting where you can grow and prosper.* I have acted as a career consultant to too many people who had to go through depression, frustration, and ulcers to realize finally that their working environment and the people in it were unhealthy for them. All the promotions in the world are not worth the price you will pay for working in such a negative climate.

WHO IS MOST SUSCEPTIBLE TO MANIPULATION TACTICS?

1. CORPORATE POLITICIANS

These individuals often go whichever way the wind blows. Since they tend to be motivated by personal gain, they don't want to lose out on any perceived opportunity. And they don't want to alienate anyone, even if this means being phony and insincere in order to further their self-serving goals. They often rely on whom they know instead of how well they do their job; this makes them prime candidates for the manipulation of others. They also tend to use manipulation tactics to get what they want. However, they tend not to resort to using a severe manipulation tactic such as intimidation because they know that the result may be that they will offend someone who might at another time be useful to their career.

2. NONASSERTIVE PEOPLE

Nonassertive individuals have a great deal of difficulty standing up for themselves. They tend to rely on other people's approval and are afraid of risky situations or of creating a conflict. As a result, they are easy prey for others who will manipulate them for personal advantage. Nonassertive types are also dishonest about their real feelings. They may go along with being manipulated while internally feeling angry or resentful. They tend to take on the role of victim or martyr and assume that they have no real choices or options.

3. AGGRESSIVE PEOPLE

These people tend to play "hard ball," and their favorite manipulation tactic is (you guessed it) intimidation. In a perverted way, they rationalize that they can get their way by intimidating others, especially nonassertive people, making this an excellent tactic for getting things done. They have little regard for other people's rights and tend to believe that the end justifies the means. They can have very short lives in an organization; they are subject to being affected by the same tactics they use. After all, as the Good Book says, "He who lives by the sword dies by the sword."

Eventually, their intimidating and aggressive style results in others gossiping about them, and this reflects badly on their image. Aggressive people find themselves sabotaged and subverted by others who get back by getting even. And eventually these aggressive individuals are overthrown or besieged with high turnover and morale problems with their staff.

4. THE POWERLESS

The powerless are a little bit like each of the first three types. They live in a constant state of fear and insecurity. They are the survivors in most organizations and will use whatever manipulation tactic seems most expedient. However, others in the organization soon become aware of the negative manipulation tactics of powerless people. Thus they are seen as even more powerless because of their reliance on such tactics.

WHO ISN'T SUSCEPTIBLE TO MANIPULATION TACTICS?

Assertive people are immune to manipulation tactics because they have the confidence and self-esteem they need to stand up for themselves. They accept responsibility for the many uncertain situations where they must act and face the consequences of their actions. They have confidence in themselves because they know that they will not be devastated permanently, no matter what the outcome. They have learned to use the skills and methods that will enable them to resolve successfully the many risky work situations they face. They realize that in an insecure world, the only security is to rely on high on-the-job performance to support their stands and actions. Above all, they know they are not victims. They make choices and exercise options. They are in control of their careers. And, not surprisingly, they are the most likely recipients of promotions, raises, and job satisfaction.

MANIPULATE OTHERS FOR WIN-WIN SITUATIONS

Here are some final thoughts that recap much of our discussion of manipulating positively for win-win outcomes. Keep these points in mind as a means for gaining the cooperation of others.

1. Be sincere.

2. Use self-interest benefits that are compelling, motivating, and relevant.

3. Suggest ramifications and implications for the other person's behavior.

4. Use positive consequences rather than flattery: "This project could bolster your confidence and show you that you can do a great job."

5. Use empathy instead of sympathy: "You can relate to the position I'm in. This cochairmanship could lead to a big promotion that I've been working for. It's just the kind you've been wanting, too."

6. Use responsibility instead of guilt: "We are colleagues who support and help each other, just as I helped you on your fourth quarter budgets."

7. Use consequences rather than intimidation: "Consider the possibility that the VP might think you are not company-minded. I believe it could count against you when he reviews your promotion recommendation."

8. Leave the other person a choice, once you've pointed out the ramifications and implications.

9. After that, respect the other's decision, as hard or as disadvantageous to you as it may seem. Though it may seem to be a difficult thing to do, it will be to your advantage in the long run.

chapter 6

Promoting Yourself with a Charismatic Leadership Style

CHARISMA: the special quality of presence that gives an individual influence or authority over large numbers of people; a special virtue that confers on the person an unusual ability for leadership; worthiness of veneration.

After talking to someone and being in his or her company for a while, you may have thought to yourself, "This person is very charismatic!" You may not have been able to describe the qualities that gave you that impression; you just had that feeling about this person. Charismatic individuals inspire trust, loyalty, and confidence. People are willing to cooperate and support those who are charismatic. History shows this to be true of generals, presidents, and even dictators.

Imagine how much more effective—and promotable—you could be if you were more charismatic. Being charismatic is a valuable quality in managing people and motivating them to produce positive results. Yet people quite often see this quality in others but not in themselves.

I want to state clearly that *you* can be a charismatic leader if you are willing to adopt some of the behaviors, actions, and styles of a charismatic person. A charismatic leadership image is produced through having attitudes and values that cause others to hold you in high esteem; by an outer appearance that includes your body language, personal grooming, and dress; by communicating in an empowering manner; and by the extraordinary achievements you perform on the job.

Leadership does not require that you have a certain number of people working for you. Any time you lead, guide, or direct anyone, you are exhibiting leadership. So don't discount the importance of developing a charismatic leadership style even if you have no aspirations to become a manager.

When you are perceived as being charismatic, you will feel more confident working with all types of personalities and in initiating actions that will advance your career. Your charismatic demeanor will result in others' having confidence in you, supporting you, and helping you to produce positive outcomes.

ARE CHARISMATIC LEADERS BORN OR MADE?

It is an easy excuse for people *not* to make an effort to improve themselves because they "just weren't born with" a particular talent or ability. This is especially true when you compare yourself to someone who does with great ease something you have to labor over. This, by the way, is one of the many reasons why comparing yourself to others can undermine your own personal growth. (If you have this habit, try comparing yourself to the many people who aren't half as skilled as you in a given area.)

My observations about the question of whether charismatic people are born or made are based on having personally trained and counseled over 25,000 business and professional people throughout the country. This experience convinces me of two things regarding charisma:

1. Yes, some people have a natural predisposition to act, look, and speak in ways that others perceive and acknowledge as being charismatic.

2. With coaching and a sincere effort, most people can act, look, and speak in ways that enhance their charismatic leadership style so that others will perceive them as being charismatic.

I say this because I believe it is time we took some of the mystique out of what is involved in being charismatic and stopped thinking that someone who has this quality comes along only once in a generation.

The benefits of being charismatic are fantastic in their efficacy. You can produce extraordinary results with people because they are so inspired and motivated by you that they are willing to give you more than 100 percent. Out of such a quality people will reach "in their gut" and give you performance and effort that couldn't be gotten if the motivation were merely money, a promotion, or time off. People who are motivated by charismatic leaders put heart and soul in what they do for them. We have seen this to be true historically with leaders such as Franklin D. Roosevelt and John F. Kennedy, as well as with dictators such as Adolf Hitler.

So when we talk about charisma, we are talking about one of the most potent and powerful of human qualities. And in your effort to enhance your on-the-job success, a charismatic style will be extremely valuable in motivating and leading people. You are a role model for others. They will show confidence, trust, and support for your undertakings. This ability to get the most from people puts you in upper management's spotlight and will aid you in winning promotions.

BEING CHARISMATIC: "MAY THE FORCE BE WITH YOU"

Now, I don't want to minimize what is involved in developing a charismatic image and reduce it to a list of foolproof things you need to do. It is more than that: Being charismatic involves personally caring about others, not just yourself. It involves your willingness to be sincere—that is, to be honest and have integrity, as opposed to conning people with a superficial image.

Consider people's responses to this question: "What is there about certain people that makes you say they are extremely charismatic?"

- "He really cares about people."
- "I can tell she has very high integrity."
- "His enthusiasm is contagious!"

- "His presence radiates love and respect for others."
- "She exudes so much confidence and ability that I would follow her anywhere."
- "I can feel his strength and dynamism."
- "She's a natural leader."
- "If you walked into a crowded room, within two minutes you would notice him."

WHAT MAKES A PERSON CHARISMATIC?

ATTITUDE AND VALUES

To be charismatic in the most positive sense (unlike Hitler, who was certainly charismatic but was also demented, with very twisted values), you have to examine your attitudes and values. Are they totally self-serving? Or do they serve everyone fairly?

People I have worked with who are charismatic truly embody many of the qualities that the list of reactions suggests: enthusiasm, caring, strength, confidence, integrity, and leadership. They don't tend to be money grabbers or backstabbers. Their motivation is win-win. They want others to share the benefits from what they are doing. They are not one-way users or self-serving opportunists. They are often very unselfish people, not "what do I get out of it?" types. While such charismatic people may be motivated by money, promotions, and power, they tend to have a higher calling, such as sincerely wanting everyone to succeed or benefit. They want to improve the quality of everyone's life, because their department, their company, and, indeed, their world works better when people are happy and fulfilled rather than excluded. Charismatic types want to make a difference!

Certainly, much of a charismatic person's motivation is based on self-interest and a desire to move people toward accomplishing their goals. So charismatic types do not need to be altruistic.

Like being powerful, being charismatic is neither good nor bad. However, we tend (rightly) to associate the positive elements that are a part of someone's charismatic leadership style. It is also essential to realize that it is not important whether a person really embodies the characteristics we associate with having charisma. *All that is necessary is that people perceive the individual as being charismatic.* This point is important in recognizing how it is possible to think that someone is charismatic, based on these qualities, only to find out later that he or she was really a con artist.

My intent is not to make charismatic types sound like saints or people of flawless virtue but to say that if these qualities strike you as corny or inappropriate for the business world, you may need an "attitude check." Contrary attitudes—jealousy, "me first," "I want to win at any cost," "nice guys finish last"—will ensure not only that you will be uncharismatic but that you will also most likely fail. At the very least, you will be unable to reach your full potential for winning promotions.

My experience in business and industry as an executive and a president, as well as a trainer and career consultant, tells me that a tremendous number of people need to take stock of their evaluations of what they want out of work and what they want from the people they work with. In fact, I personally believe that psychological counseling ought to be an integral part of every executive's working life. It is unfortunate that there are so many troubled, frustrated, and angry people in decision-making positions who affect the products and services we buy and the working lives of millions of people.

So in evaluating your own charismatic style, ask yourself what your real attitudes and values are. And consider any growth experiences, such as seminars and workshops, or therapeutic counseling that might help you discover unproductive values and attitudes that may be holding you back from promotions you are seeking.

If you aren't getting what you want in life, it may be because your misperception of yourself is getting in the way of your own success and achievement. Have the courage to examine what makes you tick and what really motivates you. Too many of us grow up with someone else's ideas of what should make us happy rather than our own.

This whole psychological mindset of having positive attitudes and values is at the heart of being a more charismatic person on the job. Because charisma makes you more promotable, your attitudes are well worth a serious self-examination.

EMPOWERING COMMUNICATION STYLE

To create a charismatic leadership style, it is extremely important that you are assertive, rather than aggressive or nonassertive. Assertiveness means that you communicate honestly and directly in an appropriate manner. Assertive people are emotionally honest; in other words, what they say on the outside is what they truly feel on the inside. We do not get double messages from assertive people. There is a congruency between their words and body language, and thus they show confidence and self-assurance in their communication style.

Assertive communicators have the highest credibility. They don't need to resort to indirect and manipulative tactics to get what they want. This is why they tend to get people's full cooperation and trust.

If you are aggressive in your communication style and you seek to vent your anger or put other people down, you will find that people are uncomfortable in your presence and will be reluctant to cooperate with you. In fact, people will attempt to sabotage you as a means of getting back and getting even.

If you are nonassertive, your communication style conveys a denial of your own rights, feelings, and opinions and a tendency to subordinate them to others in the hopes of avoiding conflict and confrontation. People will see you not only failing to stand up for yourself but also being unable to stand up for them, either. The result is that they will not respect you or willingly follow you. This leads to your being branded as unpromotable.

Being assertive lets others know that they can trust you. You aren't the corporate politician who speaks out of both sides of his mouth. You are willing to take a stand on issues. You stay with even unpopular positions. And if you have made a mistake, you are not afraid to take responsibility for making it. People believe that they will at least be treated fairly by an assertive person.

Assertive people inspire others because they know they have choices. They are not victims, as nonassertive types tend to be. Assertive people take full responsibility for themselves; they do not relinquish their power to others. Your assertiveness contributes to other people perceiving you as being charismatic. *When you practice being assertive, you practice being charismatic.*

EXTRAORDINARY ACHIEVEMENTS

One of the ways to increase your personal power, which is really what being charismatic is all about, is to make every effort to undertake tasks, volunteer for meaningful projects, and do exemplary work that will show others your talents—for example, turning around a losing product line, opening up a new branch office, increasing sales, reducing costs, or being the first to occupy a new position. These are ways to engage in activities that—if you are successful—will be considered extraordinary achievements. This can be risky, of course, but the rewards are great, often beyond your imagination. (For more on extraordinary activities, see Chapter 11.)

PUBLICITY AND VISIBILITY

People who are charismatic are in the public eye. It is next to impossible to be charismatic unless you are visible to others. This gives people an opportunity to have a sense of you and feel your presence. Chapter 9 discusses how you can publicize and make yourself visible in the organization through your achievements and accomplishments.

DRESSING CHARISMATICALLY

You have no doubt heard a great deal about dressing for success. Writers such as John T. Molloy, author of *Dress for Success* (Warner Books, 1976), deserve credit for emphasizing the importance of creating a favorable professional image through dress and appearance. There is no question that the right clothing can show you as someone who communicates authority, trust, and presence, all of which are charismatic qualities. The wrong clothing can show you to be unsavvy, out of step with the times, someone not to be taken too seriously, and certainly not someone whom others want to follow.

So there is no question that appropriate dress is very necessary in helping you feel charismatic as well as causing others to see you that way. Fortunately, there is plenty of information in books that will guide you on how to dress for success; there are image and fashion consultants who can literally scrutinize your closets and take you shopping; and there are color consultants who can help you pick the colors that look most appealing on you. Take advantage of advice offered by professionals in this area.

FIVE GOLDEN LAWS FOR YOUR CHARISMATIC LEADERSHIP STYLE

1. STAFF

Always surround yourself with the brightest, sharpest people you can find to perform a task or project or to be on your team. Only insecure, easily threatened executives concern themselves with being shown up by gifted staff members. Charismatic leaders instead harness the power and abilities of their staff or team members. Results-oriented staff can only make you look good because you are associated with their success. And you are credited with having chosen them and having empowered them to produce superior results. In addition, practicing this philosophy further establishes your charismatic image as a leader who is so secure in his own talent that he eagerly seeks out talented staff.

2. DELEGATE

The ability to delegate is one of the most essential qualities of a successful manager. Anyone can try to do it all alone. But by delegating, you give yourself more time to solve problems rather than fight fires, (i.e., constantly facing daily crises or emergencies), which is often the case for managers who believe that they must be directly involved in everything their staff does. By delegating, you will become "big-picture-oriented"—seeing your work in a larger perspective—rather than getting mired in all the small details that nondelegators get stuck in. As a manager, your job is not necessarily to do the work but to see that it gets done. Chapter 8 explores the many ways in which to delegate, which will help you attract the company's most talented people to your department. They will want to work for you once the word gets around that your staff is challenged and given responsibility.

3. PRIORITIZE

As part of your big-picture orientation, it is vital that you and your staff set priorities so that goals and objectives are agreed upon, acted on, and completed by a given deadline. By having your staff turn in priority schedules, you will begin to see who is doing what work. It will often help you to discover someone who is not producing the tangible results you feel are necessary. You can then decide what is the best way to help raise this person's productivity.

4. ACKNOWLEDGE

One of the secrets to motivating people you work with is to acknowledge them for a job well done. Most people in business do not get enough strokes or compliments that show appreciation for their excellent effort. Insecure executives worry about complimenting staff and coworkers out of some fear that the employees will get swelled heads and think they're too valuable. Some managers are afraid that compliments encourage employees to ask for raises.

This is as antiquated as subscribing to the motto "No news is good news." This implies that if you don't hear anything bad from your manager, it must mean you are doing a good job. This reminds me of the one spouse who says to the other, "You never tell me you love me." The other spouse replies, "Well, I married you, didn't I?"

The point is that nothing replaces the wonderful feeling of someone verbally acknowledging or complimenting you. This is why, whether you do it in person or through a memo, you can motivate people to produce greater results by letting them know you appreciate their best efforts—not just at annual salary reviews but on a regular basis throughout the year. This further establishes you as a leader and positions you for future promotions.

5. FOLLOW UP

The three things to keep in mind in properly following up are follow up, follow up, and more follow up. Whenever anything is to be done, establish a date for completion and write it down. Insist that others do the same. Much productivity is lost because of not following up *enough*. The only way you can tell whether you have followed up sufficiently is to have the results you intended to reap. This is especially true for sales people who must continually call up and call back prospects and customers. Show this same tenacity when you find that your telephone call has not been returned or when someone who promised to turn in a report has not done so. If you do this, you will find yourself getting your work done and will not be disappointed by others. It is the best way to feel in control and take responsibility for producing results. It will also go a long way toward giving you the charismatic reputation of someone who gets the job done!

IMAGE KILLERS

Many people kill any chance of being charismatic or being perceived as such because they seem to be hard at work ruining their own image. There are a number of image killers to be on the lookout for:

1. Gossiping	5. Messy office
2. Excessive anger	6. Nervous behavior
3. Low energy projection	7. Being out of fashion
4. Guilt by association	8. Improper handshake

Check this list and if you are guilty of any of these, you are working directly against a charismatic leadership style. Desist immediately!

1. GOSSIPING

"Never gossip, always listen" is a motto an old colleague used to say. Actually, even listening to gossip can detract from the charismatic image you want to project. So be careful not to devote too much of your time to such chat. You may think, "Well, it's the other person who is talking, not me. I am just one of the group who is here." That is precisely the problem: People see you as being there, listening. It is similar to not being willing to rob the bank but deciding that you'll wait in your bank robber friend's car until he is finished. Guess what? That makes you an accessory to the crime. So don't aid and abet a gossip.

Instead, encourage people to communicate their differences or conflicts directly to the person they are gossiping about. I find it very effective to deter gossips by pointing out why their gossiping is not in their self-interest. For example, I may say to Gus the Gossip: "Gus, I know you may have no intention of gossiping about Alex, and yet it sounds that way. And the result is that I believe it undermines your image of being an up-front and direct person who says what's on his mind. I suggest you take this matter up face to face with Alex."

Gossips are not charismatic. After all, if they are gossiping about one person today, tomorrow they may be gossiping about *you*. That is always the underlying fear of people who see you gossiping.

2. EXCESSIVE ANGER

Have you ever noticed how angry some people get when you disagree with them about something at work? Or how some people get inordinately upset over what seems to be a rather small mistake? There may be an incongruity in their anger—that is, their anger is out of proportion to whatever they are angry about. The anger that is being projected in the current situation may actually have its origins in a previous situation in which they could not express their feelings directly and completely. Such people are really angry about something else.

If you are prone to excessive or incongruent anger (where the anger "doesn't fit the crime"), you will find that people will avoid you, won't work well with you, will feel uncomfortable around you, will sabotage you to get back and get even, will gossip about you, and may even overthrow you as they do dictators, despots, and tyrants.

If you find that you are experiencing excessive anger, you may have some unresolved psychological issues that you should seek immediately to resolve. Next time you become very angry, ask yourself, "Do my anger and upset match the situation that made me angry?" I have heard executives complain and get almost violent about their spouses' habits (say, leaving the cap off the toothpaste or not putting the toilet seat down). You don't have to be Sigmund Freud to know that their excessive anger is out of proportion to their complaint. Something else is bothering them.

If you experience this, consider getting professional help by going to a psychologist or therapist. This anger problem is robbing you of your charisma, among other important things. It won't just go away in time.

3. LOW-ENERGY PROJECTION

Many people show their enthusiasm in a low-key manner. That's their style. However, many people are afraid to show their enthusiasm at all, because if something goes wrong with their idea or project, they will be held responsible, and all the world (so they reason) will remember their enthusiasm. So they are often very guarded about how well their ideas will work or what results to expect. They often play the CYA (cover your ass) game. Basically, they are afraid things may not work and may even result in failure, so it's best to play it safe and conservative.

Unfortunately, this low-energy posture ensures that no one's expectations will be too high. However, people who have to work with low-energy types find that their enthusiasm is greeted with icy caution. Thus they too can become low-energy and find their original enthusiasm waning. Low energy is the antithesis of charisma, because charismatic people are alive with enthusiasm about their ideas and work, and they aren't afraid to let people know it. Sure, it's a risk to declare your interest and excitement about an idea or project. But that enthusiastic and confident style is what makes a charismatic person's attitude so infectious in a group or organization.

Low energy projection indicates caution and conservatism to others. When that is appropriate, fine. When it is a general operating style, however, it is not charismatic. It is motivated out of fear of failure.

To break the low-energy-projection pattern, suggest ideas and projects that you can endorse wholeheartedly and involve others in. Of course, even great ideas are filled with risks. People want to work with leaders who have conviction and strongly believe in what they are saying.

4. GUILT BY ASSOCIATION

The choice is always yours to associate with whomever you want to in your personal life. And it is also yours at work. Unfortunately, at work some terrible consequences can come out of your associations with the "wrong kind" of people. In fact, this is precisely where hidden agendas can come into play because all the experience, expertise, and competence can count for naught if the higher-ups in the organization prejudge you because of the company you keep. And make no mistake, they can and they do. You can be the loser. Note the following examples:

• Bud is one of the new, bright managers. He's very friendly, especially to a number of the different executives' secretaries. He tries to socialize with them and is often seen taking them to lunch.

• Marlene is one of the few executive women in the organization. The only other women are clerical staff. Marlene tends to seek the others out for informal companionship at lunch. She feels more comfortable with them, because they are women, than she does in trying to break into the company's "old boy network" filled with middle and upper-level managers.

• Manuel is the company's only Hispanic executive. He feels much more comfortable getting together with other Hispanics in the company. The fact that they are engaged in very low level positions in the company doesn't bother him. He shares a certain rapport with them that he doesn't have with most of the stuffy executives in his accounting department.

• Thomas makes a relatively good salary, yet he figures, "Why not save a few bucks and 'brown bag' it in the employee cafeteria?" even though none of the other executives and managers eat there, let alone bring their lunch to work.

• Betty enjoys getting together with Tim and Audrey for lunch on a regular basis. Tim has been disciplined on several occasions for tardiness and insubordination. Audrey has been in her position for over six years, and she has let everyone know that she has no interest in being promoted.

Bud, Marlene, Manuel, Thomas, and Betty have one thing in common: They may be "guilty by association." Of what? Of being identified with the negative qualities and behaviors of their colleagues.

Now, you may be thinking, "No one is going to tell me whom I can have for a friend or colleague!" You're right. And probably no one will. But in many organizations, there is a hidden agenda that says, "Don't associate with the wrong kind of people if you want to be promoted in this company."

You must know the consequences of your behavior if you are dedicated to rising in your organization. If you aren't happy with the unfairness of such hidden rules, perhaps you can change them when you are in a position to do so. First get into that position. You can't do that if people discriminate in such a way. And you will certainly not accumulate any charismatic points by such associations.

Let's take a closer look at the perceptions that each of these people's associations foster.

Bud. What are the chances of Bud being considered as a serious prospect for weighty responsibility when he focuses such obvious effort on being the office Romeo, attempting to date all the secretaries? Bud's actions bother other executives, who find it hard to meet with him to discuss business over lunch because he is always tied up with someone else. His behavior raises questions about his priorities and the sincerity of his interest in being a "company man" instead of a "company stud." The result is that Bud is not seriously considered for promotions.

Marlene. Marlene is in a difficult position because she is lonely when she doesn't have a number of colleagues to get together with over lunch and socialize. But rather than risk initiating lunch invitations with male executives, she would prefer to be comfortable, even if it means fraternizing exclusively with lower-level females in the clerical department. Marlene is a staff executive who should be "socializing up," not down.

This is, in effect, what you do when you spend an inordinate amount of time at lunch and at after-work cocktails with people at hierarchal levels far lower than yours. My saying this has nothing to do with casting any aspersions on clerical staff. I am a firm believer that most of these professionals have never gotten the credit they deserve for the tremendous asset they are to their organizations. What I am referring to is the *perceptions of others* that may significantly affect your upward mobility and your prospects for future promotional opportunities.

Many higher-ups evaluate your readiness for higher leadership by the company you keep. This is not to say that Marlene should *never* have lunch with a secretary. It is just that it should be an occasional get-together, not a continual practice and not a crutch to avoid getting together with other executives. Marlene's regular companionship with her clerical friends shows management that she is unable to establish important relationships with her peers and superiors.

Manuel. Manuel, too, would rather seek the company of fellow Hispanics because it is comfortable. In his case, he is proud of his management position, even though he far outranks his friends in the company. His associating with others in his own ethnic group only serves to fuel the fires of people who stereotype ethnic groups such as his, reinforcing the beliefs that they are clannish and not upwardly mobile. Manuel can leave some time for his buddies but should concentrate on developing relationships with executives at and above his level. It will help him get known and get greater cooperation to perform his job well and advance his career.

Thomas. Thomas is penny-wise and pound-foolish. In the short run, he may be saving a few dollars bringing his lunch, but he is showing others that he's a "nickel-and-dimer"—someone who thinks small. Thomas should be concentrating on getting together and forming relationships with others at lunch where such meetings could result in personal support, ideas, and information that in the long run could reap him great monetary rewards. His lunches with the right people could be worth thousands of dollars to his career.

Let me expand on this point about lunching with lower-level employees in order to save money. I know some readers will indignantly say, "What's wrong with trying to save a few bucks?" Nothing! But why not concentrate on ways that will result in making big bucks? Let's say that Thomas makes $26,000 a year. Let's say that the employees who typically brown-bag it make a salary in the range of $12,000 to $18,000 per year. At their salary level, it is perhaps appropriate for them to save money and bring their lunch. But for Thomas, doing the same thing sends a message to his fellow and more senior executives that he must be really broke, that he's so small-time he can't even afford a sandwich in a restaurant.

Thomas loses not only the esteem of the other executives but also the money-making opportunities that would accrue to him if he went out with them. Eating lunches out with more upwardly mobile executives could result in his hearing about investment tips, privileged information about the company, promotional opportunities in the company, and tips on how to negotiate for higher salaries or perks with the company.

The moral is to "socialize up" in your company at lunch and at other informal get-togethers. The information you will gather will be worth more than any money you could save taking the "brown bag" route. And, of course, you must be sensitive to the hidden agendas in your company, which might suggest that anyone who brings lunch and eats it in the company cafeteria is either paid by the hour or not going anywhere in the company.

Betty. Betty is insensitive to the fact that the managers who have disciplined Tim—as well as anyone who knows of Tim's disciplinary problems—are going to have a rather jaundiced view of Betty: guilt by association. People know you by the company you keep. To make matters worse, Audrey may be thought of as doing her job well, but the entire management group knows that she lacks any real ambition and is going nowhere in the company. Are these people Betty's role models? Again, while she may want to get together with them occasionally, she is doing what is comfortable rather than developing other relationships that would draw primary attention away from her friendships with Tim and Audrey.

Since the thought of anyone telling you whom to eat with may be so emotionally charged, let me repeat: Eat with whomever you want. Just be aware of the fact that in the real world, there are consequences related to whom you fraternize with that may affect your success and upward mobility in your organization. Other people's perception of you impacts on your success and promotability in the organization. If you don't believe this, you are in for a rude awakening!

So, enjoy being with whomever you want to be with at work. But try not to use familiar relationships as a crutch to avoid initiating relationships with other peers and higher-ups. Initiating new friendships and social relationships is also a risk—but one worth taking. Remember that there are great benefits to broadening your network of contacts and influentials in your organization. This is a prime way of hearing about promotional opportunities.

5. MESSY OFFICE

I once heard an executive brag about how he liked the fact that his office was messy: "After all," he would exclaim, "everyone can see how damn busy I am." He was very wrong. All people could see in his office was that he was disorganized and unable to prioritize his work. There was absolutely nothing about him or his office that inspired charisma.

Neatness and order inspire confidence and a sense that you have everything under control. This gives you charisma points. It makes a favorable impression on anyone who passes by or stops in your office. A good habit to form for yourself and with your staff is never to leave your office in a messy state. Before leaving, clear everything off your desk and sort it, file it, put it away.

6. NERVOUS BEHAVIOR

Nervous tics detract from your charismatic leadership image. They make other people uncomfortable and even anxious about you. If you fidget, bite your lip, twirl your hair, fiddle with your earring, stick your hands in your pockets, or pick at your fingernails, you are detracting from your image. Appearing nervous, unsettled, and perhaps out of control sends a message about you that will cause others to have less confidence in you and what you do. People who are charismatic generally show a relaxed presence. They may also show a high-energy side, but this is quite different from nervous behavior, which suggests upset or frustration.

7. BEING OUT OF FASHION

We have talked about dressing for success. However, a more subtle variation in your dressing can rob you of any hope of being perceived as charismatic: being out of fashion. If you do not look contemporary, you are perceived as being out of tune with the times or unaware of what is going on around you. This is evident with people who wear wide ties when the style is narrow ties or who wear bell-bottom slacks when straight-leg slacks are in.

You don't have to make yourself crazy worrying about what is the hottest designer label or spend all your paycheck on the most current fashion, but don't go to the extreme of being out of fashion. At least pay attention to fashion trends. By doing so, you signal to others that you are in tune with the times. If you expect to win promotions, people have to be able to relate to you. They can't if your clothes make you look like a throwback to a different era.

8. IMPROPER HANDSHAKE

You can tell a great deal about a person by the way he shakes hands with you. Leonard gives a "fish shake": His fingers come together limply when he shakes hands with people. This does not inspire any sense of his being charismatic. In fact, people often think of him as being a wimp. They have no confidence in him as someone who could stand up for himself—let alone others. His handshake is working against his future promotions.

Phyllis shakes hands with her fingers pointing down to the ground, presenting the back of her hand to people she shakes hands with. I call this the "contessa shake." The result, especially with men she shakes hands with, is that they don't know whether to kiss her hand or shake it. Instead, it communicates fragility and delicacy—not prime qualities in a future manager.

A solid handshake inspires confidence and gives you presence. Now there is no need to shake hands in a way where you break the other person's fingers in an effort to show how macho you are. The key is that a good, firm handshake is part of a charismatic demeanor. As the commercial says: "Don't leave home without it."

Each of these image killers can detract from your overall charismatic image. Charisma is made up of both the tangible (extraordinary achievements and outer style) and the intangible (assertive communication style).

This reminds me of a story that makes this point: A rabbi and a priest are seated ringside at a boxing match. They are both watching the fighter in front of them as he makes the sign of the cross before the fight begins. The rabbi excitedly looks over toward the priest and says, "Father, Father, what does that mean?" The priest replies, "Not a damn thing if he can't fight."

Moral: To be charismatic, style is not enough. You need to produce results.

chapter 7

Using Your Manager and Your Staff to Win Promotions

There is no question that your relationship with your manager is the most important relationship you will have at work. It directly affects your job success or failure, as well as your future promotability. And almost as important is the relationship you have with your staff, because they can either support you as a rising star in the organization or contribute to your downfall. Even if you don't have a staff working for you now, you may have one working for you in the future. Either way, much of what will be discussed in this chapter regarding staff is equally pertinent to your relationships with your coworkers.

It amazes me that in most colleges and even inside most organizations, little education or training is made available on establishing productive and satisfying relationships with our manager, staff, and coworkers. Everyone is just expected to get along and to work things out. Yet in the real world, most of the problems people encounter can be traced to poor or uncooperative working relationships with others.

In personal relationships with friends and loved ones, we can seek out a therapist or counselor to discuss any problems or disharmony. But that option is generally not available in the work setting. In fact, many managers will (fairly or unfairly) use their anointed power and offer you the door "if you don't like the way we do things around here."

So it is imperative, before you work for someone or with others, that you consciously consider a number of factors that will have a direct bearing on whether you are destined for a productive relationship and support for the future promotions you want. While there are no guarantees, to be sure, you can at least increase the odds of having a good relationship, if not a great relationship, by carefully reading the material in this chapter. Your career and promotability will depend on this special attention.

YOUR MANAGER

Probably the most sacred and important relationship you will have in the world of work is with your manager. Your manager can usually either make you or break you. Since most organizations still abide by the chain-of-command structure modeled after the military, there is a great deal of respect and deference invested in your manager as your leader. It may seem scary, but your manager has incredible power over your future and success in your organization. It is nearly impossible to have a successful climb to the top without having an excellent working relationship with your manager.

A good relationship with your manager can mean big raises and perks, challenging responsibilities, recognition and acknowledgment of your best efforts, exposure and visibility to high-ranking executives, and exciting promotional opportunities—perhaps even a special mentorship relationship.

A bad relationship with your manager can mean small and infrequent raises, unchallenging and routine work, little cooperation or recognition, even for work that is well done, low visibility or exposure to important decision-making individuals in the organization, a stagnated career with few promotional opportunities, and very little personal attention beyond what is absolutely necessary.

If this seems like a shocking contrast or a black-and-white perception, let me assure you that it is very real. One of the main problems that has brought hundreds of otherwise competent professionals into my office for career consultations is a frustrating or stifling relationship with their manager. Some individuals don't even realize that this is the root problem—why they are not getting acknowledgment and recognition from their organization for their hard work, why they seem to have to fight to get even a small raise, why they never feel challenged by their work responsibilities, or why they are not given fair consideration for promotional opportunities. It all goes back to their relationship with their manager.

Certainly one of the biggest decisions you will make in your career is deciding whether to take a job and work with a particular manager who probably doesn't know you very well or has little experience with you. And let me assure you that, just like the old adage "You don't know someone until you live with him," this is especially true once you decide to work for your manager. This is true even if you think you know your new manager because, for example, you worked in another department and therefore had some dealings with that manager before. Or you may feel secure because you have heard from others that "he's a great guy" or "she's a real people person."

YOU AND YOUR MANAGER:
A MAIL-ORDER MARRIAGE

Positive comments from others may be reassuring, but usually such indirect experience or general comments are superficial. Most important, they leave out the one factor that you *can't* know the answer to: discovering the kind of chemistry your personalities will produce, either a healthy, supportive relationship or a stagnating or even destructive one. In many ways, it is just like a marriage—a mail-order marriage. You don't really know each other until you meet and "marry"—that is, take the position and begin working together. This is truly risky. Just like any marriage, your working relationship with your manager is often filled with great expectations and the highest and most honorable intentions.

But this marriage doesn't even start out as one of equals. You are the subordinate, and you will have to earn your manager's respect and high regard. If you do, this could be one of the most dynamic and valuable relationships in your career and, indeed, your life.

HOW TO DETECT A BAD RELATIONSHIP

Your relationship with your manager may vary from the extremes of being excellent or destructive. Obviously, when you have an excellent relationship, you and your manager support each other and you are challenged in your work and rewarded for high performance. Promotional opportunities are inevitable.

Other types of relationships are usually tolerable, but two—the destructive and the stagnating—are the kiss of death.

THE DESTRUCTIVE RELATIONSHIP

In a destructive relationship with your manager, you do not get the acknowledgment and raises or consideration for promotional opportunities that you would like. However, what is good about this extreme is that by experiencing this kind of treatment and disregard by your manager, you are being told, perhaps in a rather obvious manner, that you are not going anywhere in your organization. If you're smart, you'll take the hint and find yourself another organization to work for. If you don't, you may very well be forced to do so.

Be sensitive to the signs of a poor relationship:

- Continually doing routine work

- Not being assigned to challenging new projects

- No raises or minimal cost-of-living increases

- Having more junior staff outpace you in responsibilities and salary increases

- Being continually passed by for promotional opportunities

You can clearly see that you have no future in this organization. Your talents and abilities are not appreciated or acknowledged. This may be based on the truth that you are not performing in a competent manner. But it is also possible that the cause is a poor relationship with your manager. *If you find yourself in this kind of destructive relationship, take action and go elsewhere.*

THE STAGNATING RELATIONSHIP

In a destructive relationship with a manager, at least it is clear what you should do: leave. A stagnating employee-manager relationship, however, is not so clear-cut. Your manager does not regard you at either extreme. As the expression goes, you are neither fish nor fowl.

Instead, your manager thinks of you as "good enough to be on the team" but not good enough to "play regularly." This is much like an infielder on a baseball team who is considered to be a good journeyman player. Such players would appear successful if you look at the number of years they are on the team. However, if you look more closely, you will see that they are used as substitutes, for example, when a regular player gets hurt and can't play for a while. Such journeymen may excel in a particular area, such as hitting, but not in other areas, such as fielding and running. They are not good enough to play regularly. They are considered reliable players to be used strictly in reserve—never as first string.

This is precisely what happens to many individuals at work who are in this stagnating role, where they just don't seem to be regarded as upper-management material or even suitable for the next promotional level. Yet they are worthwhile employees, as long as they don't demand responsibilities they are not considered suited for, large raises that would seem inappropriate, promotional opportunities they are not deemed qualified for.

Most people are familiar with this journeyman type of individual, who has been in a position for a long time and whose career seems to be going nowhere. Such individuals hang on to the illusion that they will one day get the recognition, financial rewards, and promotions they believe they deserve. Some of these stagnating types are, like the veteran journeyman in baseball, happy just to be on the team, even if they don't get to play in the game every day.

For some, though, the illusion occurs when they confuse the way they would like to be regarded with the reality of how they really are regarded by their manager and their organization. I recall one such individual, Vic, who was always looking to be recognized and considered for more challenging opportunities. One day he came into my office and told me that he was asked by his manager to fill in for a coworker, Don (who was regarded as a rising star in the department). Vic was told to begin gathering statistics and data for a special report normally done by Don. Vic erroneously saw this as his being "chosen" for this special responsibility. In reality his manager had no choice on this particular occasion but to delegate this work to Vic so that the report would be in process and no time would be lost due to Don's absence. Don was the one who always did this report; that was the manager's choice.

If you are in a stagnating relationship where there is some appearance or even the illusion that you are well regarded and have a bright future, you must make an honest assessment of how you are really regarded by your manager. Otherwise, you will set yourself up for disappointment and frustration when you finally realize that your future is playing second string for your manager.

Here are some signs of a stagnating relationship with your manager:

- Continual reassignment to the same kind of work while peers at your experience level are offered more challenging assignments
- Being left out of important meetings and special events that fast-track peers are invited to
- Not being given exposure and visibility to high-ranking individuals that other staff are encouraged to interface with
- Not being given the same information about plans, policies, and projects that other coworkers are informed of
- Finding out that your salary raises are continually less than those of peers or that peers are getting perks that you aren't
- Observing that peers are given serious consideration for promotions while you are only given lip service

There are many indicators that will validate your nagging suspicion that you are not perceived by your manager as being one of the rising stars on the team and that in reality your job may be secure, but you may have little chance for upward mobility or will move at a much slower pace than you had planned. You will want to pay serious attention to your ten-year career plan (discussed in Chapter 16) so that you can keep yourself on target and achieve your goals.

CAN YOU CHANGE YOUR RELATIONSHIP WITH YOUR MANAGER?

Can a bad relationship change enough to become dynamic or even positive? It is unlikely. My own observation, based on years of working inside different organizations and counseling many professionals, is that only through extraordinary achievement can a destructive or stagnating relationship be transformed.

It is much easier for managers to collect evidence that supports their original perception, whatever that may be, than to be open to viewing an employee in a new light. Of course, whatever your manager's perception is at first, transforming the relationship from good to great, from destructive to stagnating, or from stagnating to dynamic must be backed up by solid and consistently high performance and results. The problem, again, is the way high performance and results are perceived.

Consider our baseball journeyman example. If the journeyman player substitutes and plays a great game (for example, wins the game with a late-inning home run), the manager's perception may only be, "He did just what we would expect from him by filling in and doing a great job while our regular player was out." This is a much more common view than the manager's having a brand-new perception because of the great game that the journeyman played. If you are regarded as a journeyman player, it may take lots and lots of extraordinary success to shake your manager's existing perception of you.

Ultimately, it is your responsibility to assess the kind of relationship you have with your manager and where it seems to be headed. Use time limits in doing so. Also consider some of the tangible signs that have already been mentioned in making an objective analysis in terms of the real relationship you share. You will want to have candid discussions with your manager about his or her perception of you, which should include discussion of the signs you observe, so that your final assessment will be accurate.

THE TWO MOST IMPORTANT CRITERIA FOR GREAT MANAGERS

You can find many books that discuss in intricate detail all the qualities and traits of high-performing managers. However, if I had to isolate the two most important qualities that the best managers had in common, they would be that managers delegate effectively and that they staff their department with the best talent they can find.

DELEGATING

Chapter 8 goes into great detail about how to delegate to and empower others. You will want to look for (and be) a manager whom you feel certain has a record of wanting to share responsibilities with staff. In delegating, a good manager can groom staff for higher leadership experience by assigning them meaningful and challenging projects. And in the process the manager will have more time to solve problems instead of fighting fires (i.e., going from crisis to crisis).

Be leery of managers who are overly detail-minded to the point where their need for control and their own personal fears of failing cause them not to delegate responsibilities to their staff. They seem to want to do it themselves or constantly look over their subordinates' shoulder.

By choosing a manager who believes in the importance of delegating and giving staff responsible work, you can count on the fact that you will have a chance to grow and demonstrate your talents and abilities. This opportunity is vital to your career advancement.

STAFFING

The best managers, just like professional baseball scouts, recruit the most talented players for their team. Insecure and threatened managers are too worried about being upstaged or fear that a bright staff person may make them look bad. Thus they tend to become competitive with some of their more gifted staff. Effective managers, by contrast, find it challenging and rewarding to find ways to harness the ambitions and abilities of talented members of their team.

If you work for a manager who is a great scout at staffing the department with high-potential people like yourself, you will reap the dividends of being stimulated by other high-achieving, ambitious, and brilliant minds. Not only can these coworkers stimulate you, but they can also be a source of learning and further development of your own expertise. In many cases, working with other goal-oriented people helps to prevent the stagnancy that comes with dull, unambitious people. Self-confident, high-producing people create a competitive environment that, when properly monitored by a sensitive manager, is healthy and motivating.

Also remember that excellent team players make the whole team look good. I know there are many fast-track types who would prefer no competition so that they could be singled out as stars. However, this small benefit is far outweighed by their losing the stimulation provided by working with superstar coworkers. Let's face it, if the only way you can look good is by playing with average teammates, you are going to be in for a rude awakening when you get into an organization where the managers have consistently staffed their departments with high-caliber individuals. Get used to playing with the best and you will be the best. If you play with less than the best, you'll always wonder how you would have performed among really challenging competition.

SEVEN QUESTIONS TO ASK BEFORE CHOOSING A MANAGER TO WORK FOR

Most people take very little responsibility for choosing the manager they work for. They will say, "What choice did I have? Even though I didn't particularly care for his style, he's the one I'm stuck having to work for if I accept the promotion."

Ironically, you might be much better off in the long run to pass up a promotional opportunity if in doing so you would avoid having to work for a manager whose uninspiring leadership style or powerless image might severely affect your ability to produce results on the job or hamper your future upward mobility in the organization.

Most people who are offered promotions do very little evaluation of the people they will be working for. They accept the position with little consideration, almost as if this important analysis had no consequences to their career. Some people have a short-run attitude of "Who cares? As long as I get a promotion, a title, and more money." This is amateur thinking and the worst kind of reckless risk taking. You may be playing a form of organizational Russian roulette by not carefully weighing the considerations. I have seen executives who were so excited about accepting a new position that they didn't even realize that they had just "promoted themselves to fail."

The point I want to make is *not* that you're taking your life into your hands by accepting a new position where you will work for a manager you may not know too well. However, you must consider the kind of manager you will be working for and whether this individual possesses some of the qualities that are required if you expect to get the challenging responsibilities you want, the raises you expect for producing superior results, and the promotional opportunities for the higher leadership positions you seek.

To do otherwise is very shortsighted. You wouldn't buy a used car or a home without having it thoroughly checked out to make sure that everything is in good working order. After all, you are investing a lot of money. Isn't your career, the promotions that you are seeking, worth that same scrutiny?

Begin by adopting a new mindset: You will choose whether or not you want to accept a promotion by carefully scrutinizing whom you will work for. In accepting a promotion, you ordinarily choose to accept a position based on such factors as the responsibilities of the new position, whether it involves traveling or relocation, and how much money is being offered. Why not check out the most important of all factors, the manager you will report to?

Here are questions in seven significant areas that you should answer when evaluating the kind of manager who is most likely to support you; give you challenging responsibilities, substantial raises, and promotions; and be gratifying and fulfilling to work for. Use the questions to evaluate your prospective manager or your current manager. Record your own impressions and ask other people their perceptions of this manager in each of these seven areas.

1. PROMOTIONS

Is your manager able to get desirable promotional opportunities for talented staff? Have many of his former staff been promoted to higher-level positions? Does he go to bat for talented staff in an effort to secure promotions? Or is he just concerned with keeping a stagnant group of staff whose sole destiny is to continue to work in that department and perpetuate his dynasty?

2. PERSONAL POWER

Will your manager intercede on your behalf if you have a problem or are in trouble with someone in the organization? Will she come to your rescue? For example, if you make a mistake, does your manager have enough power and influence to smooth any ruffled feathers? Or is she likely to disavow any concern for you at the first sign of trouble or conflict?

3. ORGANIZATIONAL CLOUT

Can your manager accomplish results above and beyond the conventional in the organization? For example, if expenditures are needed beyond what is budgeted, can he obtain them? This clout can save you a great deal of frustration when you know that you can't accomplish a certain task unless sufficient "beyond the budget" funds are available. Or, if you need a new item added to a meeting agenda, does your manager have the influence with higher-ups to get this done so that you will be heard?

4. CONTACTS AND RAPPORT

Does your manager have good connections with high-ranking executives, either formally or informally? Does he get invited to social events that include mingling with the high-echelon executives? Does your manager have a good rapport with key managers and influentials in other departments? Such contacts can help you cut through red tape when you need to get things done.

5. AWARENESS

Is your manager informed of key decisions and major policy shifts? Is she in the know, formally or informally? Does she have a good source of information through the grapevine? Is she savvy to what is going on politically?

6. CHARISMATIC LEADERSHIP

Is your manager considered a bona fide leader, someone who has charisma and a bright future in the organization? Will credibility accrue to you from being a member of his team? Or does he have a recognized expertise that will benefit you? Will you be perceived as an heir apparent?

7. COOPERATION AND LIKABILITY

Do people like your manager? Do they seem to willingly cooperate with her, even if there is no line relationship? Do people and departments seem to go out of their way to help and support your department because of their high regard for your manager? Or do people grimace at the mere mention of her name?

It is not necessary that you get yeses in all seven areas for you to choose to work for a particular manager. However, each set of questions covers vital information that you will want to consider in your decision to work for him. An accurate assessment can make the difference between career stagnation and career momentum.

DETERMINING YOUR MANAGER'S ATTITUDES AND FEELINGS TOWARD YOU

Important as it is to consider your own and other people's perceptions of a new or current manager, it is just as important to have face-to-face discussions. I suggest that you actually conduct an interview to get your manager's views on all areas affecting you personally in order to make an intelligent assessment of how challenged, fulfilled, and financially prosperous you can expect to be as this person's subordinate.

Whatever you do, do not use the "stick your head in the sand" approach and decide that it would be better not to broach certain topics. If there is potential for a problem, clash, disagreement, or difference in how your talents and future are perceived, let it be known now, not after you have committed to working for this person.

There are two main purposes in interviewing your manager. First, discover his general attitudes and philosophy on areas of importance to you, such as delegating or merit raises. Second, bring to light your manager's attitudes, feelings, and perceptions about you in particular.

Look for congruency between your manager's general attitude toward an area and his perception of you in relationship to that area. For example, an incongruity would occur if your manager told you that he believed strongly in delegating and then warned you not to expect to work on your own because you lack enough knowledge of the organization. You are on notice that you should not expect to be delegated to, despite his general belief in the importance of delegating.

With this in mind, let's take a closer look at key areas you will want to cover when you interview your manager.

RESPONSIBILITIES

Does this manager believe that it is important for staff to be exposed to many areas of work or just to specialize in areas they have particular talents in? Can you expect your work to be filled with variety, or will it settle down to a general routine? Will responsibilities be shared, or can you expect to be working alone a great deal?

Which kinds of responsibilities does your manager believe should be delegated to staff at your level of expertise? How long will it be before you can be assigned more important or challenging work? How much personal assistance and direction does he like to offer staff? Does he believe in letting you off on your own without too much structure? This is your chance to ask your manager which responsibilities you may be involved in over the short, medium, and long term. The answers you get will give you a strong indication of whether you can expect to be challenged and stimulated or bored and stagnating.

SALARY

Find out what your manager's attitudes are toward salaries, salary increases, and perks for people in general and for you in particular.

Nothing is more frustrating than working for a manager who is cheap or who has very traditional attitudes and will not approve increases because "you're already making pretty good money compared to what I got when I was your age." Or you may find out that your manager is not personally motivated by money and assumes then that you aren't either.

Recently I counseled a woman who had a position as director of marketing for an old, established engineering firm. During her two years of working there, she had received lots of compliments on her superior performance but had obtained only modest raises. So she confronted the partner in the firm who reviewed her salary. She said that she had been disappointed in the size of her raises. He told her that since she was married and her husband had a great job, she didn't need to be making any more money.

She was shocked, despite the fact that her manager had made a number of very telling remarks regarding his chauvinistic attitudes toward women. He couldn't accept a woman's being equal to a man and had twice commented that her salary was excellent, "especially for a woman." Such remarks should have put her on notice as to what she could expect with regard to the size of future raises.

In another instance, I once had a discussion with a prospective employer about salary for a job I was considering. He asked me what kind of money I hoped to be making in the next five years. When I told him, he almost choked! He said that he had been with the company for over 20 years and was still not making anywhere near that amount. He almost reprimanded me for having such high aspirations. As he told me to lower my sights, I got the distinct feeling that he would project his low-salary attitudes on me. Since his experience and expectations were so low, it was bound to affect the kind of money I could expect to make working for him.

These situations should help make the point clear that your manager's attitudes toward money will directly affect how much or how little you make—often with little relation to what the company can really afford. So don't be afraid to ask direct questions about getting top money for high performance. Don't ever apologize or minimize how much you "like money and all the wonderful things it can buy."

As I discussed in my book *How to Ask for a Raise Without Getting Fired* (Harper & Row, 1980), giving raises is very subjective. Don't underplay your desire for money. If you give your manager the impression that money is OK but what really motivates you is being fulfilled on the job, you may find that your manager will give you lots of opportunities to be fulfilled at the expense of receiving modest salary increases for your best efforts.

PROMOTIONS

It is important that you find out how your manager sees your future. Find out if he is willing to give you informal assessments on your readiness for promotions other than annual reviews. When is it likely and reasonable to expect a promotion? Some managers are very rigid and have already decided that no matter how competent you are, you have got to be in a position "for at least two years" before they will consider recommending you. By contrast, an intelligent manager can give you the typical range of time that others who are in your position stayed before being promoted to another position.

Part of being groomed for a promotion usually involves being given exposure and visibility to others, especially powerful or high-ranking individuals. Having favorably impressed these influentials, you are more likely to be promoted, and your promotion will receive the support and blessings of these higher-ups. If you are working for a manager who wants all the credit or is insecure that mistakes you make in front of others will reflect badly on him, you may find that your visibility will be very limited, making it more difficult for you to receive a promotion.

Also ask your manager how many people have been promoted in the department. Find out how long current staff have been working for this manager. You will want to make sure that working for this person is not a "sentence to Devil's Island" where you can expect to spend the rest of your organizational life.

LEAVING A BAD MANAGER RELATIONSHIP

After making an assessment of a manager, it is important to be realistic and honest with yourself. If a prospective manager doesn't measure up, don't accept the job. Likewise, if you have a stagnating or destructive relationship with your manager or are aware that your stock is pretty low in his eyes, you have three options:

1. Get Out!
2. Get Out!
3. Get Out!

A bad relationship—whether because of a personality clash, a lack of appreciation, or any other legitimate reason—must be cut out as if it were a cancer. Even if it has taken years to discover that your relationship or your manager's attitudes or powerlessness has thwarted your progress, go. No one said it would be easy or comfortable to leave. However, you must if you sincerely want to advance in your career.

You may be able to transfer to another department, but unless you work for a very large organization, your past will travel with you. You may also have to leave if you have a bad relationship with your boss's boss. That individual may block raises and promotions that your manager may recommend you for.

Why not start out new and fresh? If you are like thousands of people who talk about their job as if it were the only one in the world they could get, you are in more serious trouble than you even imagined. Leaving may not be a comfortable option for you, but it's a necessary one. I have rarely met an individual who left a bad manager-relationship situation and later regretted it. Almost everyone—including myself—when I decided to leave a company because of a bad manager relationship—imagines the worst and feels terrible about leaving friends and colleagues and having to face the trauma of searching for a new position and adjusting to a new organizational environment. But the odds are that you will be much happier and far less likely to make the same mistakes that were responsible for your previous dilemma.

MORE ON SELECTING THE RIGHT MANAGER FOR YOU

VALUES

Often people like their job and their work responsibilities but don't respect or like their manager for a very special reason: The person is dishonest or unethical.

If you are discussing your salary and desire to make more money and your manager says, "Hey, don't worry about it. Just make up some additional expenses on your expense report and I'll approve them. That's how you can make an extra few thousand a year," you now have some insight into this manager's dishonest values. You may end up despising yourself if you work for someone who is dishonest in this manner. And even if you don't plan on cheating on your expense account, the very fact that you work for someone who does makes you equally culpable if your manager's dishonest practices are ever discovered.

WORKING HOURS

In your zeal to get the job, you may not be too concerned with your working hours. Or you may take it for granted that most organizations have a standard workday. This can be a very unfortunate mistake—

especially if you like plenty of personal time for recreation, socializing, and being with family and friends.

Don't ever take your working hours for granted. Ask your manager directly how many hours you are expected to put in on a weekly basis. You should be able to get a ballpark range, such as 40 to 50 hours a week. Don't ever be foolish enough to buy the trite line "We don't pay our people by the hour—we pay them for results. It doesn't matter to me how many or how few hours you work so long as you deliver results." These are the words of someone who is consciously or unconsciously trying to manipulate and exploit you. This manager *does* care how many hours you work, even if you are producing results. (Just try finishing your work by noon and announcing that you've decided to relax and take the rest of the day off!)

Of course, you should be paid on performance. And especially at the executive level, individuals should be paid on the basis of results, not just time. However, what is exploitative about the above line is that it is a clever way of leading you to believe that you will work a reasonable week (for example, 40 to 50 hours) when the manager already knows in advance that to achieve results you will have to work much longer than that.

So acknowledge the fairness of being paid for producing results, but be sure to ask, "In order to deliver the necessary results, what is the typical amount of hours I should plan on working in this position?"

If you value your private time outside of work, I strongly suggest that you go one step further and state the number of hours you are committing to. In making such a statement, use the concept of anticipation. For example, in order not to give the impression that you are a "clock-watcher" who plans on leaving at 5:00 P.M. "even if the place is on fire," anticipate this manager's concern that you might be inflexible by saying, "Other than in emergencies, I would like to plan on being able to produce superior results in this job by working a forty- to fifty-hour week. Do you agree that this is a realistic time commitment to this position?"

It is important and appropriate that you let your manager know then and there that you have a life outside of work. Don't make the mistake of trying to impress your manager that the only thing that matters in your life is work. If you aren't honest about your interest in having a life outside of work, your dishonesty will come back to haunt you. Establish a common agreement with your manager as to what your basic working hours will be.

BEWARE OF THE WORKAHOLIC MANAGER

If you work for a workaholic manager, within a few months you will think you are doing hard labor at Leavenworth Penitentiary. You will feel driven, pressured, and exhausted. Workaholism is a disease, just like alcoholism. Workaholics will tell you that they love their work, so they don't mind working so hard. More often than not, the truth is that workaholics either have a poor private life or none at all. They take refuge in their work. The organization is their family. Often individuals with emotional or psychological problems hide out in their job. Life for them is much more manageable if all they have to do is to get to work early, leave late, go right back the next day—and not face or resolve their personal problems and relationships.

It might not be so bad if someone you worked for was a workaholic in a vacuum. After all, if that's what he wants to do, so be it. However, workaholics tend to have similar expectations of others. They will not feel good about their working extra-long hours every week while *you* go home at 5:00. This is the danger that workaholics present as managers. They transfer onto their employees their expectations that everyone should be as willing as they are to devote 12 or 14 hours a day to the job.

If you don't share this same devotion, you will be looked upon as not being committed to the department or company. Coworkers who succumb to the long working schedule of such managers will begin to resent you for leaving at a reasonable hour. You may begin, unnecessarily, to feel guilty. You will feel pressure to conform. Or you may eventually be invited to leave. Errors in your work may be attributed to the fact that "you aren't willing to put in enough time on the job like the rest of us."

I define a workaholic as someone who consistently works 12 or more hours a day, on a regular daily, weekly, and monthly basis at the cost of having any other life interests or relationships. Such an individual usually works in this fashion not so much out of some special love for the job but out of unresolved emotional or psychological issues (bad marriage, fear of failure) that are the real impetus for his excessive work behavior. Workaholics are often among the first to burn out or frazzle due to the tremendous pressures they or their outside relationships put them under.

It is extremely important to refresh and renew yourself. This is impossible if you are constantly working. Workaholics may work hard, but they don't work smart. Your productivity level increases tremendously when you have taken time out to recharge your batteries and get your creative juices flowing again. Workaholics have no time for doing this.

Let's face it: The coffee break did not come about because a group of presidents got together and decided to be good guys and give everyone a chance to grab a cup of coffee. It came about because empirical research showed that worker productivity after a short break from work increased far beyond the time given off. There is absolutely no justification for chronically and consistently working long hours without some real breaks. Too many negatives counterbalance the few short-term benefits of working long hours. Workaholic executives suffer from job burnout, poor health, high turnover, low morale, and decreased productivity.

Always ask your manager the hours in a typical workweek—for the manager and the staff.

HIDDEN AGENDAS

When you interview your manager, ask about the organization's hidden agendas (see Chapter 2). What are some of the informal dos and don'ts for anyone who expects to be promotable and achieve success on the job?

If you don't believe that your manager will be totally candid in discussing the organization's hidden agendas, ask hard-hitting questions under the guise of information. For example, Margaret said to her prospective manager, "Stewart, the job sounds great, but I have something to ask you, off the cuff. In most companies, informal information is dispersed outside of work. How many times a week do people meet over at the local pub after work to discuss business? How much time should I expect for after-work socializing if I take this position?"

Stewart replied, "Well, I'll have to be honest with you, Margaret. The guys get together after work around six and we all go out to

Joe's Pub for a couple of hours, sometimes more, at least twice a week."

"Oh, really," said Margaret, thinking to herself, "I really don't want to work here."

This conversation is in contrast to Perry, who is naive. "Stewart, the job does sound quite good, I have to admit. It sounds like a very challenging position, but I hope this isn't one of those companies where they discuss work and important information at some bar outside regular working hours . . ."

Stewart replied, "Oh no, we tell our employees everything they need to know between regular nine-to-five working hours."

So keep in mind, if you have an open mind and a savvy attitude, people will give you the information you want if you ask in a non-threatening manner. Once you have the information, you can decide for yourself what is best for you. Remember to become aware of the particular hidden rules for success in your manager's department. You may also find that there are hidden rules for being successful and well regarded by your manager. Ask current staff members what these rules are.

JOB DESCRIPTION

Discuss your job description with your manager carefully so that there is real agreement on what you will be doing. This is also an excellent time to establish an understanding that the job you are accepting is based on the responsibilities included in the description. Therefore, if it changes, you would like to rediscuss your current title, responsibilities, and salary.

Also, if there are areas of your job where you will need special assistance, such as in statistical computation or data processing, make sure that you are honest in saying so. This way, you won't have to apologize about getting assistance when you officially take on the job. Avoiding discussion of your need for help can make you seem dishonest when your manager finds out about your inability to do something. This can cause your manager to cultivate negative opinions about your truthfulness and your ability to do other things you have said you could do.

ESTABLISH JOB LIMITS

SET LIMITS

We have discussed the concept of setting limits: letting others know what you can and will do and what you expect of them. This is especially important when you start a new position. If there is anything you won't do or don't feel comfortable doing, set your limits immediately.

Jan's manager, Miles, thinks nothing of asking the secretaries—"his girls"—to get him coffee. Fearing that Miles might ask her to do similar errands, Jan set her limit with him. She said, "Miles, one small detail that I want to be clear with you is that I am not willing to get coffee for you. It's not a good use of my time, and I wanted to mention this now [anticipation] so that you don't think my refusing such a request is because I am trying to be contrary."

Here's another example of limit setting. You may take a job where the amount of travel is somewhat vague. The job may call for "25 to 50 percent travel." You will definitely want to clarify the extent of traveling. If the job calls for travel 50 percent of the time most of the year, you may be very upset if you are thinking you'll be away 25 percent of the time. Set limits on what you will and won't do.

If there is anything you won't do or have considerations about, make sure you say them up front or at least bring them up for discussion. Many people don't want to do this; their thinking is, get the job first and handle these other things later. If you practice this dishonest policy, later you won't have a leg to stand on when you are forced to be honest about your discontent or unhappiness.

REVEAL YOUR AMBITIONS

Whatever your hopes or dreams, feel free to discuss them openly. See if you can detect any positive or negative signs or reactions from your manager. Be candid about the kind of responsibilities and promotional opportunities you are interested in. And, as mentioned before, discuss your salary requirements. If you have some particular philosophies, bring them up for discussion and observe the reactions and conversation that they foster with this manager. Most of us are afraid of revealing too much. Ironically, just as in a marriage, you will eventually end up revealing those interests, concerns, considerations, and aspirations. Your candor is also an excellent way of promoting a positive relationship with your manager.

INTERVIEW OTHERS

Before you accept a position in your current organization or a new company, it is mandatory that you meet and interview at least several people in the department where you will be working. They will be an excellent source of information on the new manager and hidden rules in the department or organization. You ought to prepare a list of questions you want to ask them. Observe how comfortable and open the employees are about answering your questions. This in and of itself will tell you a great deal about the atmosphere you will be working in. Find out about the responsibilities, promotions, and salary experiences they have had. Find out about their goals and interests.

If your prospective manager won't let you speak to other people because "they are so busy" or because "we like our people to join our group before we get down to socializing," beware! There is absolutely no excuse for not letting you talk to other people in an organization. In fact, it's good business. Not only can you assess them, but they can assess you. By being open you have a better chance of making the right decision from knowledge and not from ignorance.

YOUR RELATIONSHIP WITH YOUR STAFF

Now that we've discussed your relationship with your manager, let's look at your relationship with your staff. Many managers, because of their hierarchical power, feel that they are in total control of their staff and have nothing to fear. Those are the managers who seem to go into shock when they realize that their staff has undermined them and caused them to look foolish or incompetent in the eyes of upper management or clients.

After all, as a manager you are responsible for both successes and failures. It is important to carry yourself as a leader at all times. If you empower your staff, stimulate them, and surround yourself with the most talented people available as well as practice good delegation techniques, you will have an organization that can be counted on to produce great results.

Much of what has been said earlier about your relationship with your manager applies directly to you if you are a manager. I will not repeat many obvious points that have already been made. Suffice it to say that your staff can make you or break you. My own philosophy as a manager has always been to do as much as I could to support and reward staff. The more you do for them, the more they will want to do for you. So often leaders are supported by their followers not so much for what they have done for them but for what their staff can see is the leaders' benevolent and willing attitude to do all that is in their power. This is another valuable by-product of a charismatic leadership style.

ASSERTIVE LEADERSHIP

To lead people effectively, they must see you as an assertive leader, one who treats them fairly and who communicates honestly and directly in an appropriate manner. The emphasis for such leaders is to encourage others to take individual responsibility for what they do and not be martyrs or victims.

When you are assertive, people have confidence that you are telling them what you really believe, not what you think they want to hear. The result is that you are not only respected but also credible. This, combined with other managerial traits, will cause others to perceive you as a charismatic leader. People want to work for you and be associated with you. They will trust you and will want to follow you.

By contrast, if you rely on manipulation and politics, the people who work for you will learn to fear and distrust you. They will devote great energy to "covering their asses" instead of taking necessary risks and producing high results.

As an assertive leader, you set the tone for your staff to communicate in an assertive fashion with others in the organization. The result is that you, in turn, will get greater cooperation and operate at a much higher performance level than people who emulate their aggressive or nonassertive managers. You are a role model for others, not so much because of your knowledge or expertise but because of the way you manage others and lead them.

ASSESSING YOUR TEAM

When you are assigned to manage a department or an organization, you will constantly encounter new situations. Handling them the wrong way could be very hazardous to your career advancement. Quite often, the first thing new managers do is to go into their department and either make lots of changes or make very few changes. Instead, the first thing you will want to do—aside from familiarizing yourself with departmental goals, budgets, and other details—is assess your staff. Once this is done, you can make decisions on whom to fire, whom to promote, where talents ought to be utilized, and what changes should be made.

PERFORMING AN ORGANIZATIONAL AUDIT AND SURVEY

It would be ideal if you had six months in which to observe your staff and discover how best to motivate them. What kind of leadership worked best for your predecessor? Did the staff do best with leadership that was filled with structure and supervision, or did they function best in a "sink or swim, you're on your own" kind of environment? It would be great to have foreknowledge of who are your strongest and most dependable staff—and your weakest.

But most likely you don't have that time. You have to make decisions, prepare work assignments, and plan—right now. Performing an audit and survey will get you the answers to many of these questions in the quickest and most accurate fashion, so that you aren't losing valuable time trying to play it safe or taking unnecessary risks in making the wrong choices.

An *organizational audit and survey* (OAS) refers to an actual survey of the people in your department (or organization) in order to reveal (1) the strengths and weaknesses of your predecessor's leadership style and (2) the strengths and weaknesses of each member of your staff. To give you a concrete example of using an OAS, let me describe how I implemented it in one organization that I worked in.

I called each member of my staff into my office and asked him to give me an evaluation of the strengths and weaknesses of my predecessor's leadership style. I told them I was looking for an intelligent assessment in order to get an idea of what each person in the department liked and didn't like. I told them I wanted to take the best elements of the atmosphere my predecessor had established and add some new, positive elements of my own. I gave them examples of what I was looking for in their evaluation, for instance: Did you find my predecessor to have a structured or unstructured environment? High or low supervision? Heavy delegation or little delegation? Long hours or short hours? Lots of personal assistance or very little? Which approaches assisted you in being the most creative and productive?

I let each member know that I was interested in practicing a leadership style that was going to be compatible with the members of my staff, not doing a 180-degree turnaround where they would be doing everything in a new manner. I wanted to do what *worked*. Also, I wanted to hear how each member viewed the leadership style of the former manager.

I heard not only their assessments of their former manager's strengths and weaknesses but also some of their frustration and anger, and well as some of their admiration and affection.

This process not only gave me tremendous insight into my predecessor's leadership and managerial style, but just as important, it also gave me a chance to observe my staff. Their responses gave me valuable insight into their own character and the leadership approaches they were responsive or resistant to. I also observed their emotional reactions to their previous manager's style. It was a very revealing and informative experience for me. And it gave me some excellent ideas of how I could integrate my own leadership style in a manner that would yield the greatest results in bringing out the best in them as a team.

In the second part of the OAS, I assessed and evaluated the strengths and weaknesses of each member of my staff by asking each of them for an evaluation of every other. After all, they have worked together and have talked about their talents and abilities. It is a natural way of gaining some valuable insight and information.

To make sure that no one saw this as some kind of Gestapo attempt to interrogate and cause dissension in the ranks, I anticipated this concern by saying to each person, "I would like your honest assessment of the strengths and weaknesses of each member of our department. I am *not* looking for gossip or anything unconstructive. I am looking for your own opinions that will help me use each person to his highest and best talents. It will also help me in further developing the skills of anyone who may be weak in an important area. My aim is to run a department where we each support one another, develop strengths, and improve weaknesses. No one is good at everything; that is what teamwork is all about."

The first staff person I asked this question said, "Well, the way I assess Carla as a team member is that she's got a very creative mind and comes up with some excellent concepts and theoretical solutions. If you are brainstorming, she's a fantastic resource. However, her quantitative skills are weak. She has no statistical background, so one of us works with her in projects requiring statistical backup."

You can see how that kind of information was useful. My own team was doing some scouting for me. It allowed me to learn a great deal about my staff.

Of course, I also asked each person to describe his or her strengths and weaknesses. But to confine my audit to just what they thought about themselves would have been too narrow and self-serving. By getting a consensus from a large group, I felt much more confident in understanding each member's strengths and weaknesses.

Naturally, I took some of what I heard with a grain of salt. I was able to distinguish assessments skewed by rivalry, jealousy, camaraderie, support, and appreciation. I could see who liked or disliked someone else. And I reserved my own right to observe each member myself over a period of time.

Now, some people might say, "Why not just start from scratch and be totally objective? After all, you will be prejudiced after having had a number of people evaluate an individual the same way." That's a fair concern. However, I have seen quite a few managers who took many months and suffered through some big mistakes and people problems that could easily have been anticipated if they had had the information that comes from an OAS. It seems to me rather silly to have to learn everything from scratch when there is no need to do so. I would rather take responsibility for being fair and coming to terms with biases or prejudices that may result in an OAS than avoid this important staff assessment process as if I couldn't trust myself because I had foreknowledge. Making necessary decisions based on an OAS is a calculated risk worth taking.

By the way, an OAS is done only once: when you first take over. Be sure to tell people this. Another benefit of using this assessment method is that it gives the players on your team an opportunity to talk to the coach in a constructive way about how to use key personnel. Staff members don't have to feel like they are gossiping or putting anyone down. Once they know that they have had an opportunity to give you input, your staff may appreciate your willingness to consult with them and gather their opinions. After all, they have some excellent insights you may not have thought of.

I personally think it is much better to be open about people's strengths and weaknesses. You are only discussing what is really apparent to everyone, anyway. Having to hide them or pretend they don't exist is the ultimate in unenlightened management.

POLITICS AND PRACTICES TO USE IN CONTROLLING YOUR STAFF

To be an effective leader who gets the job done and produces excellent results, you must be in command of your staff. To be responsible for your staff, you need to be in control. There is no greater fear for a manager than to have his staff engaging in activities, making key decisions, or involved in confrontations—and not be aware of their staff's actions. No manager wants to feel a lack of control over staff.

As a manager, you are expected to be "in the know" at all times and fully informed by your staff. Your own manager and those in upper management positions will quite often ask you about activities that your staff may be involved in or even controversial positions they have taken in an organizational matter. You must be aware, lest you appear to be an out-of-control manager who is acting more like a figurehead than a leader.

One of the first acts you will perform upon taking over your new department or organization is to call a staff meeting where you can openly present policies and practices that you expect your staff to abide by. This can also be an opportunity for them to raise questions or discuss your policies further. You will no doubt want to communicate some of your own special ideas and philosophies on how you will run the show.

Here are seven special policies and practices that will help you in taking responsibility and controlling your staff. Adherence to these will minimize unnecessary problems for you and for your staff. Each of these policies is intended not only to keep needed control over the troops but also to help you manage people constructively.

1. THE NO-SURPRISE RULE

This is a rule for your staff to follow and one you will want to follow with your own manager. *If at any time you make a significant mistake or are involved in a major altercation with someone in your organization, you are responsible for telling your manager about it at the earliest opportunity.* This is the essence of the no-surprise rule. It is meant to keep your manager apprised and in the know at all times. This is especially important if you have made a major blunder, whether it's an altercation at a staff meeting or a mistake in an important report. Nothing makes a manager feel more out of control than hearing from someone else's lips, "You'll never believe what your staff person, Ken, did at today's meeting!" After all, as manager you are responsible for your staff's actions, which reflect on you. If you haven't been personally prepared so that you can react or cope appropriately, you can appear foolish or incompetent in the eyes of others.

So it is important to encourage your staff to get there first and "fess up," even if they are afraid of being reprimanded. I tell my staff that any mistake they make is compounded if I have to find out about it from someone else. This policy will go a long way toward ridding yourself of the Watergate mentality that believes covering up is better than owning up. I further explain to my staff that by my being in the know I am in a better position to stand up for them or at least mitigate the damage of their action [self-interest].

The no-surprise rule is just as important when it comes to alerting your own manager to your activities. Suppose that you've been invited to lunch with the vice president of a rival company, simply to discuss mutual interests in your industry. It may be perfectly innocent and possibly even beneficial to your firm in terms of what you might learn, but if you neglect to inform your boss, your rendezvous could be misconstrued as a get-together with baser motives in mind. You would indeed be taking a very dangerous risk that might jeopardize your future in your organization or undermine your manager's confidence in you.

Or, suppose the head of another department requests your assistance on a project that could be viewed as competition to what your department is working on. You may have the time and inclination to help out, but it's simple courtesy and basic business smarts to inform your manager and perhaps even point out how your department might benefit if you accept the assignment [self-interest].

2. THE CHAIN-OF-COMMAND RULE

This rule has its roots in the military. The logic is simply that there is a hierarchy of power. Each person in the hierarchy has specific responsibilities and authority in particular areas. The problem occurs when someone tries to break the chain—for example, when an individual "goes over the head" of the person who is in charge and responsible and approaches this person's boss directly (usually as a way of getting something he or she may not have been able to get by going directly to the manager in charge).

Powerless managers have this happen to them all the time. Their subordinates may feel frustrated in not getting the results they want from their immediate manager, so they decide to seek relief by going directly to their manager's manager.

You can see clearly how this leaves the manager in question out of control and not in the know. The result is predictable because your manager is called in by his manager and made aware of the fact "one of your employees came to see me directly about a matter that is really under your jurisdiction."

Here is a classic case from my experience as a product manager. A sales manager, Eric Brown, met my boss, the VP of marketing, at a headquarters meeting. They hit it off, discovered they both went to similar East Coast schools, played football against each other, and had great chemistry between them. Eric, the sales manager, said,

"It's been great meeting you!" and the VP of marketing said, "Hey, same here. Next time you need anything, call me. If you're ever in Chicago, stop by, we'll have a couple of drinks. If you ever need anything, you call me, you hear?"

That particular social relationship can produce formal results, as I saw in my career. Eric called me up and asked for a dollar a case promotional discount in his territory in Omaha, and I said no. In this company, sales people were in charge of selling; marketing people were in charge of making sure that sales were profitable.

However, this sales person was only interested in making his sales budget, so he went "around" me and called my manager, the VP of marketing, and said, "You told me to call you any time I needed something. Guess what? I've got to have a dollar a case discount in Omaha to meet my sales budget."

My boss said, "No problem, you got it." Then he called my office and left a message with my secretary: "Make sure Schwimmer authorizes a price change immediately and gives one dollar a case off to Eric Brown, the sales manager in the Central Territory. I want it done by Wednesday." And then my manager went out of town.

I gave the dollar a case off, as I was told. What else could I do? The implications of this are dangerous. One of the inviolate rules is never to break the chain of command, never to go above your boss's head. You must make sure everyone respects the chain-of-command rule, that no one is ever to go above your head without your authorization. When that happens, as it did here, you must make sure to resolve the problem that has been caused by both power centers, the one who violated the chain (Eric, the sales manager) and the one who authorized the violation (the VP of marketing). So here's what I did. I went to my boss, the VP of marketing, and used some of the concepts discussed in Chapter 3: "I" versus "you" language and self-interest.

"Excuse me, Mr. Vice President, I wonder if I could just talk with you for a quick moment about the dollar a case discount that you authorized for Eric Brown in the Central Territory. I want you to know I complied with your authorization, but I also wanted to let you know that in doing so we are going to be losing a quarter of a million dollars on the order Eric has placed. I know you are responsible to the president for profitability, and I wanted to make you aware of the ramifications of granting that particular request [self-interest].

"I also want you to know that the scuttlebutt in the sales department is that if you want to get something done, don't bother to go through the product managers, go straight to the VP of marketing instead. I suspect you'll be getting a lot of phone calls, and I really believe that's going to hurt morale because many of our product managers, including myself, are extremely concerned about having our authority undermined [self-interest]."

He gasped, "A $250,000 loss!"

I said, "Yes, I believe that's the figure we'll be losing, based on Eric's projected sales. To correct this problem I'd like to suggest that we remove one dollar per case promotional allowance in the St. Louis market for him and thereby make up the shortfall of $250,000.

"Second, I've written a memo that I'd like to recommend you consider sending out to the national sales force, making them aware that the proper procedure for getting promotional allowances is to go directly through the product managers and not to go through you unless it's an emergency."

He said yes to both of these suggestions, especially when I gave him the specifics. Then I called the sales manager. "Hello, Eric? Eric, you devil, you went over my head to my boss, huh? You got the dollar a case, huh? Well, I want you to know that I've met with him and we're withdrawing one dollar a case from your St. Louis market."

He sputtered, "You can't do that. I'll never make my sales budget!"

I replied, "I understand that, but quite frankly, I have the responsibility of making sure everything you sell is profitable, and I would like to recommend that in the future if you need any special allowances you talk to me about it and not go over my head. The VP is in charge of the big picture, not my individual product line. I'll be happy to work with you, but please come to me directly in the future. Good-bye."

You might say I issued a consequence, of sorts, to this salesman. But it becomes important to realize that if we don't want people to go around us, we must use self-interest and consequences as a means of compelling them.

It's the same situation when someone such as Marv, a manager in another department, goes to one of your staff people, Doris, to get her to do something for him. You eventually find out that Doris is now doing work you don't want her to do for someone else. You must make sure that Marv is not violating the chain-of-command rule. All you have to do is tell your staff people, "You are not to do something for somebody without my authorization. If someone outside our department asks you to do something, I would like you to do one of two things: (1) Come to me directly and tell me before you begin. (2) Tell that person to come to me directly because I authorize your work load and set your priorities."

Then go directly to Marv, the person who violated the chain-of-command rule, and tell him, "Marv, Doris told me this morning that you asked her to do a particular project. I want you to know that I insist that you come to me directly any time you need something and I'll be happy to get it done. You see [self-interest], I can't take full responsibility for work you've asked my department to do if I don't know what is going on. And it just so happens that Doris was working on another project that had to be done, and now she can't complete it on time because she's working on the new project you've asked her to do. So for me to take total responsibility for my priorities, I need to know what's going on. I've asked my people to come to me directly any time you or anyone else comes to them for help. I'd like to ask you to comply with that policy."

This is a simple example of how an assertive, fast-track person takes control.

The purpose of the chain is to provide order, structure, and an organized way in which to divide responsibilities and authority. Obviously, if people decided to go to whomever in the organization they wanted to about any matter that they couldn't resolve through their immediate manager, we would have chaos in our organizations.

Thus, to be in control of your staff, it is absolutely necessary to make sure they are aware of the fact that they are to see you first on any matters relating to you, your department's operation, or the organization. This is my policy, even if they have evidence of some sort of illegal or unethical activity. The rationale is that this way you can help them, direct them, or at least prepare yourself for any explanations that will be required.

Staff should be reminded that any exceptions to this rule show disloyalty and disregard for your leadership in your current position. It is just plain impossible to run an organization if there is no orderly reporting relationship for activities and functions in the organization.

3. NO MEMOS WITHOUT COPIES

I like to have a written record of all correspondence that my staff sends out. I may even delegate the responsibility of reviewing such documents to someone else. The point is that if I am going to be responsible for my department, I must know (or have access to knowing) what is going on. Now, if you have hundreds of people working for you, you can adapt this by having other managers appointed to receive memo copies of correspondence from their staff.

By obtaining copies, you will be in much greater control. And the fact that your staff people have to copy you makes them especially responsible for what they may say in writing.

4. NO POLITICS

Of course, there will always be some sort of politics in any organization. But in some organizations the atmosphere is filled with constant jockeying for position and an emphasis on style rather than substance. There can also be minimal information about pressing issues or concerns (losing a big contract, an incoming vice president, an impending firing). This creates a highly charged political atmosphere where people live with the fear of the unknown. The result is that people become embroiled in speculation, gossiping, and unproductive anxiety. This creates a bad environment for work to be done.

This is usually brought about by unenlightened management that looks at its employees as unimportant and has a condescending attitude: "We'll tell them when we are good and ready." I have been in organizations where hardly any real productivity occurred during a three- or four-week period because people were too afraid to do anything until the news broke. So assure your staff that as their manager you will make every effort to keep them informed so that they need not be concerned about their job or their future. I go one step further and invite my staff to bring to my attention any political rumors that they would like clarified.

5. DELEGATING AND RESPONSIBILITIES

It is important to encourage your staff to develop their talents by letting you know whenever they feel capable of taking on tasks that they are not currently involved in. It is also important to instill a sense that they are responsible for their own results; you will not tolerate blaming others for their lack of achievement.

For example, one of your staff disappoints you by getting a report to you late because someone else didn't give him the information he needed on time. Your staff person must be reminded that being responsible means that he follows up in a manner whereby he produces results, rather than using others as the excuse or justification for failing to deliver on his word.

This "delegation with responsibility" philosophy encourages staff to work to their highest level and not assume that they will have to live with the routine of an everyday job. It gives them an active role in being responsible for challenging themselves. It also motivates them to be creative and innovative in finding tasks that will give them variety and keep them fresh.

6. CRITICIZING AND COMPLAINING

Obviously, no one agrees or supports everything that the leader does or, for that matter, what others do in the organization. However, the problem with most criticizing, complaining, and gossiping is that it does nothing to solve the problem being discussed. It only tends to undermine morale and the efforts of others.

An excellent policy to ask your staff to abide by is that they agree only *to complain directly to the person who can do something to correct the problem.* Further, they are to agree that if anyone complains to them about a matter that they have no control over, they will agree to redirect that person to someone who can do something about the problem.

Instituting this policy cuts down on wasteful complaining and gossiping that does nothing to solve or remedy a problem. If adhered to, problems are properly directed, and the chances of resolution are increased tremendously because solutions are sought from the appropriate people responsible for solving the problem.

7. PEER MENTORING

Chapter 13 discusses this concept in depth. In establishing peer-mentor relationships, you are encouraging staff to help each other based on their special, individual talents. The idea is to use members of your team who have special strengths to act as resources for each other. As the leader of your organization, it is important that you set the tone in letting others know that you encourage and support their assisting and improving each other and that you will even allow company time for peer-mentoring agreements. In fact, as a manager, you may want to implement this program directly with your staff once you have become more familiar with each individual's strengths and weaknesses.

By letting your staff know that they have no need to hide areas where they are weak or deficient, you will find that you have created an atmosphere where people are not afraid to seek help and improve themselves. You'll have a stronger team as a result.

By using these techniques, you will build a strong department, establish constructive relationships with your manager and staff, and assure your continued success and upward mobility.

chapter 8

Delegate or Stagnate

DELEGATE: to designate a person to act or represent another; to commit powers or functions to another as agent

EMPOWER: to give power or authority; to authorize; to enable or permit

Delegation is one of the most important traits that you, as a promotable executive or manager, can develop. It is also one of the riskiest, because when you delegate you are no longer in total control. However, to be seriously considered for promotions, you must learn how to delegate and empower staff, coworkers, and even people whom you have no authority over. Upper management looks at this skill as a necessary prerequisite in considering you for promotions.

Many people restrict their promotability by trying to do everything themselves. Anyone can try to do the job alone. People who do not want to risk delegating are small-minded, overcontrolling, detail-oriented individuals who are usually insecure and have great difficulty in relinquishing control and responsibility to others. Those who effectively delegate are among the most productive people in any organization. They get the big jobs done, and they involve others in the process, thus gaining their support and cooperation. Delegators are the "can do" people, the team leaders in a company. Like a great quarterback, they call the plays and suggest the right strategy to win the game.

If you are interested in promotions, higher leadership positions, and greater responsibility, you must feel comfortable and competent in your ability to delegate and empower others to produce results for you and your organization. While there are definite risks associated with the process of delegating, the information in this chapter will help you produce the positive outcome you are seeking.

TO WHOM DO YOU DELEGATE?

When you ask most business people whom they delegate to, they respond either by saying they do the work themselves or they have their staff do it. So the first thing you must do to be an effective delegator who empowers people at work is to develop a new mindset: *The entire organization is available to you to delegate whatever you need done.*

Having this mindset, you will begin to use others as resources to assist you. You will stop yourself from the tendency to feel like a lone wolf who's handling everything single-handed. People who delegate only to their staff assume that as soon as their staff is overloaded, that's it. But it isn't. There are many other options for delegation beyond staff. The foremost rule in delegating and empowering others is to *appeal to their self-interest as a means of motivating them to assist you.* Remember the definition of self-interest: the reason why somebody will want to do or give you what you want. Using the self-interest of the other person is the best way to motivate the person whose help you want. Consider the variety of people you have to delegate to:

1. YOUR MANAGER

That's right, your manager! Every manager has a special area of expertise. Often managers become generalists when they take on managerial positions and thus rarely get an opportunity to use directly their expertise. So sometimes the opportunity to return to one's roots can be a welcome and refreshing task.

For example, I once worked for a customer service manager who, prior to his promotion to this position, spent all his time out in the field calling on both small and large accounts. After his promotion, he no longer did this. Instead, he had field customer service reps—like me—to do this.

During a month when the company was running a special sales promotion, I knew I would never be able to contact all the accounts in my territory in the allotted time. And the other field reps had a similar problem. I decided to see if I could delegate some of the customer service calls to my manager. Keeping in mind his self-interest, I approached him and said, "Fred, I know you rarely go out on customer service calls, because you've got people like me to do that job—and [anticipation] I know how busy you are doing your own work. Yet I have about six accounts [limit setting, so he doesn't think I have dozens of accounts] that I will not be able to service properly. I know you used to love doing field work. Would you cover these accounts for me this month only? It would give you a nice break from your usual grind here at headquarters [self-interest], and I think it would impress some of the top brass to see that you are still interested in what's going on out in the field."

He said, "Yes, of course, that would be a great change of pace!"

Now, I'm not suggesting that your manager will help you every time you ask. After all, he is your manager and has priorities and responsibilities. But if I had decided that about my manager in advance, I would have never approached him about delegating some of my work.

2. OTHER DEPARTMENTS

Often when you think of whom you can delegate to, you think only of your own staff, over whom you have authority. Or you assume that other departments are too busy to help you. This narrow thinking is a crucial mistake, because it deprives you of getting assistance that will lighten your busy load and thus allow you to do a more competent job on other work. Not delegating can result in depriving yourself of a specialist who might be far more competent than even your own staff.

For example, in one company I worked for, my entire staff in the sales and marketing department was busy putting together data for a major budget report. Despite late working hours, it appeared as if we would never complete the project. Then the thought struck me that we should be delegating part of this work outside our own department. The perfect people to delegate to were in the statistical services department.

Traditionally in the company, only my department gathered sales and marketing data. No one had ever thought of asking statistical services for direct assistance. Many of the company's "corporate politicians" rationalized that they weren't going to give away any of their responsibilities to another department, even if it meant being burdened with an excessive work load.

I decided to be unorthodox and unconcerned with the insecure and antiquated thinking of my peer department heads. I made an appointment to see Al, the manager of the statistical services department. Using self-interest, I said, "Al, as you know, the sales and marketing department does its own statistical data gathering. Yet your department's expertise and available computer time would be invaluable in helping us gather some important sales and marketing data for a special budget report we are doing. You've said to me in the past that since sales and marketing run this company, you wished you had a more direct involvement in what we're doing. This could be your chance [self-interest] to gain some well-deserved recognition and visibility in the company."

Al said yes. He wanted to help and knew what I was saying was true and in his department's best interest.

Again, my point is not to make this sound easy, because I've had many noes thrown at me, even after I've appealed to someone's self-interest. But I've successfully delegated quite often and gotten quality results in the process. Best of all, I've saved time and gotten the expert assistance I needed to get the job done.

3. SUPPLIERS AND VENDORS

Many of us allow our suppliers to play only the exclusive role of shipping us a specific product or supplying us with a special service, without giving thought to how they can be a resource to us in other ways. Yet we can delegate projects and assignments to our vendors and suppliers merely by catering to their self-interest and taking advantage of their natural willingness to maintain good business relations with us.

For example, when I was in the food service business, one of my tasks was creating new menus for our institutional food service accounts. This often included creating new sandwiches and meal entrées for hospitals and cafeterias. After much effort, I realized that I was already overcommitted to other facets of my business operation. So I contacted several of my food suppliers and asked them if they would be willing to develop a list of new food entrées and sandwiches that my company could produce for our customers. Both suppliers to whom I delegated this project not only came up with new menu ideas but were also willing to come to my food plant to help make up the original menu items. They even set up the weights and specifications for each item.

Now, their obvious self-interest was that by creating new food items, they could encourage me to buy additional ingredients from their companies. However, many of the items that they came up with were not items that their companies sold! I delegated this project very successfully, got tremendous assistance in the process, saved time, and impressed my customers with some very original and delicious food creations.

Always consider delegating and asking assistance from suppliers. They often have research and data that can save you from reinventing the wheel.

4. CLIENTS AND CUSTOMERS

We are often so busy doing things for our clients in order to serve them and sell them more products that we forget that we can delegate projects and work to them. Many times these projects will ultimately benefit them and in the process allow us to sell them even more of our products or services.

At one company I worked for, I was tearing out my hair trying to gather sales data on the ten biggest users of the automotive products my company offered. I was spending a great deal of time going through sources, reading magazines and periodicals, and contacting companies to get the sales and marketing data my manager had delegated to me to research.

Then I got the idea of delegating this project to one of the larger companies that was currently an account of our company. I had a good relationship with one of the buyers at the company, so I simply offered him the opportunity of helping me look like a real star. I asked if he would be willing to get me a copy of a marketing demographics study that his company had done on its competition (their nine major competitors). His report was invaluable and had the exact data I needed.

Once I had that report, along with the other information I had already gathered, I produced an excellent research report. This impressed my manager, not only because of its content but also because of the speed with which I got it assembled and the resourceful way in which I got the information.

5. TRADE ORGANIZATIONS, AGENCIES, AND NETWORKING GROUPS

Frequently, much of the work that we undertake has already been done partially or totally by someone else. This is certainly the case with trade organizations, which gather for their membership just the information they want. With that in mind, you can arrange to have such an organization do a lot of the work you would have had to do yourself.

For example, I was once asked to put together a report on growth trends in a particular industry. I had no staff to assist me in gathering this information, and I was told, "Just do the best you can." I called up two trade organizations that had a large membership of professionals in that industry. I wrote a special questionnaire and got the education chairperson to administer it to her membership. To appeal to the group's self-interest, I told them that in return for their help, I would send copies of the final trend report to them for distribution to their membership. They were thrilled about the prospect of having this information for their members.

The key was my mindset that I wasn't the only person who could do the job. Instead, I had a whole host of resources and people that I could empower to assist me in getting the job done. Once I had this attitude, it was easy to come up with a self-interest reason for why they would want to assist me.

6. TEMPORARY HELP AGENCIES AND INDEPENDENT SUBCONTRACTORS

As obvious as this delegation resource may be to most people, I am always amazed when I go inside companies and hear executives talk about how much work has piled up. "We're so busy, our secretaries don't even have time to file!'' Or I've heard executives complain, ''We just don't have enough data processing people to do all our inputting.'' Yet it doesn't occur to many people to use temporary help or subcontractors who have the required expertise.

Of course, there are executives who love to excuse themselves from using temporary help services by saying, ''There is no money in the budget.'' And while this may be true some of the time, this excuse doesn't address the other question, which is, What is it costing you and your organization for this work *not* to be done? It destroys morale when the staff is continually overloaded and overworked because management is reluctant to delegate work overloads to outside sources.

A long-term delegation value comes from using subcontractors who have a special expertise, such as independent data processing professionals. By using them periodically, you begin to develop them as support staff who are somewhat familiar with your operation and can help you during future overload periods.

7. FAMILY AND FRIENDS

Again, it is important to include family and friends among your delegation resources. They have jobs and contacts too, which can be useful in gathering information or assigning tasks. I worked for one advertising specialty company where I was required to distribute samples all over the city. My time was limited, so I called up ten friends and a couple of family members and asked them to drop off samples at particular locations near their homes or jobs. Not only were they happy to do me a special favor, but they also appreciated my giving them a few free samples.

The key to successful delegation and empowerment is to open your mind and be creative in using all the delegation resources available to you.

BENEFITS OF DELEGATING TO AND EMPOWERING OTHERS

The benefits of delegating to and empowering others seem obvious, yet many people are unaware of them. When you understand and appreciate the benefits, you will think in terms of delegating beyond just yourself or your staff.

TIME

Delegating to others saves you time. Just make sure it is not at the cost of efficiency. Often managers have staff members do work that is within their ability, even though they are not the most competent or efficient individuals for a particular task. Delegating should not be done just to save time; it should be done in a way that uses people to accomplish tasks to their highest and best ability.

EXPERTISE AND VERSATILITY

Another benefit of delegation and empowerment is that your staff develops greater expertise in whatever they do. This can be done by having more experienced staff working with less experienced staff so that you, in effect, make your weaker players stronger. In many organizations, specialization is emphasized excessively, to the point where people become one-dimensional and can only do certain jobs. In fact, it can breed the divisive "it's not *my* job" mentality. By having stronger staff empower weaker staff to learn and master different jobs, you end up making the whole team stronger and more versatile. In the process, you minimize mistakes that happen when people are bored or are doing too much routine and repetitive work. This also prevents job burnout. Even the car manufacturers in Detroit have learned this with their assembly-line workers. They now have programs that allow workers to rotate jobs on the line to increase productivity and improve morale.

LEADERSHIP DEVELOPMENT

By delegating to others, particularly staff, you end up developing people for higher leadership positions by seasoning them for a variety of work and jobs. Thus you are developing people's talents as well as their leadership capabilities. This is also of special value when key staff people leave your company or when you have temporary gluts in the work load.

CREATIVITY AND INNOVATION

By varying your delegation resources and involving different people, you get fresh input and new approaches to doing work that regular staffers may have overlooked because they've habitually been doing it the same way over and over. The by-product is creativity and innovation. By using many delegation sources, you can build up a support staff for work you are doing because a larger number of people, not just a select few, will be knowledgeable about a task or project. In this process, you are causing your organization to have greater depth instead of relying only on a few people. This approach to delegation helps rid you of prima donnas in your staff. These are people with a special expertise who have developed an inflated value of their self-worth, thinking they are the only ones capable of doing a certain job or task.

MONEY SAVINGS

By allowing others to contribute, they find greater challenge and satisfaction in their jobs and thus are less likely to leave the company because of boredom or lack of job challenge. Thus you reduce costly turnover and retraining expenses.

PROBLEM SOLVING

In this process of delegating to and empowering others, you will have more time to focus on the big picture, instead of being overly detail-minded or obsessed with staying on top of everything. And by seeing the big picture, you will be in a position to solve problems instead of fight fires. The difference is that, for firefighters, every other day is a crisis or emergency. They don't tend to do very much delegating, whatever their excuse or justification. They are poor planners. By contrast, problem solvers have the time to relax and plan solutions thoughtfully. Unlike firefighters, who are constantly reacting, problem solvers are prepared to respond with creative solutions to special problems that arise. They aren't alone in facing a situation because they have previously delegated to and empowered others who can now remedy the emergency or crisis.

GAINING PROMOTIONS

This, of course, is your greatest benefit as you become a recognized delegator and empowerer of people at work. You will be seen as a more powerful and authoritative individual because people around you know that you are willing to give them fresh opportunities and challenges. You are not insecure or threatened by others doing work for you. The ability to delegate to others is what makes certain managers so successful in producing results in their organization and thus more likely to be given promotional opportunities.

BLOCKS TO DELEGATING: WHY PEOPLE DON'T DELEGATE

You may be asking at this point, if there are so many sources to delegate to in getting a job done and if there are so many benefits to delegating, why don't people delegate and empower others more often?

People use a variety of negative attitudes, erroneous beliefs, and excuses to explain why they find it so difficult to delegate. To feel comfortable and develop a natural mindset to delegate, you must confront the fears you may have about delegating to others.

The first step in this process is awareness of mental blocks that get in the way of your delegating to others. Once you have become aware, you can reexamine the irrationality of your fears and overcome them. Let's explore 12 beliefs that prevent people from delegating. Put a check mark by each one that inhibits you from delegating to others.

___ *"I don't know how to delegate."* Most people don't know how to delegate. They think delegating means telling someone to do X, Y, and Z. Good delegating begins with empowering—enabling someone to do the job you've delegated to them. Specifically, this means that you determine what resources and talents the person needs to be successful to complete the desired task. A general who wants to send soldiers into combat doesn't just say, "Charge the hill and get the enemy!" A good general makes available all the necessary resources to ensure the maximum chance of success in the task he's delegated to his soldiers.

Here are three steps for delegating:

1. Make a checklist of each step involved in completing the work you plan to delegate.

2. List the resources or skills required.

3. Choose the individual who appears best qualified to do the assigned work.

By creating an organized method for delegating, you will quickly learn how to delegate to and empower others effectively. If you do this, you will feel more comfortable and confident about delegating.

___ *"I must be perfect; you must be perfect."* If you've ever worked with people with this attitude, you know that they do very little delegating because their staffs are not encouraged to try new things and develop themselves. Instead, they are being encouraged *not to fail.* Thus perfectionist employees or managers set up an environment where they take a long time to "get it perfect" before going on to another task. The result is that this fear of failure keeps productivity low (and slow) to ensure that no mistakes occur.

We should all strive to do a job with pride and excellence. But what the perfectionist does is to operate defensively without any appreciation for the value of making mistakes, which are an integral part of doing any task to a level of excellence.

Be aware of the "I must be perfect" syndrome and what it costs you in wasted time and minimized productivity. Perfectionists breed a CYA mentality because people become terrified at the thought of trying something new or difficult and making a mistake. In extreme cases, this kind of fearful environment results in people constantly making excuses and blaming others when things go wrong. This can cause morale problems.

You can always identify such people because they proudly justify their behavior by saying, "Well, I can't help it, I'm just a perfectionist." (This reminds me of people who tell you that the worst thing about them is that they are "too good" or "too honest.") It's as if they

The Mistake Chart (from Lawrence D. Schwimmer, *How to Ask for a Raise Without Getting Fired*, New York: Harper & Row, 1980).

think that because they are striving to do a perfect job, there can't be anything wrong with being a perfectionist. There can and is, as I have pointed out. The benefits of perfection are negated when the by-product of this perfection is low productivity, insecure CYA-minded staff, and an anti-risk-taking environment that hampers creativity.

By understanding more about the process of mistake making, you will be better able to rise above this perfectionistic syndrome. The "Mistake Chart" shows how professional growth occurs when you take the *risk* of trying anything new.

Notice particularly these points:

• You decide to take a risk in doing a new task.

• An unfamiliar task involves practice.

• Practice can lead to making errors.

• Errors furnish the experience of growth and proficiency.

• This develops your confidence and expertise.

• Thus you are more willing to take other risks.

Delegating to others and encouraging them to take risks, even though they make errors along the way, results in their gaining self-confidence and the expertise to do an excellent job. You, in turn, will find yourself with staff who will be a far greater resource to you in the future.

___ *"I can do it faster myself."* Maybe so, in the short run. But if you invest time and energy to train an individual, you may find that this other person's speed and efficiency may surpass yours. The "I can do it faster" rationale is firefighting talk; you feel you are in such a crisis over a project that you focus only on getting short-term results instead of considering the need to invest in developing your staff for the future.

___ *"No one will do it as well as I."* Watch out! This fear is born out of a perfectionistic attitude that can cause you to be so critical of others that no one will meet your standards. People with this attitude operate out of their own insecurity. They tend to focus on times when someone didn't do the job as well, and they make those experiences the rule. Ironically, if you empower people and invest in their doing something for you, they may very well end up doing it even better— which brings us to the next irrational fear.

___ *"They may end up doing it better than I."* A classic reason why competence and excellence are not passed on to others is the fear of being shown up by the person delegated to. This fear comes from thinking someone else's superior performance diminishes you. In reality, it suggests that you must be very perceptive to know a talented person when you see one. It also suggests that you are probably an excellent motivator and teacher of this capable person, who is producing such great results for you. The essence of delegating is that you are eager and willing for someone to do it better than you.

___ *"I'll lose control if I delegate."* Loss of control is the concern of the insecure individual. Skilled professionals who need a legitimate degree of control get it within the context of delegating, not by refusing to delegate.

If you require control in order to be comfortable delegating to someone, you have the option of having this person report to you during each stage of the work. You can carefully observe what the person is doing and still feel you're in charge. Another way you can satisfy the need for control is to have a trusted senior member oversee the work of the individual you have delegated to.

___ *"People will think I am not doing my job."* This consideration is often based on confusing the difference between dumping and delegating. You may indeed be dumping your work on someone else, *even though it is specifically your responsibility,* if, for example, what you are really trying to do is leave work early to go on a ski weekend. So be clear whether your motivation is to dump or to delegate. When you delegate, your intention is not to avoid responsibility for doing your own work; it is to get the job done most efficiently, whether in the short run, because you legitimately need assistance, or in the long run, because you are trying to train and develop someone for future responsibilities.

___ *"I will have to do too much follow-up."* The concern for having to follow up on the work you have delegated is born out of the same fears as "I can do it faster." It is also based on thinking that you are the only one who can do the follow-up. It does take time, and follow-up is a necessary part of the delegation process. So be creative. Delegate follow-up to someone at your level of competence in whom you have confidence. Have one of your experienced staff or coworkers check out the project periodically and follow up with the individual you have delegated to.

___ *"I'll no longer be as important or needed if people knew what I know."* Just like cowards, insecure people die a thousand deaths every day on the job. Their fear is that they might be easily replaced if others knew or could do what they do. Ironically, such people suffer the most because they are so busy with old tasks that they are unable to take on new tasks. If you are one of these people, be aware that this myopic attitude causes job stagnation and prevents progressing to new responsibilities. It stunts your growth as a leader because one tenet of successful leadership is to empower others to do a job and *not* continue to do it yourself. In this process, both of you are able to increase your abilities. In addition, having trained others to do your job tasks well makes you far more promotable in the eyes of upper management.

_____ *"I will have to be responsible for someone else's mistakes."* This is a legitimate concern. When you delegate, especially if you do so as a manager, you must be responsible for someone else's mistakes. This is why delegating requires the willingness to take a risk. And you should delegate knowing that you can expect first-rate results. However, this may require extra supervision and training. Being responsible for someone's mistakes is an opportunity to develop your ability to manage people and projects. You can minimize the possibility of making mistakes by having someone's work reviewed in stages. When delegating to someone for the first time, assign someone to work with the person.

_____ *"If I delegate my work, what will I do?"* Believe it or not, one of the reasons people are unwilling to delegate is that they feel they will be giving up something that is theirs. They feel territorial about their work. However, when you delegate work to others, you can begin to use the time you gain to solve problems and plan more challenging projects that will increase your value to the organization and put you in a prime position for promotion.

_____ *"If I delegate, I will lose visibility, status, and credit."* There are some special political considerations associated with delegating that you should be aware of. For example, doing a particular project may give you some desirable visibility or status because of the nature of the work.

This was the case in one organization where I prepared a special monthly report for the president of the company. After a while, I realized that the report was cumbersome and routine. The only reason I continued doing it was for recognition from the president. However, the truth was that in continuing to do this report, I was not using my abilities in the best way. Clearly, I should have been delegating this work to my staff.

Then I realized a way in which I could have the status and visibility I wanted, as well as gain more, by delegating the monthly report to others. I informed the president that I was taking full responsibility for the report by overseeing it but that I would be having various staff members prepare it. I further explained to the president that this would be an excellent way for him to have periodic exposure and interaction with some of my key staff members, which would be valuable if he wanted to use my staff for other projects [self-interest]. This also allowed me the opportunity to give my staff special visibility so that I could promote them more readily. It also gave me a more powerful persona with my staff when I awarded them the honor of doing this report for the president. (This, by the way, is an excellent example of reward power, which is discussed in Chapter 11.)

THE HOWS OF DELEGATION: LET ME COUNT THE WAYS . . .

We are now ready to look at some of the specific tools and concepts you can use when you want to delegate to and empower people who work for you or with you.

1. SELF-INTEREST

This is the reason why someone will want to do or give you what you want. By appealing to the other person's self-interest—what they want—you will find them most receptive to being delegated to. When I delegated the president's monthly report, I offered my staff high visibility and exposure to our president. I was appealing to their self-interest because such visibility could result in a possible promotion or merit raise. So, first and foremost, in delegating ask yourself, "What is the self-interest of the other person?" By doing so, you'll always be relevant, motivating, and compelling to others.

2. LIMIT SETTING

This is defining the parameters of what you want done. When this simple technique is *not* used in delegating, the result is frustration, usually on the part of the delegator.

Bernie's boss, Carl, says, "Bernie, I'll be needing that report next week." On Wednesday, Carl says to Bernie, "Where's that report you were going to have for me?" Bernie is upset and confused because he thought he had all week. And Carl is upset because he needs the report and thinks it should have been completed by now. Carl now feels he can't depend on Bernie.

When you want anything done, define the time parameters so that both you and the other person know when something is expected to be done. Don't ever assume that something is obvious. If your manager doesn't give you a limit, initiate one yourself.

Bernie could have said to his manager, "Carl, I'll be happy to get you the report next week. If it's OK with you, I'll plan on having the report completed and in your office no later than nine Thursday morning."

If you have the kind of manager or staff who forget easily, send a follow-up memo (discussed in Chapter 10).

3. FOLLOW-UP CALENDARS

One of the best ways to delegate effectively and be successful at anything you do in business is to learn the four steps involved in follow-up:

a. Follow up

b. Follow up some more.

c. Follow up even more.

d. Don't stop until you've followed up to completion of the task.

Ironically, most people don't really know what follow-up is. They think follow-up means you ask someone for something and if the person doesn't do it, you ask again. If the person still doesn't do it, you forget about delegating and either do it yourself or just let it fall through the cracks. That's not follow-up.

Follow-up is an unrelenting and high-intentioned effort to do whatever is required to complete a task. It is knowing that you will not quit following up, despite what may appear to be a lack of co-operation on the other person's part. The highest-producing sales people are absolutely tenacious at follow-up. If you want to delegate and produce results, follow-up is mandatory.

You can use limit setting as the backbone of your follow-up effort. If Bernie's manager didn't receive the report he had been promised by 9:00 A.M. Thursday (their agreed limit), he would automatically have known when to follow up. *Successful follow-up is a direct function of having previously set limits.* Once you know what the limit is, you will either have the result you were promised or have a specific time in which to investigate the problem of not having the agreed-upon result.

In other words, when you establish limits to ensure precisely when something will be done, you are at the same time establishing when to follow up if it isn't done. To aid you in this process, use your calendar. This means that you write down all limits—dates on your calendar. When you delegate, ask the person to whom you delegated to mark the dates on his calendar as well, so that you are assured that he has a reminder. Once you have the dates and projects to be done committed to a calendar, you can have your assistant or someone else follow up for you (you can delegate follow-up).

Writing down completion dates on a calendar also has the psychological effect of making people feel more responsible for what they're committed to do because "it's in writing." It helps them to organize and prioritize the work they promised to get done. Because it is written down, it adds a tangibility that is missing when you have only a verbal agreement about when something will be done. When nothing is written down, it is much too easy for each person to have a different recollection about the same discussion.

4. COMMUNICATION SKILLS

Using empowering communication skills makes a tremendous difference in your success in delegating. Skills such as "I" versus "you" language, anticipation, consequences versus threats, and metatalk are discussed in detail in Chapter 3 and should be part of your daily communication style at work. Your ability to communicate and motivate people is one of your most important assets in delegating to others. This skill is the cornerstone of promotability.

5. CLASSES, WORKSHOPS, AND SEMINARS

As professionals, our business and professional education never stops. Information and technology are changing so fast that each person in your organization should be required to attend several workshops, seminars, or classes every year. Such seminars are investments in your most valuable organizational resource, your people. This results in many dividends: increasing people's promotability, reducing employee turnover, raising productivity, and increasing profits as well as personal fulfillment on the job.

6. STAFF TUTORING ASSISTANCE

One of the best ways to strengthen staff and coworkers is to provide training and assistance on the job either during or after working hours. As simple as this idea may seem, very few organizations empower staff by using experienced staff to develop less experienced staff. People are expected to be proficient from the moment they take a job. Whether you are a manager who wants to develop one of your staff or an employee who needs to gain a greater competence in an area, consider staff tutoring.

In Chapter 13 the concept of peer mentoring is discussed in detail; this specifically deals with using the talents of peers to increase your level of expertise and information.

7. MOCK PROJECT

Often in delegating work there is a sink-or-swim ethic: The individual is told just to do the work. That may be appropriate in certain work or projects, but it can be a bit of a shock the first time. It can also make the individual feel pressured. He can become anxious, and make errors in an effort to do the job perfectly, which can undermine his confidence level.

An alternative is assigning the work on a mock project or trial basis. In other words, he does not have the responsibility to do, for example, the April financial report; someone else with the necessary experience will do it. However, the individual will be assigned to do the mock April financial report, a chance to practice preparing that same report as if he were the person responsible. This removes any pressure to be perfect the first time he does the report. You can even have the person who normally does this report critique the individual's effort.

This allows you to delegate at no risk in a situation where you can later review and critique his work also. At the same time, you are empowering someone to whom you will be able to delegate confidently in the future. This builds confidence in the individual you are delegating to and is at the same time reassuring to you.

8. HIDDEN RULES AND AGENDAS

Often in delegating you may forget that to accomplish a task, you may need more than skill, competence, or expertise. When delegating to and empowering others to do a task or project, you must make them aware of any hidden rules or agendas that might make it difficult or frustrating for them to accomplish the task you have assigned. Here are some pointers on common hidden rules associated with delegation:

• If you want special information, make sure the "right" person is asking for it (e.g., sales person, accountant, vice president, or director).

• If you want cooperation, make sure you "copy" the right people and keep them informed so that they will support you, not resist you.

• If you want assistance on a project from any department, don't break the chain-of-command rule (i.e., you must not go over someone's head if you need help or assistance; go only to the very next person in the chain).

Not being sensitive to such hidden rules means that you could sabotage either the success of someone to whom you delegate or your own success in accomplishing something that has been delegated to you.

9. REVIEW THE COMPLETION PLAN

On any project or assignment you delegate to someone, make sure the individual supplies you with a brief outline of how he is going to accomplish the task you've assigned. This is especially important with newer staff or coworkers, with whom you may want to meet in advance to see if they have any specific questions on implementing the plan. The key is that they have organized their thinking about the project sufficiently to complete it successfully.

Delegation's rule of thumb: The newer or weaker the individual to whom you delegate, the more progress reports you should schedule in order to observe the various stages of work leading to successful completion.

10. BACKUP BUDDY

Make sure that on special projects or with less experienced people, you have a backup person specifically charged with the responsibility of overseeing the less experienced person to whom you have delegated. Here's a good self-interest point you can say to the individual whom you have chosen as a backup buddy: "This person's success will be an indication of your strength and prowess as a future manager." This is both true and highly motivating!

11. MEMOS

Memos can assist you in delegating to and empowering your staff to do a task or assignment for you. Use memos to accomplish the following:

- Find out your staff's opinions on what you can delegate to them.
- Get other managers to cooperate with your staff when you are away.
- Acknowledge and thank others for a job well done.

Chapter 10 discusses these and other types of memos you can use to delegate successfully.

12. INTERVIEWING BEFORE DELEGATING

It is important to assess strengths and weaknesses of staff and employees in order to find out where their talents lie. Chapter 7 discusses how managers can perform an organizational audit and survey to help them decide what tasks they can delegate and in what areas their staff needs to be strengthened.

Exercise: DELEGATING TO AND EMPOWERING OTHERS

Directions: Delegate to and empower an imaginary person in the following scenarios. Decide what skills you will use to accomplish this. Use the list of skills and ideas to assist you in filling in the blanks of the scenarios you choose. Then say out loud what you would tell someone else in delegating a task.

SKILLS AND IDEAS

Anticipation	Limit setting
Calendar	Memos
Classes or seminars	Metatalk
Consequences versus threats	Mock project trial
Follow-up	Self-interest
Hidden agendas	Staff tutoring assistance

"I" versus "you" language

1. You have to ask a very defensive person to do a report in the specific format you want.

SKILLS: _____

2. You have to empower Bruce to get work done for you by a certain date. Each time he has agreed to do so, at the last minute he asks for additional time. Now you have to rely on his completing this work on time with no excuses. You have no reporting relationship with him.

SKILLS: _____

3. You have explained to Jill on three separate occasions how you want work done for you, yet she continues to make errors. Obviously, she still does not understand. Establish a means of delegation and empowerment whereby she will successfully do this work for you. She reports to you.

SKILLS: _____

4. You need the cooperation of Henry, who works in another department and over whom you have no direct authority. You need some information from him by a certain date. You're afraid he will not give your request top priority.

SKILLS: _____

5. You have a staff person, Kim, who is very weak "quantitatively" (i.e., she doesn't have a very good math, statistics, or numbers background).

You need to improve her skills level. Meet with her to resolve this problem.

SKILLS: _____

6. One of your staff, Kirk, wants to be responsible for doing a monthly project report. You don't think he can do the job according to the standards you want. Establish a plan for delegating this project report to him that will make you feel reasonably confident that he will succeed.

SKILLS: _____

7. You need to delegate more of your work. Meet with Loren and interview him to determine his strengths, weaknesses, and attitude. Your objective is to determine what work you can delegate to him.

SKILLS: _____

8. Nanette has recently done an excellent job on work you asked her to complete. Have a meeting to let her know how you feel about her accomplishment, and let her know how you will reward her.

SKILLS: _____

9. Your boss has not delegated much of her work to you that you could do. Yet she has complained of being overworked and not having anyone to help. You would like to be of service to her by taking over some specific work (projects, reports, meetings, etc.). You believe she doesn't have the confidence that you could handle the work. It's up to you to convince her to delegate work to you.

SKILLS: _____

10. You have to get some vital information from Mark, who works in another department over which you have no authority. He does not return your phone calls in a timely manner. Even though you have mentioned your frustration to him, he still fails to return your calls promptly.

SKILLS: _____

chapter 9

Publicizing Yourself: Letting Your Star Shine

Most people are afraid to publicize themselves, to be visible in the organization. By contrast, motion picture stars will do practically anything to seek recognition for a superb acting job in a movie. Yet most business and professional people do little to publicize their accomplishments, publicly take credit for having made the right decision, or seek recognition for accomplishing an extraordinary achievement. Most people would rather play it safe. They are content to wait to be discovered, yet they wonder why promotions are so few and far between. Publicizing yourself is a vital ingredient to advancing your career and letting management know that you are a star player on a fast track to the top.

People often fear public exposure in the organization and are concerned that it could make them unpopular or even get them fired. This is the root reason for not taking credit for their ideas or positions until they are *sure* they will be well received and the outcome will be successful. Unfortunately, by the time they feel secure enough to take credit and remind everyone that "it was my idea," it is too late to gain very much credible publicity value. People often lack an appreciation for the importance of positive publicity to their career advancement—and for the fact that they are the ones in charge of publicizing themselves. So, while there are obvious risks to seeking publicity and making yourself visible, the benefits to you are enormous in ways you may never have imagined. Some years ago, a talented quarterback named Joe Namath publicized the fact that his football team, the New York Jets, was going to upset the much favored Baltimore Colts. Joe took the risk of looking foolish or embarrassed and losing a great deal of credibility by taking this stand. Yet when he and his team beat the Colts as he said they would, he was acknowledged not only for being a talented player but also as someone who delivers on what he promises. In his case, it launched him as a national celebrity. For you, it could result in rapid promotion.

Tremendous power and success are in store for you if you are willing to take on-the-job risks and simultaneously seek to publicize and gain recognition for what you do, believe in, and stand for. This is true whether you stand up for a person, an idea, or a project.

WHY SEEK PUBLICITY AND VISIBILITY?

Visibility will make you powerful, promotable, productive, wealthy, supported, and satisfied! To be sure, we are talking about the publicity and visibility that you deserve as a result of your superior achievements, extraordinary performance, and distinguished service to the organization. In perhaps a less dramatic way, this may be the publicity you deserve for simply being right about something or someone by taking a stand before knowing the exact outcome.

People generally do not want to publicize mistakes in judgment or errors in their work. However, there may even be circumstances where it could prove beneficial to their professional image to do so. For example, one executive I worked with introduced a new product line, only to find that it was discontinued within six months due to insufficient sales volume. Rather than hanging his head low, making excuses for his failure, or blaming other people, he did just the opposite. He put together a presentation called "Six Ways to Fail at Marketing a New Product." He suggested to the president and several of the senior vice presidents that rather than sweeping failures under the rug, many of the company's marketing, sales, and research executives could benefit from understanding how new product failures occur. He made a brilliant case for how studying his failure could prevent such future failures and instead help to improve the possibilities for great success.

He presented his talk at several company meetings and eventually at a few of the company's national meetings. People were impressed with his honesty, creativity, and willingness to take full responsibility for his failure. Eventually, all this visibility and publicity over his presentation on failure won him the confidence and admiration of many key executives in the organization. They didn't see him as a failure. They saw him only as someone who had once failed. He was perceived as a success: "a savvy pro who won more than he lost, but at least when he lost you could rely on him to be a straight shooter and not make the same mistake again." He became so popular over all this publicity that pretty soon no one remembered his failure. They just remembered his wisdom and leadership ability in wanting to see to it that others didn't make his mistakes. It wasn't long before he was promoted to a position of higher leadership.

YOU AS A COMMODITY

When you are working in an organization, particularly a large one, it is easy to feel like a small fish in a large pond. You can use publicity as a way of positively differentiating yourself from everyone else. This is true even if you work in a two-person office. It is also true if you work alone, because you can use publicity to gain the attention and recognition of other people in your industry, as well as potential clients. This, in turn, can lead to a promotional opportunity with a new company.

The purpose of publicizing yourself and being more visible in your organization is to bolster your perception as a person of value— a resource to the organization, a prized member of the team. Once people take notice of you and your achievements and successes, you will be inspired to other achievements and successes. Public recognition is a fantastic personal motivator. Everyone likes a winner, and everyone wants to be on a team with winners. But there are even more tangible rewards for you if you learn how to make yourself visible.

Many people become miserable, resentful, and ultimately apathetic because they believe that they haven't been properly acknowledged or recognized for their superior achievements. In most cases, it's their own fault. They were waiting for someone else to blow their horn. *In the real world, it is up to you to publicize yourself and gain visibility in your organization.* That's not to say that you can't ask for assistance in doing so. It's just that it is your responsibility. Knowing this will prevent you from having naive expectations that someone else is in charge of publicizing you.

Organizations that publicize their employees don't do so solely to make the employees feel good. They often do so because it confers positive publicity and visibility on the organization. Therefore, the individual being publicized is merely a tool to benefit the organization. Let me illustrate this point with an experience I had. In one company I worked for, I received a large cash bonus for breaking a long-standing sales record. I received all kinds of publicity and recognition from top management for this achievement. While the company was genuinely pleased with my high performance, the sales manager later told me that the company's hidden agenda was "to let the entire sales force know how much money *they* could make" if they performed as well as I did.

BENEFITS OF PUBLICIZING YOURSELF

POWER

A number of factors are involved in people's perception of you as a powerful person. (We will explore the whole topic of power more fully in Chapter 11.) Power is the ability to act, to get things done, to accomplish and produce results. One of the necessary ingredients of being powerful is that you engage in activities, projects, or ideas that give you visibility. When you do something well and you attract the attention of other people, you are perceived as being powerful. People see you as being able to produce results and accomplish things. The very fact that you are distinguishing yourself from others is part of their perception of you as important.

When you publicize yourself, have visibility, and develop this image of power, people tend to cooperate more with you. They tend to defer to you and support you. They see you as an influential whom they want to have as an ally and supporter. You have instant credibility. People have confidence in you.

PROMOTIONS

Another benefit that can come from your publicity effort is that you will be considered for promotional opportunities far more often than people who have low visibility status. The reason for this is that when only a few people know of your achievements and accomplishments or even your innovative talents, you lessen the likelihood that those few voices will be the ones who make the promotional decisions affecting you. The more people who know of you from your publicized accomplishments, the more opportunities will be available to you for promotional advancement.

When you have broad visibility in the organization, your name will more likely be brought up or considered when promotional opportunities occur. Also, as a result of being publicly known, you will find it much easier to approach people directly about positions you would like to be considered for. Just like an actor whom people have seen do a great acting job in a movie, you will be similarly viewed as someone whose past achievements will inspire the confidence that you can do the job in other, more responsible positions. You won't need to continue to prove yourself because only the people in Department X know you and your work. Instead, many departments will be aware of your superior work or creative ideas.

MONEY

When you become a visible star, you are a very valuable commodity. You are a treasured prize to your organization, not only because of your high performance but also because everyone knows about it. This is an important distinction for you to grasp. There are many high performers and achievers in organizations, but not many people really know and appreciate fully just how well they are doing. So these high performers get very little mileage out of their accomplishments, certainly far less than they are entitled to.

The result of the perceived value you have created through publicity and visibility is that you are worth more money. You will find it much easier to get raises and merit increases than other people who are competing for the same chunk of the salary budget that you are.

Another reason why you are likely to make more money is that no one wants to lose a team star. It hurts morale. It raises questions as to why the rising star left the organization. Your visible and successful persona symbolizes a great deal to the organization. You are an investment—one to be protected.

OPPORTUNITY AND EXPOSURE

One of the most exciting facets to your publicized achievements is that you are considered for opportunities that other people never even get to hear about. You might be invited to attend exclusive meetings and company affairs. You get exposure to high-ranking executives and clients. You are often chosen for select committees or special projects that you would not ordinarily be a candidate for.

You will also be hearing of other job opportunities through phone calls you'll be receiving from executive searchers who, because of your high visibility, will have heard about you and will let you know about other companies that are interested in your being a star on *their* team, often at a much higher position and salary level.

SATISFACTION AND FULFILLMENT

The recognition and acknowledgment that coworkers and high-level executives give you is often worth even more than monetary rewards. It feels great to be publicly rewarded and recognized for your superior talents and achievements. Often your visibility will extend to trade associations or network organizations that you belong to. It can be very fulfilling to achieve recognition by a group of peers within your industry, too.

RISKS OF PUBLICITY

Any discussion of the benefits of publicizing yourself would be incomplete if it didn't also address the risks related to visibility. So, let's take a closer look at some of the negatives that visibility can bring you.

Like any public figure, you may be the object of close scrutiny and rival jealousies on the part of people who would like to be regarded as positively as you. Also, when you are visible, your mistakes and general conduct can draw far greater attention than the mistakes of a person with a very low profile in the organization. And your public image will call for you to show a higher standard of performance and conduct than other people in the organization. But so what? There are inevitable risks in standing up and being counted when you publicize your best efforts. However, the rewards are so great, so exciting, and so fulfilling that they far outweigh concerns you might have over the negatives that could occur. The unfortunate mindset of many CYA types is that they are overly concerned about protecting their backsides and avoiding being associated with an idea or project that doesn't work. Consequently, they don't derive the full benefits of their excellent work.

Along with the general concerns that people have about being too visible, there are many considerations, or blocks, that inhibit them from taking the risk to publicize themselves in their organization. After all, the first step in removing such blocks is being aware that they exist. Once you have confronted that block, you can decide whether the costs of having it are worth the expense of it. More simply put, once you see the tremendous value you are passing up (i.e., career advancement possibilities) because of your fears and considerations, you may be willing to face your fears and take the necessary risk of being visible. Here are some of the typical concerns people have about their own publicity and visibility.

"I HAVE TO PROTECT MYSELF FROM FAILURE"

This is the number one concern of CYA employees. These people live in constant fear that they might support an idea, person, or project that does not turn out well. Thus they will be blamed in some way for the lack of success. The result is that they stay away from being visible; it is too much exposure with too great a possibility of a negative outcome. They will not take the risk.

Worse yet, people who invest their energy in their fears of failure inflict their paranoia on those they work with. CYA types often look for others to blame and are forever coming up with excuses for possible failure. For them, the game is "not losing," whereas promotable types play the game more positively, with the outlook, "How can I win?"

Quite often, CYA types have suffered from having made mistakes in the past. So they decide to be very careful in the future. They often contribute to a low-productivity environment because of the "I must be perfect" syndrome they create around themselves (discussed in Chapter 8).

The positive strategy for overcoming fear of failure is taking small risks and letting at least two people know beforehand what you are going to do. You see, CYA types want to keep a lid on failing, so there is little chance they will publicize their work until they know it's successful. Even then, they still believe there is risk involved because they rationalize that what looks like a success today may be viewed as a failure tomorrow. Their credo: "No news is good news."

To deal with this irrational fear, consider all the positive benefits that you are not getting because of this fearful mindset. And be willing, slowly, to take more and more risks that you will publicize. The rewards can reform even a CYA individual.

"THEY'LL DISCOVER HOW INCOMPETENT I REALLY AM"

The motivation of many people for not seeking publicity and visibility for what they do is that they are afraid someone will take a close look and see that they are really not all that competent. To protect anyone from making that discovery, these people assume a low profile. They may appreciate the compliments, but they don't want anyone scrutinizing their work too closely.

I once knew a very capable manager who didn't have much of a technical background. But he did have a great talent for choosing bright, talented, technical staff. He suffered from feelings of inferiority because he never had a technical degree or background, so he delegated a great deal to his staff. The work done in his department was of high quality and well respected, and he, as manager, was given credit. However, he lived in fear that too much visibility or publicity for his department's work would show that he did very little of it himself and that he relied tremendously on his staff.

What he failed to realize was that the best managers *don't* do the work themselves. They get other people to do it, making sure that they oversee that it is done well. This is the essence of empowering and delegating to others.

This manager's self-image, like that of many people who suffer from this fear, was very low. He erroneously believed that competence meant he should be able to do his staff's job, when in reality he had great competence in the areas of motivating and managing people and mobilizing their best talents.

If you find that you have the same rationale as this manager for why you don't seek to publicize and make yourself more visible, then be open to reexamining your definition of competence. The manager in this example measured his competence as if he were one of the staff, instead of viewing his competence from the position of being a manager.

"I'LL HAVE TO BE RESPONSIBLE FOR PRODUCING SUCCESSFUL RESULTS"

One of the big reasons people avoid publicizing their work is that they fear having to be responsible for producing successful results. Their concern is obvious: If they publicize the work they are doing, they will then be *expected* to come through with a superior performance. For those who are confident risk takers, this public declaration of their successful intentions makes them look like real winners, when they do the excellent job they had forecast. However, such publicity is a scary risk for people who want a way out in the event that their optimistic predictions go awry. This thinking is the essence of the CYA mentality. Many people fear that having achieved *one* success, others will then expect regular successes from them.

This was the case for a schoolmate of mine, Norman, who after lots of hard work finally got an A on a history exam. When I started to congratulate him boisterously, he practically put a muzzle on me. He didn't want anyone to know how well he had done. Norman rationalized that if people knew he had gotten an A, they would always expect him to get A's. He feared publicity because he thought it would result in expectations that he could not live up to in the future.

As adults, many people have this same rationale for not seeking publicity for even their best achievements. Unfortunately, this self-defeating attitude causes people to focus on future outcomes that may be negative instead of seizing the splendid opportunity to publicize the positive outcome they have presently achieved.

Keep in mind also that there is a strong "commitment psychology" associated with letting others know what you are accountable for and what results you intend to produce. It tends to support you in being a person who keeps his word. This is the case for people who decide to quit smoking: They are advised to tell everyone that they are quitting smoking. By doing so, they tend to be more responsible for keeping their word, since they know that others will be watching how well they keep to their commitment. This is an excellent way to support yourself in taking the publicity risk: Be 100 percent committed. Let people know your positive intentions in advance!

"I DON'T WANT PEOPLE TO THINK I'M BRAGGING"

This is one of the biggest considerations that people have about publicizing themselves. Mohammed Ali, the great prize fighter, once said, "Bragging is only when you *can't* do something you *say* you can do."

Fears about the acceptability of self-acknowledgment go back to our childhood, when many of us were told to be humble. Praising our own achievements was considered bragging, and having an appreciation of our own talents was considered conceited.

When people have an exaggerated opinion of their own abilities or importance, they are indeed conceited. And when they boast, particularly for effect, you can be sure that is bragging. However, the ability to acknowledge your talents and abilities and have pride in your accomplishments is very healthy. In fact, most of us need to practice letting others know what we do well. Saying something positive—self-acknowledgment—is one of the most difficult problems people have. In one workshop I conduct, one exercise has people form pairs and take turns telling the other person one thing they like about themselves. People are quite often embarrassed and uncomfortable. By contrast, when I ask them to say something negative about themselves, they seem to be able to go on forever. After all, no one is going to be too disapproving about your putting yourself down.

My point is that for most of us, it is uncomfortable and even unnatural to tell someone directly how good we are or how well we do something. If you are to publicize your achievements and best efforts and gain visibility, you must overcome this block. In the real world of business and industry, you have to learn to blow your own horn—not as a phony braggart or a conceited bore, but out of self-appreciation for your many talents and abilities. This is what it means to have self-esteem.

You can try to rid yourself of the notion that you are bragging or that you will be seen as conceited by telling at least three people a day something about yourself or something you have done that you are proud of. Watch their reaction to what you have just said. If you have any doubts about their reaction, ask them for feedback as to whether you sounded like a braggart or just someone who has pride in his achievements. At the same time, find three people whom you can acknowledge for their talents. Believe it or not, you will find it much easier to compliment yourself if you are able to compliment others sincerely. If you want the cooperation of people you work with or who work for you, try complimenting them for their talents or successful efforts. You will be amazed at the esprit de corps and high morale you can create by doing so. This suggestion ties in with the next irrational fear.

"IF I PUBLICIZE MYSELF, PEOPLE WON'T LIKE ME"

Some people want to be liked and have the approval of others so much that they are willing to subordinate themselves and even pass up the recognition they are deserving of. Some are even willing to be martyrs about doing so. "I do a great job, day after day, and no one here seems to notice!"

Others are afraid that people will not like them because they are bragging. Many people are fearful that publicizing their best efforts will cause others to become jealous of them, with devastating results. If others are jealous of you, they may undermine your work and gossip behind your back. Or people may think you are trying to "kiss up to" upper management.

If other people's opinions are more important to you than your own, you may be too dependent on other people's approval. People who care about you and want you to be successful are happy to see you receive recognition for your superior efforts. Ironically, most people who like you do so unconditionally. And if you publicize yourself in a positive manner, people will like you even more because you are a winner! Your celebrity status confers an "honor by association" on them.

"IF I DO A GREAT JOB, OTHER PEOPLE WILL
AUTOMATICALLY RECOGNIZE AND PUBLICIZE ME"

And perhaps the tooth fairy will leave a million dollars under your
pillow for one of your upper molars, or perhaps you'll be able to buy
some cheap swampland in Central Park. As the comedienne Joan
Rivers says, "Oh, grow up!"

In the real world, major achievements are often recognized.
However, many semispectacular and minor achievements go unrec-
ognized or are acknowledged in a very low-key way.

*Don't ever make it someone else's responsibility to acknowledge
your superior efforts.* You may be lucky and find someone who will
do it for you, but the surest way is to assume responsibility for publicizing yourself. This will allow you to position your publicity in a
manner that does you and your career the most good.

For example, I knew a woman at a food processing company who
worked into the wee hours of the morning in a very innovative detective effort to track down a lost truckload of perishable foods that
had a value of $250,000. When she finally located it, her boss thanked
her for a great effort. That was the end of it! No one else knew, other
than a few people in her department who had the curiosity to ask her
why she looked so tired the next day.

You might say that she did get recognized, but in such a low-key
and nondescript way that it was in inverse proportion to her mag-
nificent money-saving effort. She should have found some manner in
which to seek publicity for her job well done. Instead, she relied on
someone else, who had his own reasons for keeping the matter quiet.

Sometimes it may not be in your manager's or another person's
interest to publicize your accomplishment (as in the case of the lost
truck of perishable food). In some instances, the very people who are
in a position to acknowledge you publicly are too busy and involved
in their own work. Or, quite often, they just don't share the same
self-interest with you that would motivate them to recognize you
publicly. For example, the manager of the woman who saved the
company a quarter of a million dollars may have thought that going
public with the matter might put him in bad graces with the higher-
ups for having lost the truck in the first place. Yet it was certainly in
this woman's self-interest to gain publicity because it could have re-

sulted in a raise, a promotion, or some sort of special commendation.

Some people may not want to acknowledge you because of jealousy or rivalry. Very few people share your desire to hear the trumpet blow your praises. That's why it is up to you to promote yourself.

Now, none of what I am saying is meant to suggest that no one will give you due credit. Or that your manager or coworkers won't pat you on the back for a great job. What I am saying is that there are special means by which you can gain the most mileage and recognition for high performance. And it is your responsibility to find those means so that you will reap the greatest rewards. Best of all, you will empower yourself so that you can go on promoting yourself in your climb to the top.

FIFTEEN WAYS TO PUBLICIZE YOURSELF

There is no best way to publicize yourself. Some ways will be more comfortable and appropriate to your organizational environment than others. For example, if you work at a staid and conservative accounting firm, you might choose a different way of promoting yourself than if you worked in the loose, more relaxed atmosphere of a recording company. So look at these suggestions as choices. You will make the final selection.

These suggestions can, perhaps even in a dramatic way, help you advance your career and give you the competitive edge over others in your organization who are vying for the same promotional opportunities as you. Here's your chance to go for it! Remember, no guts, no glory.

1. Send memos about your special achievements or successes. People often ignore the personal publicity value of their everyday achievements on the job. You may tend to look at only your most extraordinary achievements as being worthy of recognition or as being appropriate to self-publicity. This is not true. Many of your day-to-day successes can be the basis for your receiving important recognition that will qualify you for special responsibilities, gain you promotions, win you raises, and bring you immense personal satisfaction. Look at your successes in a new light and take note of them. Here are examples of publicity-worthy events:

- Capturing a new account from the competition
- Being elected to an executive office in your industry's trade association
- Coming up with an innovative idea (e.g., an ad campaign)
- Any special achievement (such as locating a lost truckload of perishable food)

Such personal victories should be publicized in a way that not only makes you more visible but also benefits you the most by gaining you the right attention from the right people.

For example, let's say that you have not only achieved your sales budget objective but surpassed it. Certainly, your manager would be happy and might even pat you on the back and say, "Good job!" And perhaps people in general would be aware that the sales force is doing a great job. But this is insufficient acknowledgment for your accomplishment. One method you can use to get the publicity you want is by writing a memo congratulating the *supporting cast* of people and departments that assisted you in achieving your spectacular results. In so doing, you would naturally copy all the important and influential people to whom you wanted to publicize this event. In the process, you would be seen not as a braggart but as a magnanimous and generous person who shares credit.

Once, when I had a fantastic sales quarter, I wrote a separate memo to the managers in sales promotion, advertising, customer service, and manufacturing. Each memo thanked influentials for their support and help in making my sales budget. And the memo let them know that they were valuable and deserved lots of credit. I also "copied" their managers and in many cases the managers of those managers. All of this acknowledgment yielded tremendous future cooperation and support from these individuals because of the recognition and credit I gave them. Of course, in the process I gained a great deal of positive visibility, too. On the next page is a sample of a memo I sent to one of the departments.

In addition, or as an alternative, you could say the same things to people personally or over the phone. You could even write up a short article for your company's monthly magazine or newsletter acknowledging all the people who were part of your success. This is just the kind of publicity the woman who saved her company $250,000 could have used. So, be on the lookout; there are many kinds of successes you can publicize in this manner.

TO: Ron Green, Manager of Manufacturing
FROM: Larry Schwimmer, Sales Rep
DATE: April 10, 1986
RE: Super Sales Budget Performance
CC: My Manager
          Ron's Manager
          VP of Sales

Dear Ron:
While I am proud of making our third quarter sales budget—which few people gave us a chance of achieving—I just want you to know that you and your people deserve a lot of the credit. Your overtime effort to expedite some of our last-minute orders saved the day! Thanks for the tremendous effort.

Sincerely,

Larry Schwimmer

2. Edit or contribute to your organizational newsletter, trade journal, or monthly magazine. In large companies, even if you aren't a big reader of your organization's news publication, rest assured that many people are! By taking on the responsibility of being one of the staff—even the editor—or merely by being a contributing story writer, you can gain great credibility and publicity for yourself and your department. After all, you will have some control and input regarding the stories that will be used. I once knew an executive in accounting who regularly took it upon himself to write stories about the accounting department and, in particular, about who was doing what. He would ingeniously relate what he or his department was doing in relation to the latest achievements of the organization.

I once knew a woman who worked for a bank and had been featured in the bank magazine column "Women on the Move." She used this as background material with her résumé when she decided to apply for some exciting job opportunities at other companies. She used this valuable collateral information to impress prospective employers with her many capabilities.

Thus the visibility and publicity you obtain for yourself have value not only where you currently work but also as a tool in finding a job elsewhere in the future. This is an excellent way to promote yourself in your current company or at a new company.

3. Suggest cost-saving or innovative ideas. Many times people believe they have a great suggestion or idea that would help someone else and, of course, the organization itself. However, people often don't make the suggestion because they are concerned that they will be offending someone who will view their suggestion as some sort of intrusion. It's as if they were sure someone would say, "Why don't you mind your own business, buddy!" Yet if you were president of a company or running your own organization, would you want your employees to be concerned or interested in helping other employees and departments? You bet you would! *Don't ever let your fear of petty egos deter you from offering constructive suggestions.* And don't underestimate the publicity value of such ideas. More often than not, it's the way the suggestion is offered that can prove offensive or disturbing instead of well received and appreciated.

This is why you will always want to keep the other person or department's self-interest in mind when you make suggestions that you think will improve something or save money. Also, use the concept of anticipation in making a suggestion; that is, incorporate it in your written memo or your verbal suggestion. If you recall, when you anticipate, you are openly acknowledging the concern or consideration that the other person may have about you or what you are saying.

For example, let's say I have no technical background but I have a suggestion to offer Matthew, a technical person. Since Matthew may believe I lack credibility because I don't have a technical degree, I will address that in my statement.

"Matthew, I know that I have no formal technical degree [anticipation], but I have several suggestions that I think would save you some red tape in doing some of your standard procedures analysis [self-interest]. Would you have any objection if I put them in writing to you for your consideration?"

Of course Matthew won't mind. Would you? Once you've gotten

his interest and approval (which isn't necessary but is helpful), you can publicize your suggestions further. And you may improve your personal relationship with Matthew when he realizes that you are someone who sincerely wants to help him.

Keep in mind that publicizing and making yourself more visible does not mean that the entire company must be aware of who you are or what you have accomplished. While in many cases you do want lots of people to know your best efforts, there are many instances where you will want only one key person to know. So we are interested in *whom* you are publicizing yourself to, not necessarily the number of people you inform. Always focus carefully on who should know your best efforts or accomplishments when selecting the method you use.

4. Give a lecture or teach a class at a local college. One of the best and simplest ways to publicize yourself is to volunteer to be a guest lecturer at a local college in your area, preferably the most prestigious college. Of course, you might be interested in teaching a full-term class, but I am referring to a very small amount of your time: one appearance at an evening class where you will be the guest instructor.

Here's how I implemented this publicity project and gained some valuable visibility. I had a marketing manager's position at a *Fortune 500* company where I was involved in all aspects of marketing, especially advertising and promotion. So I called up a professor at Northwestern University who taught an advertising class and told him I would like to share some of my experiences about our company's TV and print ad campaigns. Would he be interested in having me as a guest lecturer for one of his classes during the term? Excitedly he said, "Yes!"

For him, it was an opportunity to have someone from the "real world" of marketing and advertising come talk to his students. I said that I would be happy to do it if he would promise to write me a letter evaluating my talk and the reaction it drew. I told him I wanted the letter sent to my business address because I wanted it for my files.

It was great fun to prepare my talk, and the students loved hearing about our company's ad campaigns and having the opportunity to ask questions of a real live marketing executive. Within two weeks I received a glowing evaluation from the professor on the eloquent and professional job I did in representing my company and discussing marketing and ad campaign strategy. He went on to credit me for "filling the students with the enthusiasm and challenge of having a career in marketing and advertising." In addition, he acknowledged me as being a real credit to my company and "truly an executive on his way to the top."

To publicize this project, I sent my boss a visibility memo (discussed in Chapter 10) that let him know I enjoy talking to others about the marketing that I do for the company. I told him I wanted to share a particular evaluation from a recent talk that I was very proud of. I sent along a copy of the complimentary evaluation letter that the professor had sent me. I also sent copies of the memo and the letter to the president of the company and to two of the vice presidents.

My boss was very impressed, especially when he saw that it was Northwestern University. And so was one of the vice presidents, who I knew had graduated from there. They saw me as a young executive with a lot on the ball and great career potential. And since the president was very civic-minded, he came over to my office to congratulate me personally and encourage me to keep up the good work!

Many people keep their achievements quiet, as if they had been sworn to secrecy. That's rarely an effective policy. Through my particular publicity project, I gained some important recognition and, in the process, enhanced my value to the company. To this day, I am convinced that this project was an important factor in the promotion I received six months later.

5. Volunteer for projects. This may seem elementary, yet most people are so busy doing their regular job that they don't want to have to do any additional work—particularly if it is after regular hours. And some of the best volunteer opportunities occur after 5:00 P.M. The visibility you can get by volunteering may be that you will be working with some senior executives and personally interact with them in ways that you would never have an opportunity to do in your usual 9-to-5 day.

Also, in volunteering you may well get a chance to do something or manage a project that you would never otherwise have been considered ready or seasoned for. Even if you are a staff person with no one working under you, you may find that volunteering to head a project will give you the valuable managerial experience of leading and managing a group of people. This can later be used as an example of your managerial experience and talents. Many people look at volunteering as doing "grunt work" without considering the tremendous self-developmental possibilities, as well as the way it can be used to advance their career.

One secretary I knew volunteered to do some nonsecretarial work that put her in regular contact with several upper-echelon executives. These executives eventually talked to some of our middle managers about her tremendous potential for a position of greater responsibility. Soon after, she became the company's first secretary to be put into a junior management training program—all because of her visibility from volunteering.

6. Become an emissary or delegate. Organizations are forever in need of someone to be a representative to the community or to another organization or agency on behalf of the company. Often the person who is the delegate acts as a liaison or gathers information and writes reports. This may be an opportunity to act in a higher-status role than your usual 9-to-5 capacity.

I had a Hispanic friend who suggested to his company that it could gain an immense amount of goodwill for the products it sold if the neighboring Latino community saw the company actively involved in community affairs [self-interest]. He volunteered to attend such meetings as a representative for the company and to report back. He obtained extremely valuable experience, contacts, and visibility.

7. Use your expertise to teach or train others. If you have some special expertise, even in an area unrelated to your job, you may be able to use it to give yourself some real visibility. I knew one employee who had worked for a federal government office that dealt with commercial regulations and laws. Although his current responsibilities had nothing to do with his former federal job, he nevertheless made great use of it and became very visible in the process.

He contacted the manager of his company's law department and explained his background in federal regulations and years of experience with the government. He offered to do an informal question-and-answer seminar with some of the company's attorneys and paralegal staff. He said he would enjoy the opportunity to be a helpful resource to their department. The manager of the law department agreed to set up a get-together with about eight of his people for an hour Q & A session with this man.

The reaction to this man's knowledge of government cases and the government's posture on various regulations was so impressive that he was asked to be a regular resource to the law department and its staff. Eventually, he was promoted into this department at a much higher salary.

One clerk who spoke Chinese fluently heard that several of the company's senior executives were going to travel to China to explore business possibilities. He wrote a letter to one of the vice presidents and offered to give him a crash course on Chinese customs and some basic greetings in the language. The VP took him up on his offer and quickly realized that the man was being underutilized in his current clerical position. Soon this clerk was promoted to a much more challenging position where he could be of greater value to the organization and be developed further.

8. Create a "Brown Bag Lecture Series." Many companies sponsor a lecture series that covers a whole host of topics during lunchtime. Employees bring their lunches and eat while listening to a speaker give a talk on a topic relevant to their personal or professional growth.

You can be the person who organizes a Brown Bag Lecture Series in your organization. Obviously, if you are one of two people in an office that measures 12 by 12 feet, this idea might not be for you. However, I know someone who works in a very small office in a building where there are many other small offices who organized a Brown Bag Lecture Series for employees from the whole building.

There are many lecturers and public speakers who want to practice giving talks at no charge. Others appreciate the exposure at your company and may waive their usual fee. I know one woman who organized a Brown Bag Lecture Series that drew standing room only crowds. She regularly approached well-known lecturers and authors and was rarely turned down because she appealed to their self-interest in speaking at her prestigious company. The series finally drew the attention of the executive board of the company, who sought her assistance in starting similar lecture series in other company branches throughout the country. What visibility she got from this project!

The result of initiating a Brown Bag Lecture Series is that you can have fun, make contacts with some very impressive speakers and company executives, and in the process carve out a name for yourself as the organizer of such an event.

9. Write an article based on interviews with the organization's key executives. An exercise in Chapter 1 suggested that you interview high-level risk takers in your company. If you want to publicize yourself even further, use these interviews as the basis for an article for your organizational newsletter or even for a local newspaper or magazine. You can see that the assignment to interview your organization's risk takers not only gives you some valuable insights and information but also gives you personal exposure and visibility to influentials. The published article can give you some well-deserved publicity, too.

10. Become an officer of a network, trade association, or civic group. You can gain a great deal of publicity and visibility from being an officer in a network or trade association. Ironically, only a very small percentage of business and professional people are even members of networks or trade groups (these groups are discussed in Chapter 14). Yet there are many benefits of a network group that can result in your being visible not only in your company but also within your industry and among your peers. Most organizations are hungry for members who will work on committees. And once people in the organization get to know you and trust you, it may take a very short time to become chairperson of a committee or officer of the group.

Any recognition you get from the group, such as your being elected an officer, is grist for your publicity mill. You can let your local company public relations office know about your new position. This lets people know that you are ambitious and that you are a leader. You are a cut above the competition!

For example, in one sales association I belonged to, I became familiar with the members and began scouting talented individuals whom I thought would make great sales representatives for my company. I gave a list of recommended people to the vice president of sales. He was delighted and impressed with my company loyalty and interest.

Another way to publicize your active involvement in the trade group and at the same time make your company visible is to invite your company president or some other high-ranking member of your organization to be the guest speaker at a monthly meeting.

But by far the biggest benefit of your having an executive position with a network or trade group is that you will make many contacts that will give you a chance to find out about new job opportunities and sometimes the latest information on trends or innovations in your field. One way to make use of this information is to write a monthly or quarterly report on trends, observations, and findings that come out of your participation in the group. Then, send a copy of that report to key executives in your company.

11. Organize a visibility event. For example, you could organize a company picnic or a company softball team. Such events often draw the interest and attention of high-ranking executives. And these are perfect events in which to become known among your company's employees. I knew one low-level supervisor in the mail room who organized a marvelous and entertaining picnic and thereafter won the admiration and cooperation of just about everybody. They really appreciated his effort. That kind of visibility resulted in his getting extra cooperation on the job. Eventually, his ability to "get things done" resulted in his winning his first promotion within the company.

The right kind of publicity exposure can result in your getting valuable support and cooperation from people in your organization. I make that point again because many people have a very narrow perspective on what publicity means. To many people, it means that you are trying to get your picture in the newspaper or in *Time* magazine. Often it just means that you hope to become visible in a positive way so that people know you, like you, and are happy to help you succeed in your job. This is one of the big reasons why publicizing yourself and making yourself visible are so important to your job success and overall career advancement.

12. Implement a visibility project. In most companies, there are needed projects that no one is presently doing. Such projects can bring you great visibility and publicize you in a powerful way.

Once as a product manager in the marketing department I attended a national sales meeting where I heard several sales people say, "You marketing managers never let us sales reps know about the new products you are working on. It would really help us sell more effectively if you could tell our customers what new products they can expect from our company in the future." I knew the sentiment of most of the marketing managers about telling the field sales force about up-and-coming products: "We'll tell you sales people when we have the product ready for introduction—and not before. We've got enough paperwork without having to generate more."

It was obvious to me that most other product managers couldn't understand why it was important for the field sales force to know about new products being researched and tested. Having spent considerable time in sales, I knew how valuable it could be to take new product information into a meeting with a customer.

The thought occurred to me that I could gain a great deal of visibility and publicity and at the same time help the sales force if I spearheaded a special "new products" status report. I decided to use my staff to assist me in compiling this report on behalf of the marketing department. The report would list each product manager's anticipated new products with a brief description of the product, its status, and its anticipated market introduction date.

When I began to approach the different product managers about this report, they said they would cooperate with me. However, they thought I was just wasting my time doing work that wasn't necessary. I told them that I thought it would promote better relations between sales and marketing. I also knew that the visibility value to me would be exceptional.

So I proceeded to put together the new products status report for the field sales force, with my name as author. Even though my product line was among the smallest in dollar sales volume to the sales force, by compiling this report I was, in effect, the unofficial spokesman in the marketing department for over $100 million of the company's products. I further publicized myself not only by sending the report to 36 sales managers across the country but also by sending copies to a number of important sales executives at headquarters. The prestige and credibility I received were fantastic!

The key is that I found a legitimate need to fill and gained visibility in the process. You can do the same thing if you ask questions and listen to what people in different departments are saying. Look for the opportunities.

13. Attend the "right" company gatherings. I have already spoken about hidden agendas in Chapter 2. Being at the "right" company event can often result in your being looked at with favor by the company higher-ups. At one food company I worked at, the president wanted *all* his key executives to turn out for social functions he arranged. He liked putting on a show, even if it meant partying and drinking until the wee hours of the morning.

There are events that you may want to attend because you will be making yourself visible, not just because of pressure or obligation. Your absence at a company picnic may or may not be seriously missed. But in order to be visible, you may need to be at informal gatherings at the local company "watering hole." Not being there may suggest that you aren't a member of the inner circle. Sometimes there are special executive dinners or cocktail parties that you may want to get invited to because of what it means to the people in attendance that *you* were invited. There are certain regional or national company meetings that may not be mandatory for you to attend but are places where you should be visible.

So visibility is not just a function of achievements and accomplishments. It is also a function of what organizational gatherings you do or don't attend or the ones you are invited to or make an effort to get invited to. Be aware of this, because it can make a significant difference in making the right contacts, in hearing important information, or just in the overall impression that your presence makes. I knew one executive who made sure to get season opera tickets because he knew that the president and vice president were season ticket holders and loved the opera. He would make a point of bumping into them. He eventually developed a very special rapport with both of them because of their common interest.

14. Take an influential person to lunch. Sometimes the key to being visible is so close that you can't see it. This is the case when you want to expose yourself to powerful people but feel intimidated or wait for an invitation to socialize that never comes. You can develop a great deal of rapport and gain tremendous visibility by using lunch or breakfast to get to know the other person and let him get to know you.

This happened with the president of a company I worked for. I wanted to meet him on a one-to-one basis, but he was very busy and not often available for a "frivolous" lunch with a junior executive, which I was at that time. However, I discovered that some of his common interests were similar to mine. He was British and I had spent the previous summer in London, so I thought that would be the perfect entrée to proposing a lunch get-together.

I called him and said, "Basil, I know how busy you are [anticipation], but I have never had an opportunity to meet with you for a quick lunch. I thought it would be especially interesting because I spent last summer in your country. I think it would be fun to talk with you about my experiences there." His whole tone of voice filled with excitement and interest. He said he would enjoy getting together one day that week, and subsequently we did.

Now, many people have decided that they wouldn't have the nerve to approach the president of their company or director of their organization. Yet what better way is there of promoting yourself and the kind of person you are than to have center stage with the president? I found a common interest that made it possible. You can, too.

There are many other influentials you can take to lunch to gain visibility. Make a list of influentials at all levels in your organization: subordinates, peers, and superiors. If you know them casually, get to know them better. One of the secrets I have found out about so many of these people is that they are often like the prom queen that everyone is sure has a date, so no one asks. In other words, despite how busy you think such individuals are, in reality these people are often free and available just for the asking. Many will be thrilled and receptive at having someone like you initiate a "let's get better acquainted" lunch. Not only does this give you exposure for people to get to know you and your talents better, but it is also valuable in gaining their cooperation down the road, should you be working more closely with these people.

I knew one individual who would make it a point to invite any new member of the organization out for lunch as a sort of "welcome aboard" gesture. It worked wonders in giving him visibility as a good-will ambassador. And the new people were very grateful for the interest and attention. The man's ability to let others know he cared was one of the keys in his ability to get cooperation in getting his job done well. This trait was one of the big reasons for the promotions he received.

15. Write articles or books. One of the best ways to gain stature, recognition, and publicity is to be seen in print. This is relatively easy to do because there are so many newsletters, trade magazines, and periodicals that need articles written by professionals in the field. The hard part is getting what you have written into a major magazine where you are especially likely to get tremendous publicity and national attention. But that can happen, even from a simple write-up about you and what you are doing that may have originally appeared in a lesser-known periodical.

For example, a few years ago when I was traveling around the country conducting "conflict management" seminars for business and professional people, I got a call from *U.S. News & World Report*. One of their reporters was on my mailing list and had received a copy of a brochure on my seminars. The reporter was interested in my work and my views on how to ensure a successful career. This eventually resulted in one of my most prestigious accomplishments, a featured interview in *U.S. News & World Report*. So there are possibilities for publicity on even this scale.

However, any article you get printed can yield great publicity and visibility for you. You can then make copies and forward them to influentials in your organization, to customers you deal with, and even to employment agencies, who can use such collateral material to publicize what a terrific catch you would be to prospective employers who might want to hire you.

As far as writing a book is concerned, I can tell you from firsthand experience that it is not easy or glamorous. But it can be challenging, and it certainly can establish you as a credible expert in your field if you have something of value to say. Almost everyone does, but most people don't take the time to put it down on paper. You might even want to write a book in collaboration with other colleagues. It might be only 50 pages long and used only inside your company. But having such a book printed (or even just photocopied) can be an impressive way to publicize your expertise and talents.

WRITE A MEMO ACKNOWLEDGING YOURSELF FOR A GREAT JOB

One of the exercises I've had people do in my career advancement groups is write a short memo that acknowledges and compliments themselves for the excellent job they did on their last project, report, assignment, responsibility, idea, or sale (memos are discussed further in Chapter 10). They then send this memo to someone they want to know of their achievements. This is an excellent way of gaining publicity. Such an exercise appears at the end of this chapter.

It is important for you to feel comfortable and confident about acknowledging yourself for a job well done. You may also become more aware of the specific blocks or fears that result from doing this exercise. When you do this exercise, include people you are going to copy; then actually send the memo to those people. Check back after several days and ask their reaction.

If you are like me, you might be concerned that others may misunderstand your intentions when all you wanted to do was let them know that when you do something well, you are proud of it and you like others to know and give you recognition for your achievements.

For example, if I were checking back with someone to whom I had sent such a memo, I might say, "Tony, I wanted to get your reaction to the memo I sent you last week on my getting that new account for the firm. I had been working on the account for the last three months. Finally, I persuaded them to give us a trial order. I was proud of the sales results I achieved, and I just wanted you to be among the first to know."

Eventually, you will plan your publicity and visibility events very naturally. Best of all, you will be sensitive to opportunities that will give you the exposure and acknowledgment you deserve for your best efforts. Doing this will make you more powerful and valued in your organization. You will find it easier to get cooperation and get your job done. And you will find that this visibility will make you a candidate for more promotional opportunities because you will have distinguished yourself from the masses.

Exercise: COMPLIMENTARY MEMO

Directions: Write a short memo complimenting yourself for the excellent job you did on your last project, idea, report, assignment, responsibility, promotion, or sale.

TO: _____ DATE: _____

FROM: _____

SUBJECT: _____

Dear _____ :

_____

_____

_____

Sincerely, _____

CC: _____

_____

Exercise: PUBLICITY PROJECT

Directions: Create an idea or project that will publicize and give you more visibility in your organization. Take any of the ideas for publicity and visibility in this chapter, or use any accomplishment for this project. At the end of this exercise is a form you can use to aid you in getting organized so that you can implement your effort for recognition and visibility.

The following sample shows the steps I followed in implementing my guest lecture project.

PUBLICITY PROJECT (Sample)

1. Create an idea or project that will publicize you or give you visibility.

I will volunteer to be a guest lecturer at an evening advertising or marketing class at one of the local colleges, preferably Northwestern University.

2. List the individual(s) you will have to contact to make this idea or project happen.

Dean of Business School

Professor of Advertising and of Marketing

3. List the main steps involved in completing your publicity/visibility project.

A. *Initial contact and approval of professor; establish presentation date.*

B. *Establish agreement for professor to send me letter of evaluation.*

C. *Prepare actual talk for presentation.*

D. *Follow up on receipt of letter of evaluation from professor due by (date).*

E. *Once evaluation is received, make copies for distribution along with any appropriate memo of explanation.*

4. In the left column, list the people who you want to notice, acknowledge, or recognize you because of your project or idea. In the right column, list the means by which you'll make them aware of your project or idea. For example, you could make them aware by

Continued

Continued

verbal presentation, memo, announcement flyer, company news magazine, company bulletin board, advertisement, or meeting.

PEOPLE	METHOD
President, vice president	*Memo with attached evaluation*
My manager	*Verbal explanation in his office*
Public Relations Dept.	*Letter with evaluation*
Editor, company news magazine	*Send article on my teaching experience*

PUBLICITY PROJECT

1. Create an idea or project that will publicize you or give you more visibility in your organization.

_____

_____

2. List the individual(s) you will have to contact to make this idea or project happen.

_____

_____

_____

3. List the main steps involved in completing your publicity/visibility project.

A. _____

B. _____

C. _____

D. _____

E. _____

F. _____

4. In the left column, list the people who you want to notice, acknowledge, or recognize you because of your project or idea. In the right column, list the means by which you'll make them aware of your project or idea. For example, you could make them aware by verbal presentation, memo, announcement flyer, company news magazine, company bulletin board, advertisement, or meeting.

PEOPLE	METHOD

chapter 10

Document, Document: Using Memos to Manage, Motivate, and Influence Others

Sometimes it seems as though the business world runs on paper. Just think of the endless stream of reports, letters, lists, and statistical analyses that pile up in your in box, clutter your desk, and overflow from the files—not to mention those ever-present office staples, memos. Some people would like nothing better than to put an end to the epidemic of memo writing.

But before you join their ranks, consider: Are you aware that the memo can be an extremely valuable tool? Memos can help you accomplish projects, present your ideas, manage people, protect yourself, and earn recognition that will lead to promotions. Memos can be the perfect vehicle to use in a whole host of situations at work, such as confirming in writing the promise of someone to help you with a project. Or you may want to test the waters on an innovative idea that you have. Or you may just want to write a memo defending an unpopular position you have taken.

Surprisingly, a great many very savvy business people really don't know how to use memos beyond the classic CYA memo. Memos can, however, serve a wide variety of purposes, and once you know when and how to use them, you may develop a new appreciation for the art of memo writing. You will also discover that it is another valuable tool to use in winning promotions.

There are six purposes for which you should be using memos.

1. TO COMMIT

Use a memo to gain commitment from someone. Whenever someone promises to do something for you or to give you something, consider sending them this memo. Its purpose is (a) to put the responsibility for keeping an agreement on the other person and (b) to formalize in writing what has been agreed on so that all parties are clear on who does what.

For example, Lorna has been asked to prepare a five-year plan for the vice president, due on April 5. She will need a special preliminary report from Carol's department, and Carol has promised to deliver it by March 15. If Carol doesn't turn in the report on time— a very possible occurrence—Lorna will miss her deadline. Although Lorna will have a reasonable excuse, she won't score any points by blaming Carol. After all, it is her responsibility to gather all preliminary data. So to combat this potential problem, a day or two after her initial discussion with Carol, Lorna should send the following memo.

Sample: *Memo of Commitment*

Objective: To get something done by a certain date.

DATE: March 1, 1987
TO: Carol Phillips
FROM: Lorna Christopher
CC: Carol's boss
           Lorna's boss

Thank you for agreeing to furnish me with the sales data from your department. This data is vital to completing the five-year plan for my manager. I will expect the information delivered to my office on the date we agreed, March 15.

Sincerely,

Lorna Christopher

Keep in mind that Lorna has the option of having the memos delivered to the respective bosses or not. What is essential is that Carol understands that Lorna is relying on her, even to the point of making others aware of her commitment.

Remember, follow-up is one of the most important determinants of success on the job. To ensure that the data Lorna is relying on are not forgotten, Lorna is having her secretary follow up one week in advance with Carol's office to make sure that the report will be there on time as promised.

There are many other key uses of the commitment memo, including perhaps the most important, getting the promise of a raise in writing. Whenever anybody promises you a salary increase but doesn't put it in writing, you have just visited Fantasy Island. In other words, you are under a delusion, and perhaps naive, to rely only on a verbal promise as being sufficient in this matter. But how do you handle that sticky question, "Why do you want it in writing? Don't you trust me?"

Here's how Helen answered that question to her manager, Darryl: "Of course I trust you, Darryl. Why, just the other day my husband and I were talking and I said what a great manager Darryl is and how much I trust and respect him. But, God forbid, what if something should happen to him? Who would know we had this discussion?"

Of course, Helen's first choice is to make sure Darryl agrees to put this in writing. But if this is not done, she has the option of putting it in writing herself. (She may also want to copy the appropriate people whom she wants to know about this promise.)

Sample: Memo of Commitment

Objective: To secure a promise of a raise (or promotion).

DATE: November 15, 1988
TO: Darryl Evans
FROM: Helen Powers

Thank you for the excellent performance review you gave me at our meeting today. I sincerely appreciate your recognition of my contribution to our department.

Based on our discussion, I understand how tight the budget is this year, so I'll take your advice on being patient regarding the raise I had been counting on. However, I will rely on your word that I will receive the $3,000 raise by no later than July 15.

Sincerely,

Helen Powers

The same applies when you accept a new position; make sure you get a written offer. If someone doesn't want to put it in writing, he is sending you an unexpressed message that translates to "I want to welsh on our agreement if I have to; I don't want to give you what I promised; I want to have a way out."

2. TO INFORM

Most of us are used to receiving and sending memos that announce information. However, a memo to inform is useful not only to make people such as your manager more knowledgeable about what you and your department are doing but also to give your manager a feeling of being *in control*. Many business people I have counseled over the years have a similar complaint of having a manager who seems to be very concerned about knowing everything that's going on. People find that such managers are likely to stick their nose in subordinates' business all too often. One reason controlling-type managers do this is that they fear failure will occur if they are not directly involved, sometimes on a daily basis, with what you are doing. Some staff invite this, either through ignorance or intentionally, because they keep their manager in the dark. This can lead to feelings of insecurity for certain bosses.

This is often the reason why such managers insist on excessive reporting by their staff. One way to help assure that you are not bothered with lots of reports telling your manager what you are doing or having him hover over you more than necessary is to learn to write memos that inform. The informing memo has certain characteristics:

- It is specific and tends to quantify information.
- It addresses only the highlights of what you are doing.
- Although you are writing it as a report of what's going on, the tone of the memo communicates that you are fully in charge and responsibly managing the task at hand.
- It shows deference and respect that can reassure even the most controlling or insecure boss that you are capably managing your operation.

• It creates a busy and involved image for you and forces you to capsulize and summarize what you are doing.

Sample: Memo to Inform

Objective: To report to your manager (or higher authority) in a manner that will make him feel in control and have confidence in your management ability.

DATE: June 6, 1986
TO: Peter Golden
FROM: Dan Adams

I wanted to keep you fully informed of my upcoming meeting with my staff on *June 12*. We are meeting to discuss *third* quarter promotional spending. I will bring up for discussion the *four proposals* you and I discussed. I will advise you of our recommendations by *June 24*.

Sincerely,

Dan Adams

Note: I've italicized some of the simple ways to quantify this memo. It might even be a good idea to spell out each proposal. The key is that the specificity and authority by which you inform are often what will give even the most control-oriented manager the feeling that he can trust you and count on you. You'll find that such managers will be less likely to be constantly asking you what you are doing about various projects and activities because they will have developed confidence in you.

Don't just send these memos; make sure you get them, too, on a regular basis from your staff. The extra quantity of paper crossing your desk will be worth its weight in gold in terms of keeping you up-to-date and keeping your staff on their toes.

3. TO GIVE VISIBILITY

A visibility memo is an excellent way of blowing your own horn or even getting someone else to blow it for you. This kind of memo allows you to seek recognition and acknowledgment for many of your superior achievements above and beyond the call of duty.

For example, in Chapter 9 I told the story of how I volunteered to give a talk to the advertising class at Northwestern University. I asked the professor to write an evaluation of my talk and the reaction of the students, and he sent me the following letter:

Dear Mr. Schwimmer:

The entire class was totally appreciative of your presentation on product management and advertising. You filled the students with enthusiasm about having a career in marketing and advertising. It is obvious that you have a tremendous command of your company's products as well as the advertising strategies used to promote them. You are certainly a credit to your organization and truly an executive on his way to the top.

I reproduced that letter and sent it with the following memo.

Sample: Memo to Gain Visibility

Objective: To gain attention and recognition for superior achievement or activities you are involved in.

DATE: March 28, 1986
TO: My manager
FROM: Larry Schwimmer
CC: President of the company
          Vice President
          Public Relations Department

Over the last several months I have been lecturing at some of the colleges in the area. I have enjoyed the experience and also feel it has helped to enhance the image of our company within the community. In fact, I am enclosing one of the letters of appreciation that I received. I thought you might be interested in some of the enthusiastic reactions from the people who have attended my talks.

Sincerely,

Larry Schwimmer

There are all kinds of options with the visibility memo. You can send it out by itself, or you can attach favorable critiques of your efforts. The people your boss will allow you to copy on correspondence is an individual matter (dictated by your manager or company policy). So you'll have to find out if you can copy higher-level executives in order to gain the maximum visibility this memo can bring you. However, if you use the concept of self-interest with your manager, you may find your manager much more willing to make an exception to his normal rule.

For example, once when I was going to send out a visibility memo, I told my boss that I thought our community-minded president would appreciate my efforts and look more favorably on me and our department if he knew about my activities. My manager agreed, and I was able to copy some of the corporate elite.

4. TO DOCUMENT

One of the biggest risks you can take in business is to take a position on a particular matter. There is always the possibility that you have chosen the "wrong" position. A document memo can assist you, even with unpopular positions you may take. What is important about this memo is not so much what you say but rather whom you say it to.

For example, how can you protect yourself when you've been overruled on a marketing decision that you believe will cause the company to lose a great deal of money and for which you will still be held accountable?

This situation actually happened to me. My manager, the vice president of marketing, overruled my objection to his marketing decision, but left me accountable for the results of that decision. This left me in a very vulnerable situation. If his decision was wrong and my prophecy came true, I might end up the sacrificial lamb. So I wrote a memo saying that I totally disagreed with him on his decision and I believed that it would cost the company millions of dollars if we went through with it.

However, if I had sent that memo to my boss, I might have

gotten fired for insubordination. But I sent that memo anyway and carbon-copied two allies, Craig in accounting and Arnold in research. When my secretary went to distribute those three memos, something quite careless happened: She "lost" the memo to my boss. I don't know what happened to it, and I didn't ask any questions. The other two memos arrived safely at their destinations.

Six months later, my manager got fired. A new administration came in, and they called me in to talk. They were reorganizing the company—that's where they fire everybody and put in new people and call it "reorganizing." Before they reorganized me out of my job, the new vice president said, "We've looked over company records and your performance reviews. It looks like you've been doing a very good job. However, we don't understand how you could have been part of the ABC marketing decision because it lost this company X million dollars."

I said, "I'm glad you asked, because I was *not* part of that decision. In fact, I wrote a strong memo disagreeing with it. Why don't you check with Craig in accounting and Arnold in research? I advised them at the same time that this was a bad decision and that I was totally against it, but at the time I was overruled by the VP of marketing."

With some skepticism, the new VP said he would check out my story that afternoon and get back to me. He did.

I saved myself a $40,000 a year job through the use of that memo, because otherwise I would have been fired.

Here is a sample of a document memo written by an employee, Leslie, to her boss after their disagreement about the LMN project.

Sample: Memo to Document

Objective: To protect yourself by putting in writing and notifying key influentials and allies of positions you've taken.

DATE: September 26, 1988
TO: My manager
FROM: Leslie Samuels
CC: R. Jones, Research & Development
   P. Smith, Accounting Department

As you know, we have been jointly working on the LMN project for three months now. I believe that current research strongly indicates that we should abandon this project and cut any further expenditures associated with it. In our meeting this week, you disagreed and said that further expense was justified. Please understand that while I will continue to assist you in any way I can, I would like you to reconsider your decision to continue this project.

Sincerely,

Leslie Samuels

Keep in mind that this is a tricky memo. So be aware of the allies and influentials you will want to see the memo. Is there anyone you want to blind-copy (send a copy without stating the name in the "cc")? Do you want *all* copies to arrive to the listed people? These are some of the obvious and yet important points that you will have to consider—and that may save you your job.

5. TO PROTECT

You can use a memo to protect your ideas. In practically every office there's someone who's mastered the technique of discrediting a brilliant idea of yours and then presenting it as their own. You know the scenario: You drop into Nancy's office to get her feedback on a new plan, and she offers a number of reasons why it's unworkable. Two weeks later you enter a staff meeting to hear the president congratulating Nancy on "contributing one of the most innovative ideas" he has ever heard. Curiously, Nancy's idea bears a remarkable resemblance to yours.

Fingering Nancy as an idea thief is not an appropriate tactic; it will only be perceived by others as a case of sour grapes. So in the future, write up all your ideas in memo form and send them to your manager, or at least file them so that there is a written record.

Sample: Memo to Protect

Objective: To protect your best ideas from idea thieves.

DATE: May 1, 1989
TO: My manager
FROM: Debby Dewing
RE: New business idea

After visiting six of our major accounts on the East Coast, I believe we can take some important business away from our competition by doing the following. . . . I will discuss these ideas with several key executives in our company. Then let's meet to discuss this further.

Sincerely,

Debby Dewing

A short memo like this will be sufficient to protect you from idea thieves. Sometimes just telling the suspected idea thief "I've already put it in writing to see if management wants to pursue it further" will be sufficient to protect your ideas.

6. TO GAIN SUPPORT

Before you begin work on an idea or a project, you should gain some support for it. The ideal situation in any organization is to get support from individuals *before* the big meeting. Then when you meet, it is merely to rubber-stamp your idea, not perform an inquisition on it. A support memo will help you do this. Fast-track people want influentials, adversaries, and allies to know their best ideas, even on the most controversial, risky projects. Only half-cocked rookies go off and try a new idea only to find out that it was unworkable and they never should have started it in the first place.

When I was a product manager at a candy company, I noticed that one of our products, Jumbo Jimmies, did not come in the miniature "fun-size" package that people like to give out at Halloween. All the other candies—Dingo Donkers, Butter Batters, and Snacker Sinkos—came in the small pack. I did some mathematics and figured out that if we sold X amount of the fun-size Jumbo Jimmies, we could make $8 million extra in sales revenues at Halloween.

Then I thought to myself, "You're not that smart. If you could figure that out, why didn't somebody else before you?" So I sent out a visibility and support memo.

Sample: Memo to Gain Support

Objective: To gather input and support for an idea in advance by contacting allies, influentials, and adversaries.

DATE: December 5, 1988
TO: Allies, influentials, and adversaries
FROM: Larry Schwimmer
CC: Other interested parties

I'd like to ask for your input on the following idea: Jumbo Jimmies in fun-size packaging. I believe we can sell X amount of cases and make Y dollars in additional revenues. I'm aware of the fact that this cannot be a new idea, so I'd like to get your support and suggestions on how we can make it a successful reality. Please let me know of any problems or issues I should be aware of before I undertake this project.

Sincerely,

Larry Schwimmer

Well, my allies were thrilled, the influentials were impressed, and my adversaries were very supportive. After all, I was asking them for help ahead of time.

The product is now available in fun-size packages because of my initiative. But do you know why they never made it in fun size before? Because no one had ever actually attempted to implement the idea! So I want to share with you the realization that CEOs and presidents are regular folks, just like you and me. They don't have a monopoly on all the good ideas or their implementation. This memo put me on the right path and paved the way to taking a risk that turned out to be a major success, which eventually led to a new promotion for me.

7. TO REWARD AND RECOGNIZE

Few of us make enough money to live without the tremendous value of acknowledgments, stroking, approval, and recognition for a job well done. You can use recognition memos to give your star players visibility. It is one of the reasons a lot of people will work for you even though they don't make as much money as they would like to. They get other things from you that make them feel good psychologically.

Leaders and influentials share credit with others. In fact, one executive I knew, who received numerous promotions (until he finally reached his goal of being division president), said to me: "There's nothing an individual can't get done if *he's willing to give the other guy the credit.*" When you share the spotlight, you're seen as a team player. Has someone done you a favor? Why not express your thanks in writing? Has David just pulled off a major deal? Circulate a congratulatory memo, with a copy to David's manager. David won't be likely to forget that he gained more visibility by your action. There are many situations in which you can reap benefits in terms of grateful support later down the road by using this kind of memo.

Sample: *Memo to Reward and Recognize*

Objective: To acknowledge others for a job well done and give them the reward of positive visibility.

DATE: August 18, 1988
TO: David Kelley
FROM: Jenny Robbins
CC: David's manager
       Jenny's manager
       Other influentials

Thank you for the fantastic job you did in planning and setting up our special display booth at the exhibition. The result was that we had 25% more sales prospects visit our display booth than last year. Your contribution was extremely valuable. Congratulations on a job well done!

Sincerely,

Jenny Robbins

These six types of memos are generic in nature—so, quite often you will be able to make minor changes without continually redrafting the memos. I suggest that you establish a memo file that contains a sample of each type of memo. If you find memo writing cumbersome or time-consuming, have your secretary or administrative assistant prepare these memos whenever you require them.

RETURNING MEMOS

A great time-saving device in responding to memos is simply to send back a handwritten or typed note on the very memo that was sent to you. Be sure to make a photocopy of it for your file. This not only saves time, but it also makes very clear what subject you are responding to without your having to explain why you are writing. Your recipient also doesn't have to go through files to find the original memo.

You will have one less piece of paper in your file, and you will have answered the memo immediately instead of delaying your response to a time when you may require a formal memo. You will also impress the sender with your quick response, and you can be brief and to the point.

It is clear that memos can aid you in your ability to manage, motivate, and influence others. This skill is one more way you can help yourself win promotions.

chapter 11

Building
a Power Base
for Future
Promotions

SITUATION

Judy has just been offered her first supervisory position, and she is delighted finally to have the opportunity to demonstrate her leadership abilities. However, her prospective boss, Ralph, informs her that she will be responsible for her staff's productivity and output, but she will not have the authority to hire, fire, give out raises, or deal with special problems her staff may have. Ralph will be responsible for her staff in those areas.

What kind of power would Judy have in that position? Should she accept such a managerial position? Not unless she enjoys being powerless and in a low-level quasi-managerial role. Why? Because without any real power (e.g., the ability to hire, fire, grant raises), she will be a supervisor in name only, trapping herself in a dead-end position before she even begins. She can most likely expect frustration in producing results and problems with staff who realize she has no power and who thus must continually go over her head to her boss, Ralph.

WHAT IS POWER, ANYWAY?

The word *power* inspires many positive and negative reactions in people. There are a gifted few who use power in a positive and constructive manner to produce results. However, most people are afraid of having power, don't understand it, or tend to abuse it when they have it. Few of us have taken courses on the actual uses of power on the job. Few of us are given instructions on how to be powerful in a constructive way. Whether you are trying to get it, to use it, or to keep it, there is much to learn, practice, and master.

Here is our working definition of power:

POWER: the ability to act, accomplish, and produce a desired result.

Rather than view power in the negative manner as the means by which someone dictates, controls, or oppresses, I am talking about power in the most positive and constructive sense, where its purpose is to accomplish tasks and move the organization to achieve specific goals. Your power in the organization is directly related to your promotability. When management perceives you as using power effectively to achieve results in your job, you are much more likely to move up to higher positions of leadership and responsibility.

Yet as positive as this definition of power is, the quest for power is still very risky. The anxiety and discomfort that many people have about wanting power is based on ignorance of what power is, lack of education on how to use it properly, and firsthand experience with it. Much of the discomfort they feel about power goes back to their childhoods and their fears and anxieties associated with standing up to authority figures.

As children, most people were taught to defer to people with greater power. It's no wonder that they bring this social conditioning to their relationships with others at work who have greater authority than they do. These fears can result in their balking at taking the risk to stand up to or question a superior in their organization. Powerless people are relegated to the sidelines, doomed to watch their more confident peers rise to positions of authority. People who do not perceive themselves as powerful usually aren't.

In a sense, power is like a muscle: If it's not exercised regularly, it begins to weaken and eventually to atrophy. You must exercise the power that you have (and you have more than you may have realized) in order to develop it and strengthen your power muscles. Before anyone gives you power, you must demonstrate that you have the capacity to use it. Your self-concept—your recognition of your competence and abilities—is the first step in establishing a powerful persona.

POWERLESSNESS

I have talked about what power is, but it is just as important to talk about what power isn't. By understanding what power is *not*, you can avoid the very behavior that demonstrates your powerlessness to others. Again, it is very important to be aware of your behavior and, if you are acting in a powerless manner, to identify which behavior is unempowering. Only then can you develop more self-empowering strategies.

People at work are perceived as being powerless when they behave in an overcontrolling, petty, and rule-minded manner. Often CYA-type employees exhibit powerlessness because they are focusing on fear, insecurity, and potential loss. Powerless people are often afraid to delegate because this means losing some control. They have a tendency to be too detail-minded. Their rationale is that if you pay attention to every detail, nothing will go wrong. Or they may reason that other people will miss details that only they would take care of. They make very unempowering leaders because they have a very low trust level and are constantly peering over the shoulders of staff and coworkers and slowing productivity in the process.

The further result of this powerless leadership style is that such individuals oversupervise. When they do find competent coworkers and subordinates, they may feel threatened by delegating or giving credit for their staff's superior work achievements. Powerless leaders tend to overpunish in their use of coercive power as a way of banging their chests and reminding others of who's in charge. Rather than lead, powerless people are bossy, domineering, and dictatorial.

Characteristics of Powerless People

- Too controlling
- Overly concerned with details
- Very rule-minded
- Bossy and dictatorial

- Tending to oversupervise
- Unwilling to share leadership
- Unwilling to share power
- Reliant on coercive power

TYPES OF POWER

When you have no ability to act to produce a desired result, you are powerless. This is the case with Judy, the new supervisor whose boss, Ralph, was going to give her all the responsibility without any authority. In Judy's case, the real power in a managerial job must include the basics of hiring, firing, and giving out raises. Otherwise, she is nothing but a toothless tiger; the real power rests with Ralph.

In determining whether or not you have power, it is necessary to examine the types of power that are available to you. In so doing, you can begin not only to be aware of the existence of power but also to examine whether you use it or whether it sits on the shelf in your office gathering dust or is used only in rare instances.

POSITION POWER

This is the most basic type of power, conferred through the bestowal of a formal title, whether through appointment, such as accepting a position with the organization, or through promotion. Based on your formal title and the responsibilities that are contained in it, many people will acknowledge you for being powerful—at least according to your job description of what you can or are supposed to accomplish.

You may note that the same is true of an officer in the military. An officer's power is based on the respect and authority that go with the rank. But the rank or position alone gives the titleholder only a minimum amount of the power that is available in that particular position. Actions and ability to produce results determine the real power of the person in a position. We all know people who have a position title that would appear to be of great power who in reality have little or limited power. Or you may have known someone who was a very powerful vice president whose successor, in the same position, seemed to have far less power.

Position power is a starting point in wielding power in the organization. The person in the position must actuate this power by exercising it in order for him to be truly powerful. Therefore, power by position is initially beneficial but not always necessary in order to be powerful in accomplishing and producing results in the organization.

INFORMATION POWER

This type of power is a perfect example of having great power without having any formal title. By having access to important information, you can be very powerful, especially if it is the "right" information. I once knew a very lowly staff person who had important contacts in the grapevine (an extraordinary source of information). This fellow knew valuable information ranging from the company's plans for expansion and building new plants to having knowledge about a certain high-ranking executive who was a lush. And he knew such information before anyone else did. He was a very powerful person who was always being asked out to lunch by senior executives, no doubt because of what he knew.

This is one important reason why you will want to have good contacts both inside your company and even outside (see Chapter 14 of networking). Such contacts aren't always conventional. For example, I knew one executive searcher who knew more about my company than I did. He foretold the leaving of our current company president and the coming of the new one. Nearly everyone else was feeling the anxiety and insecurity of not knowing what would be happening. I was able to use this information and was of service (and relief) to several senior vice presidents, who were very impressed and very appreciative of my relating this special information to them. They accorded me a deference and power status far in excess of my actual titled position. They were willing to exchange useful information in return, as an added benefit for my information.

NEED POWER

One of the many definitions of power is the ability to control something that is needed by someone else. If you are the secretary who is in charge of the keys to the executive washroom and people have to come to you "before they can go," you are a very powerful person. Though there may be some humor in this example of need power, there also is a great deal of truth in reality.

I have known administrative people who controlled access to select information files. This was their only responsibility, and they had the authority to permit easy access. A bad relationship with them meant that you might be granted conventional access to information only between 9:00 A.M. and 4:00 P.M. A good relationship with them meant you had more convenient access before 9:00 A.M. and after 4:00 P.M.

I also knew a woman who was in charge of requisitioning office supplies. If executives in other departments were not helpful to her, she used their need for office supplies to wield her power. She could stick by the book and give them just enough to comply with the proper requisitioning of pens, pencils, paper, etc. Or she could open up the floodgates and get them quantities of sample pens with the company logo, which they could give away and be an instant hit with all their customers.

RELATIONSHIP POWER

Quite often, there is some excellent chemistry between you and someone in a much higher formal position. You may lunch frequently or otherwise spend time together. Because of this relationship with someone of much greater power, there is a transference of some of this person's greater power to you. The effect is that you derive some of his power as a result of this relationship.

I knew one junior executive who was a star tennis player in college. He struck up a relationship with one of the senior vice presidents who was interested in learning more about tennis and improving his game. They became great friends outside of work. The result: The junior executive gained informal power because of his special relationship with the high-ranking executive he played tennis with.

There are several reasons for this. First of all, the relationship became known to others in the organization. Second, out of this close relationship the junior executive had regular and, since the two played tennis quite often, frequent access to this important decision maker. Eventually, the junior executive's manager was asking the junior executive to discuss important projects and information with his high-placed tennis buddy. This junior executive had a tremendous amount of power based on the key relationship he had formed with this high-ranking executive.

This is why, as I have already mentioned, it is of tremendous value to identify your talents and interests with those of more influential executives (see Chapter 2). By doing so, you might find an excellent opportunity to develop a close relationship—one that may result in your gaining not only an ally but perhaps even a mentor (which we will talk more about in Chapter 13).

OTHER SOURCES OF POWER

There are many other sources of power available to you once you are conscious of them. Social researchers Bertram Raven and John R. P. French have delineated five classifications of social power, which I have adapted for use in a business setting. Let's take a look at each one. Be thinking of your own examples of the power you have or *don't* have or that you aren't *using* in each area.

REWARD POWER

This type of power involves controlling various resources that could be used to reward others. Some simple examples of reward power are

- Getting a promotion for an employee
- Giving someone a raise
- Sending someone to a trade show in a favorite city
- Sending someone to a special seminar or prestigious executive training program
- Getting someone a plush, new office

When I worked in Chicago, one of the rewards I gave my staff was sending high-performers to warm-weather plant sites during the cold and snowy Chicago winters. To reward another employee who was paying $80 a month for private parking, I arranged to get him an indoor parking spot inside the company garage. (I had to exchange favors with the parking attendant who controlled the availability of spaces in the company garage.) Not only was this employee thrilled about an indoor space, but he was equally excited about saving almost $1,000 a year.

These are just a few examples of reward power. I want to make two important points about reward power. First of all, be creative. If the only rewards you can think of giving people are promotions and raises, you will soon find yourself running out of promotional slots available to people who work for you. When budgets are so tight that salary increases are frozen, you will cease to have any reward power and will soon appear powerless. If you are a manager, there are many ways to show your power through rewards beyond the conventional.

I once had a secretary who worked overtime on Sundays whom I couldn't pay because of company policy. So I gave her one Friday afternoon off every month. I gave one engineer who worked for me the reward of taking a "night course" on company time at 3:00 P.M. so he could spend more time with his family.

By the way, if you are thinking, "Well, this is great if you are a manager, but I'm just a staff person with no one under me," my answer is that you are missing the point of reward power. You may have resources that you are not aware of that you can use to reward others. Using this form of power is not contingent upon being some big shot with a staff of hundreds.

For example, I had a coworker, Jerry, who went out of his way for me on a number of occasions. So I went to a colleague of mine who had information power. He always had the list of new position openings two weeks before anyone else knew about them. He told me of a new position that I thought would suit Jerry. I rewarded Jerry by letting him know about this new position so that he could be among the first to be considered.

Second, in using reward power (and some of the other powers we will be discussing), be sure to reward others as often as possible, letting them know that you strongly believe in taking care of high achievers. Some managers and employees who have many opportunities to use reward power are stingy with their rewards. I favor an image (which ties in very well with developing a charismatic leadership style) of being generous and benevolent and happily rewarding the people around you. This tends to make you very popular as well as powerful.

COERCIVE POWER

The flip side of reward power is coercive power—controlling resources that could be used to punish. Some examples are

- Docking someone's pay
- Firing someone
- Not recommending someone for a promotion
- Not choosing someone for a high-visibility project
- Sending someone to visit an unpopular city or locale

Just about all examples of reward power can be turned into examples of coercive power. For example, I can choose someone whom I don't think is doing his best as the one to visit our new plant location in Anchorage, Alaska, in January (where you need a flashlight to see where you are going at noon). I can see to it that someone gets assigned an office with no windows. (You get the idea.) Again, don't look at coercive power as power that is usable only by managers with lots of staff. I know secretaries who punish their bosses by careless screening of calls and visitors. I have known staff who were aware of urgent news that would help a coworker who chose to withhold or delay relating it as a way of punishing the other person.

EXPERT POWER

If you are able to control necessary information or knowledge, you have expert power. For example, if you are the only one who knows anything about the company's sophisticated computer system or the only one who understands the government's complicated affirmative action policies, you have expert power. Having this necessary knowledge helps you build a power base as someone very valuable to the organization.

I once worked with an older gentleman, Richard, who was a national accounts manager for the company. He would come to work about 9:00 A.M., leave for lunch three hours later, and never come back. Some young rookies in our company complained, "It's so unfair that Richard can get away with working only half a day. Who the hell does he think he is, anyway?"

After overhearing their remarks, I walked up to them and said, "Let me tell you who Richard is. For the last thirty years Richard has cultivated personal relationships with the head buyers for every major food-buying chain in the country. Because he is such an expert in his area and so well regarded by these chain buyers, he can place ten phone calls in half a day and write ten million dollars' worth of product orders! When any of you can match his expertise, I am sure I can talk to the president about arranging a 'half-day' workday for you, too!"

These rookies walked away embarrassed, like dogs with their tails between their legs. They didn't realize how powerful a person who has the right knowledge or expertise can be. Ironically, Richard had told the president that he was thinking of retiring early because "working a whole day was just too much." It was the president's idea for Richard to go home after lunch. The smartest leaders pay you for results, not for just putting in time.

The right knowledge can give you tremendous power. You can often acquire such power by volunteering to learn about information or projects that not too many people are interested in. For example, I remember a group of executives being asked if they would like to volunteer to go to a special symposium to discuss some very esoteric research that admittedly was going to be complicated and boring. No one volunteered for this research symposium. Finally, Wilbur came forward to attend the symposium. Based on this initial knowledge and further independent work on his own, within six months Wilbur was the only one in the entire company with this special expertise. He had no one working for him, but he had a great deal of expert power going for him. He had become extremely valuable to the organization.

REFERENCE POWER

This is based on being personally attractive to other people to the point that they are likely to identify with you or want to seek a relationship with you—often because of your charisma. This is the flip side of relationship power, in which you seek a relationship with influential people.

When you are personally attractive to others, people are attracted to you. Often they have a vicarious desire to be like you by associating with you. Reference power is based on being physically charismatic to others. This is why dressing for success and taking special pride in your personal grooming are so helpful in building your reference power.

The benefits of reference power are that you have a greater choice of people to develop relationships with at work. People have an automatic confidence in you and tend to want to include you in meetings, projects, and special tasks.

An excellent example of this is the jock type of executive who is tall, dark, and handsome and fits everyone's picture of what a superstar executive ought to look like. Many people in an organization are very attracted to, and do identify with, such figures. This may strike you as being superficial, yet it is a reality and a true source of power for those who have this physical persona.

Reference power also accrues to the chic-looking woman executive who dresses well and looks the part of the woman on the fast track. This profound effect can be seen in the academic world. Research continues to show that good-looking people receive preferential treatment in the form of higher grades in school than less attractive people. And the special preference that good-looking people get for job openings is well known. Right or wrong, our society places a high value on people who take care of themselves and look great!

I know one sales manager who went out of his way to recruit sales people who were big athletic jocks. He put together a cadre of good-looking Ivy League football types who wore blazers, rep ties, and penny loafers. These sales people had instant credibility with customers who appreciated having them call to service their accounts. It may sound amazing to you, but this sales manager broke all records by recruiting these jock-type role models. He was using reference power.

Now, don't think that the only way to have reference power is to be a tall, good-looking Adonis or Venus. You can gain reference power by having a charming personality or making people comfortable in your presence and feeling they can trust you. Having been a great football player in college or having gone to the "right" East Coast preppy school is another source of reference power. Anything that makes you so personally attractive that people either identify or want to seek a relationship with you constitutes reference power.

LEGITIMATE POWER

Position power comes strictly from the title and responsibilities of a position. However, legitimate power can mean that you may have the power even though you don't actually have the formal title. In legitimate power, authority and power are invested in a position or role and accepted by others as being appropriate.

For example, at XYZ Corporation it is understood that the assistant to the director is traditionally the heir apparent. So you, as the assistant to the director, will find people according you the power of the director's position, even though you are not yet the director. I have seen more than one fast-track executive pass up an heir-apparent position because he did not take the time to look at where that position could lead him. They just assumed that such a titled position would make them a "perpetual number two person." They didn't appreciate the legitimate power that would accrue as a result of their inevitable promotion.

DISCOVER WHY YOU ARE POWERFUL

The first step in being more powerful is to be aware of power and ways to be more powerful. Many people are powerful by accident. In other words, they do something that suggests how powerful they are without appreciating that they are perceived by others as acting powerfully. This is much like people who don't know why they are successful, but they are. That's great when things are going your way.

But when these successful people go into a slump, they often don't know what to do about getting themselves out of it. When they were on top it was because they were really "tripping over their own success." My point is that to be consistently successful, you have to be aware of *why* you are successful. In the same manner, to be powerful, you need to be aware of what you are doing that promotes your persona as powerful. This way you can consciously plan strategy and use the right resources to be successful or powerful. If you do this, you will win many promotions in your career.

Exercise: The Power You Have

Directions: List at least three specific examples of the power you have (or would like to have) in each classification category. If you are having difficulty coming up with examples in any category, think of people who you believe are powerful. How do they wield power in each of the areas listed?

POSITION POWER

1. _____

2. _____

3. _____

INFORMATION POWER

1. _____

2. _____

3. _____

RELATIONSHIP POWER

1. _____

2. _____

3. _____

NEED POWER

1. _____

2. _____

3. _____

REWARD POWER

1. _____

2. _____

3. _____

COERCIVE POWER

1. _____

2. _____

3. _____

EXPERT POWER

1. _____

2. _____

3. _____

REFERENCE POWER

1. _____

2. _____

3. _____

LEGITIMATE POWER

1. _____

2. _____

3. _____

POWER THROUGH ACTIVITIES

One of this country's most respected experts and researchers on the topic of power in the organization is Dr. Rosabeth Moss Kanter. Her classic book, *Men and Women of the Corporation* (Basic Books, 1977), talks about how to build power effectively in the organization. I will combine some of the main points she makes in her chapter "Power" with some of my own personal experiences to illustrate with graphic clarity how you can increase your power in your organization.

Dr. Kanter's research indicates that one of the key ways to increase your power in the organization is through the activities that you involve yourself in. For an activity to build power for you, it must meet three criteria:

1. The activity must be *extraordinary* in nature.

2. The activity must be *visible.*

3. The activity must be *relevant.*

Let's take a closer look at these three criteria. By prequalifying activities you engage in or volunteer for with these three criteria, you will be more likely to choose activities that will enhance your power than ones that involve just as much work without the potential reward of building your power base.

EXTRAORDINARINESS

It is true that many people are not in a position to accumulate power through extraordinary performance because they are carrying out ordinary or routine jobs, even if they are doing them extremely well. But by taking major risks and succeeding, you can add the extraordinary dimension to the activity and thus have it be power-enhancing for you. Here are four examples:

- Coming up with a brilliant ad campaign
- Turning around a losing product line
- Volunteering for a brand-new position
- Taking a big account from your main competitor

The next time there is an opportunity to work on or volunteer for an activity or work assignment, ask yourself if this project will allow you to take a risk in which success will be considered extra-ordinary. If so, its extraordinariness will go far in helping you build your power base.

VISIBILITY

The activity that you engage in must attract the interest and attention of other people. This again is why being able to publicize yourself, as we discussed in Chapter 9, is extremely important. If you recall, in that chapter I related the story of how I came up with a project idea to supply the sales force with a new products report. It gave me visibility throughout the company. If I had done it without getting the attention of other influential people in the organization, it would have never been as power-enhancing as it was.

RELEVANCE

Many times you may work on a task or project that may be important to you and even minimally important to the person who assigned it, yet such work may not be power-enhancing. For an activity to be power-enhancing, it must be considered relevant to the organization and identified as a solution to one of the organization's pressing prob-lems, such as the new products report which was relevant to the entire corporate sales force.

Before you undertake new projects and tasks, keep in mind these three criteria. Of course, you may not always have a choice of which projects you can or can't take on. Yet by being aware of these three criteria, you will be more likely to volunteer for opportunities where succeeding will bring you the power you deserve for the results you produce.

POWER THROUGH ALLIANCES

Dr. Kanter's research indicates that the other way to increase your power base in the organization is through the alliances you form with the different levels of people in the organization. These alliances should be with:

- Sponsors
- Peers
- Subordinates

Dr. Kanter goes on to say that power through alliances occurs in the organization via the social connections one makes that go above and beyond one's immediate working department. These connections have to be long-term and stable, and they should include a whole array of sponsors, peers, and subordinates.

SPONSORS

The first way your power is increased is through sponsors. When you think of sponsors, you think about people who can train, develop, educate, and guide you through the system. But they can provide other advantages beyond just giving advice. Sponsors are in charge of sponsored mobility, that is, controlled selection by the elite. They decide who will get what position before anybody else does. In contest mobility, it's an open game: The company is interviewing 3,000 people—would you like to be one of them? I don't need to tell you which is more preferential to your own career and advancement.

Sponsors are the rabbis, the high priestesses, the Godfathers: artificial bestowers of power. They can be people whom you can ask support for a job you want. "Look, I'm interested in getting the position of assistant to the director. Can you go to bat for me? I want that position." Sponsors provide you, as a lower member of the organization, the opportunity to bypass the regular hierarchical chain of command. They give you a chance to cut through cumbersome red-tape procedures to get inside information.

Sponsors can provide a certain reflected form of power. This is an important signal to people that says, "There is a more powerful set of resources backing this relatively junior person." You can see how this translates in terms of your being considered more powerful, not because of your own power but because of the credit that is extended to you.

Fast-track people develop a special social relationship with a powerful person that allows them to go directly to that person, even though there is no formal interface. That social, informal interchange can often produce formal results.

This was the case for a junior executive named Steven. He had developed his speech-writing skills as a result of working on a number of political campaigns in college. He volunteered to write a few after-dinner speeches for the president of his company. Eventually, the president was so impressed with Steven's writing talents and willingness to donate time that he and Steven soon developed an informal friendship. The president began to show a special interest in Steven's job success and encouraged him to "come see me anytime you have a problem." This special relationship with someone of power aided Steven in getting cooperation and support from others in the organization.

PEERS

A second way that power can be increased through alliances is through peer relationships. These relationships can be enhanced by sharing successes: direct exchanges of favors helping your peers. This also builds your personal power in the eyes of others. Here is a tactic I used when I worked for a large corporation.

Positions that were going to be opening up within the company were posted in the mail room so that employees could make arrangements to interview for them. The personnel department would originate the new positions sheet and have the mail room copy and distribute it companywide. I would go down to the mail room before they did the mass mailing and take the new job list back up to my office. After carefully looking through the list (and deciding that I didn't want any of the positions), I would look into the organizational directory and find somebody—friend, influential, ally, adversary, it didn't matter—that I thought would be perfect for a particular position that would be opening up.

"Hello, Dick," I'd say. "I know we don't have a chance to speak to each other very often, but I've heard some scuttlebutt, very confidential, that there's a special position opening up as the assistant to the director. They are going to be interviewing soon, and you'd be perfect for it. It pays $36,000 to $42,000, I understand. You've got your MBA and you've got the support of this person and that person. I just wanted you to know about the position in advance of everyone else."

Dick would reply, "Gee, Larry, this is terrific news! How can I repay you?"

I'd say, "I'm sure I'll think of something you can do for me in return. 'Bye."

If Dick got the position, my power was enhanced even further because I could say I was the one who told him about the position first. If Dick didn't get the job, at least he appreciated the fact that I was watching out for him and willing to share some important information. That's a simple way of promoting positive peer relationships.

SUBORDINATES

The third way to increase your power is through your subordinate relationships. Because people advance at different rates, those who are your subordinates or peers today may become your superiors tomorrow. That's why you must make downward alliances with people who look like they are on their way up. It is vital to gain the loyalty of others to assist you in implementing your plans and projects. No leader can be successful without the support of his or her team.

This is one of the reasons you must cultivate good relationships with secretaries in your organization. If your secretary (and other secretaries) aren't willing to give you informal information, it may be because you are being isolated. One of the first ways of finding out that a "corporate hit" has been put on you is to be isolated from information. So don't tamper in any way with one of the most important uses of the grapevine, your organization's secretaries.

To build power through your alliances, form relationships not only with sponsors, who are quite often superior to you in position, but also with coworkers and subordinates. Having a broad base of support will enable you to accumulate the power and assistance you need to accomplish your goals and to take on the challenges that are an inevitable part of being successful and promotable.

BEING POWERFUL

Being powerful starts with being aware of what power is and the kinds of power that are available to you. You can be powerful based on the activities that you are involved in as long as these activities meet the criteria of being extraordinary, visible, and relevant. This will be useful in deciding what projects to be involved in. To gain and maintain power, it is important to seek out publicity and make your accomplishments visible. And power will also come from the right associations with sponsors, peers, and subordinates.

But perhaps the most important ingredient in being powerful is *your attitude.* Your attitude toward being powerful will largely determine whether or not you will do things that are power-enhancing or whether you will perpetuate your own powerlessness. One of the best things you can do is to examine how you really feel about being a powerful person.

In the following sentence completion exercise, there are no right or wrong answers. But your answers will provide you with some real insight into your own attitudes toward how you feel about power, what you believe you could do if you were more powerful, and even how you think others would view you if you had more power.

Many people don't want power; they are concerned that they won't be as well liked by others. If this is the case with you, it is likely that you will stay away from strategies that could make you more powerful. Your attitude makes the difference as to whether you will ultimately be a powerful person.

You have to want power to be powerful. And the best way to want power is to see the positive results that come from having it and using it wisely. To get power, you may have to confront the fears and considerations that prevent you from attaining it. Power rarely comes to people by accident. Most powerful people quest for it and make a concerted and often planned effort to obtain it. Once they do, they use it to win future promotions.

To become more aware of your attitudes and beliefs about power, complete the following exercises.

Exercise: COMPLETING SENTENCES

Directions: Fill in the blanks to complete these sentences. The first three blanks contain sample answers.

1. "If I had more power, people would . . ."

2. "If I had more power, I would . . ."

respect me

get things done

do what I wanted them to do

make more money

dislike me

fire incompetent people

Another exercise to make you more comfortable with power is to talk to people who are very powerful. Ask them what excites them about power, what they have achieved through the use of their power, and what their fears and considerations about power are. You may develop some new insights about the whole topic of power. If you do this exercise, you will find out a great deal about yourself and the nature of power. In so doing, you will be more likely to build a power base that will make you productive, successful, and promotable.

Exercise: INTERVIEWING POWERFUL PEOPLE

Directions: Pick out three people you consider powerful. Arrange to interview them on their thoughts, attitudes, and ideas on being powerful. Tell them you are doing a research paper for a course, or tell them, truthfully, that you are curious about learning more about power. I've provided some sample questions you could ask them; add your own questions to the list. Be sure to write out your questions beforehand so that the people you interview will understand that you are gathering information in a sincere way.

Note: This is a fabulous way to gain access to high-level and powerful people in your company. Usually such people are flattered at being selected as authorities on something as appealing as power. Some of the people from my career advancement groups actually got appointments with the presidents of their companies. That's visibility!

PEOPLE I WILL INTERVIEW

1. _____

2. _____

3. _____

"ON THE SUBJECT OF POWER, I WOULD LIKE TO ASK YOU":

1. What do you like most about being powerful?

2. What do you like least?

3. At what point did you begin to feel powerful?

4. Do you think your position makes you powerful, or is there something else that gives you power? If so, what do you think it is?

5. What is your biggest fear about being powerful?

6. How do you feel about other powerful people?

7. What are the attributes you need to develop in order to become powerful?

8. How do you increase your power?

9. What accomplishments do you believe you were able to get done because you were powerful?

10. What powerful people do you respect?

11. What kind of people in this organization do you think are best suited for power?

    Add your own questions.

chapter 12

Selling Your Ideas— or Yourself— Persuasively

- "I wasn't cut out for selling."
- "I think most sales people are BS artists."
- "I don't know the first thing about sales."
- "I hate selling."
- "I wish I had more confidence in my selling ability."
- "I don't need to 'sell' for what I do."

Do any of these statements sound familiar? Most people do not recognize how vitally important it is for them to be great sales people. Part of what creates this attitude is that they look at selling in its most traditional form: selling a product or service. This is a very narrow view of what selling really is and the many instances in which selling is required for those who want to win promotions.

For example, have you ever walked away from a job interview with the uncomfortable feeling that the position wouldn't be offered to you, even though it would be perfect for someone with your background and skills? Perhaps you believed that your qualifications and abilities would speak for themselves. If so, it's time you realized what most savvy professional people have always known: It is impossible— and potentially disastrous—to minimize or underestimate the value of a strong sales pitch or presentation to produce the outcome you want.

Selling yourself and your abilities effectively can make the difference between receiving a job or a promotion and being passed by. Ignorance of selling skills may be undermining your attempt to advance your career, have your ideas adopted, or receive salary raises you deserve.

No matter what kind of work you do, you will always have to sell yourself or your idea—at an interview, at a board meeting, at an informal brainstorming session with your manager or staff. This kind of selling is a skill that is easily mastered. Once you know the basic concepts, you may be surprised to discover that you are a natural sales person. And you'll certainly be delighted to see the positive effect it can have on your career.

Most people grow up with many stereotypes and attitudes about sales people and the whole notion of selling. Usually, these beliefs are based on some negative experience where people felt pressured to buy something they did not want. Or they ran into an unethical sales person who made exaggerated claims that simply were not true. Or they may have had the experience of talking to sales people who were insincere and did not have the customer's best interest at heart. These sales people were only looking to make a sale.

Fortunately, the image of the phony, backslapping sales person who will say anything to make the sale has changed a great deal in recent years. Yet many people still have an attitude of suspicion and distrust regarding sales people and the whole area of selling. Whether or not you like selling, it is vital to your career (and life) success for you to appreciate the value and importance of becoming an excellent sales person who can sell an idea, product, service, or yourself.

THE IMPORTANCE OF SELLING

By overcoming your fears or negative attitudes about selling, you will increase your confidence in presenting yourself and producing the results you want in many work situations. Your mastery of basic selling skills will enable you to advance your career and ensure a high degree of success in any job you do. You need selling expertise to present proposals; to interview; to persuade and influence staff, co-workers, and upper management; and to sell yourself as the best candidate for a promotion.

It is obvious that persuading and selling go far beyond conventional sales. Consider these situations:

SITUATION

To assure the success of a project you are implementing, it is vital that you get the support and cooperation of other departments. The project could fail because people are not properly sold, convinced, and committed to your project's success.

SITUATION

You are having a salary review with your manager to assess your performance and discuss your salary increase for the coming year. If you are unable to persuade your boss of your exemplary achievements and high performance throughout the year, you might get far less of a salary increase (and perks) than you had expected.

SITUATION

You are trying to get the executive committee to grant you additional funds beyond your original budget for research that is vital to your department's operation. Failure to persuade and sell the committee on your additional budget needs could jeopardize the success of research projects you are attempting to complete.

ARE GREAT SALES PEOPLE BORN OR MADE?

Unquestionably, great sales people are made! Certainly, there are some individuals who have natural qualities; combining these with bona fide sales skills, they become great sales people. These people were not born with these skills—they developed them. The best and most successful sales people are indeed made.

The key is for you to know that even if you consider yourself the most introverted person in the world, you can be a very effective sales person. In fact, some of the highest-producing sales people I have ever known were the antithesis of the stereotypical salesman.

They were low-key, had superb product knowledge, and soft-sold their products or services.

Realize once and for all that to become an effective sales person, you must get rid of the negative models and points of reference you have about sales people. From here on, you will be a great sales person with your own selling style—looking, feeling, and sounding nothing like your old idea of a sales person.

BEING A GREAT SALES PERSON

The highest-performing sales people got to be that way by (1) learning basic selling skills, (2) practicing the application of these skills in a variety of selling situations, (3) getting lots more selling experience, (4) anticipating and overcoming a wide variety of customer objections, and (5) recognizing the need for unrelenting follow-up.

You can incorporate everything we will talk about into your own style of selling. There are no concrete rules about selling; there are only tools and approaches that you should use if they work for you. Obviously, some work better than others.

YOUR SALES ATTITUDE

It is important to have a positive attitude in selling, not an attitude that is phony or conjured up or just a cover-up for negative feelings about selling or feelings of inferiority. My selling attitude has always been, "I have never lost a sale. Some just aren't closed yet!" I say that not out of some attitude of braggadocio but because I have seen over and over again that an idea, project, or account I couldn't get today could be gotten tomorrow or at some time down the road. This comes from being persistent. It also comes from understanding the *process* of selling, which includes the ever-present possibility that the *no* you receive from a customer (or coworker) today may, through your efforts, turn into a *yes* tomorrow.

It also comes from having an attitude that selling is just one more professional skill at which you must be proficient to be competitive with others who are trying to advance their careers just like you. It is a necessary component in your professional package. Another part of having the right attitude is knowing that it is important to *initiate*.

You will often have to bring forth your idea or proposal; you will have to find your own prospect to sell; at a promotion interview, you will be the first to mention the reasons why you are the most qualified for the position. This is in contrast to someone who thinks that selling consists of someone coming to you to buy what you have. This may happen; however, in the real world it is generally called "order taking."

An order taker is the person you see sitting behind the counter at your favorite clothing store waiting for you to hand over whatever you have decided to buy. He will then ring it up on the cash register. A sales person, on the other hand, would be out there on the floor, helping you pick out what you want, answering questions, making suggestions, and giving you important information on colors, styles, and sizes. Sales people know how to initiate. It is a big part of the attitudinal mindset of selling anything.

Another part of the sales attitude you will want to cultivate is coming to terms with the "Big R": *Rejection*. No one likes rejection. Yet one of the differences between the most successful and the least successful sales people is the way they view rejection. Sales people who produce poor results take any failure or rejection as something personal against them, as if the rejection were a statement about the kind of person they are. Such people generally have a pretty low self-image to begin with. It is easy for them to gather inconclusive proof that they are failures by using situations where they have attempted to sell someone and had their sales effort rejected. Notice that I didn't say, "They were rejected." What they had to sell—proposal, idea, product—was rejected. You must make that distinction.

Your attitude for successful selling has to be, *"I may fail, but I am never a failure."* By having this mindset as part of your selling attitude, you will be less likely to take personally any (temporary) rejection of your ideas, proposals, or sales presentations. It doesn't mean anything more than that your presentation in its current form is incomplete and insufficient to compel the other person to buy what you are attempting to sell. It should result in your redirecting your sales effort. In doing so, you will begin to hear what others say not as rejection but as feedback. You will then be able to use this feedback to sell them in a manner that relates to their needs. This will produce the sales results you seek.

Another important part of your selling attitude is never, ever underestimate the amount of *persistence* necessary to sell anything. I have had to place dozens of telephone calls to convince people to buy things that they had already told me they wanted. That's right! Just because the person to whom you are trying to sell wants what you have doesn't mean that you will automatically get the order. The person may have obtained a 95 percent commitment to what you have to offer, but the remaining 5 percent reservation may get in the way of your closing the sale. Later on, I will talk about dealing with that 5 percent which is called a consideration or objection.

For now, just appreciate the fact that *you will know that you have persisted enough when you finally get the permission, approval, go-ahead, or the order that you were seeking.*

LEARNING THE SKILLS FOR SELLING ANYTHING

It seems that every successful sales person has some deep, priceless secret that he will share with you to make you successful. It is wise to learn as much as you can about skills, tools, and approaches that other successful people use. Just don't get taken in believing that there is only one way to do anything.

In fact, I have seen the same sales principle work wonders for one person and fail dismally for another. The message is clear: Take in suggestions for successful selling, adapt them to your own use, and apply them in your own way. You'll find that such skills or strategies will be more natural and comfortable for you and consistent with your own personality and selling style. Don't rely on or search for the one sales guru you think has the answer.

My experiences and observations have shown me that there are eight basic skills that—though needing your refinement, creativity, and adaption—are standard elements used in selling anything: your ideas, proposals, products, services, or, most important, YOU. These skills may make the difference between a promotion and being passed by. Learn, practice, and master them and you will be able to succeed at many of the challenges presented to you in your job.

Step 1: THE ART OF LISTENING

The process of selling anybody anything begins with listening, which is a radical notion for people who are not listening but only waiting for you to stop talking so that they can begin. You cannot find out what the other person wants or needs (which is one of the major ways to sell someone) if you are talking.

If you are trying so hard to talk or to sell that you forget to listen, you will turn your buyer off. It is very easy for any potential buyer (of your idea, your proposal, or yourself) to get an immediate sense as to whether you are sincerely interested in finding out what his need is so that you can fill it or whether you have a one-track mind hell-bent on trying to make the sale. (This, by the way, is one of the pitfalls of the canned sales spiel, where the sales person lacks spontaneity and instead just wants to get through with the pre-rehearsed sales pitch.)

Listen consciously to the person to whom you are selling, and from time to time acknowledge their statements to you with nods or remarks such as "I see," "OK," "That makes sense," and "Right." This will help you establish one of the single most important elements to successful selling: *rapport*—a connection, agreement, and harmony with the other person. In so doing, you are at the same time establishing credibility along with an image of sincerely being interested in what the other person is saying. I often start off a presentation by saying: "First of all, I'd like to begin by listening to what you have to say about . . ."

When you listen, try to relax and get comfortable. People who aren't listening often fidget and have an expression on their face that indicates impatience. This may telegraph to the person to whom they are trying to sell a message that says, "Hurry up and finish so that I can begin selling you." If this is the feeling that this person gets from you, count on the fact that you will not only have little rapport but practically no credibility or trust.

Don't assume when you are listening that you can't ask questions. Questions are an excellent way not only to establish greater rapport but also to clarify a problem, need, or issue that you must understand fully to sell effectively. When I need to ask a question, I will often simply say, "Excuse me, before you go on, I want to make sure I am clear on the point you just made." This is much better than abiding by some rule you learned as a child that said, "Never, never, interrupt." If you interrupt politely and respectfully without being excessive, you will find that your listener will appreciate your honest interest. Sometimes I will literally say, "May I interrupt you? I want to be sure I understand what you have just said." Or you can make a note or two and then ask all your questions at the end.

Personally, I have found that you can create excellent rapport by having a dialogue in which the other person does the majority of the talking and you do the majority of the listening, at first. Intelligent questions let the person to whom you are trying to sell know that you are sharp, alert, and eager to understand what is being said. In fact, I often will make up questions in advance so that I am less likely to forget to ask an important question whose answer might be instrumental in selling that person.

Step 2: INTERVIEW AND ASSESS

While you are listening, you may want to jot down a key word that relates to questions you will want answered by the other person. I will often say to the person I have just heard speak, "Now that I have had a chance to listen to what you have said, I would like to ask you some questions" or "informally interview you." This builds credibility and confidence for you in the mind of the person to whom you are trying to sell. Rather than acting as if you already know the solution to his problems, you show your willingness to do some investigating and research firsthand.

As you ask questions, you will begin to assess the other person's wants or needs. For example, you must find out how he evaluates ideas such as yours, other candidates for the job, or the criteria established for buying what you have to sell. You will also gain some insight into his self-interest: the reason he will do or give you what you want. You will discover what benefits to his self-interest would be relevant, motivating, and compelling.

All this information will help you in composing a presentation that will get him to see your product or idea in the most positive light. In this interview, you should begin to get an idea of his objections, problems in the past, and considerations—the nagging concerns that are holding him back from giving you what you want. You will also get insight into his approach to buying and making decisions. Does he seem to require lots of analytical data? Is he quantitatively or qualitatively oriented? Is he the chief decision maker, or must he get an OK from his manager?

This information will be extremely valuable to you in finding the best way to sell him and make him feel comfortable and confident in his decision to buy. For example, he may tell you, "Before I make any decisions, I want to get a preliminary reaction from a number of the field service managers." So, you know that as part of your homework you may need to do some advance selling to field service managers to, in effect, get their views and endorsements.

Interviewing and assessing goes far in establishing rapport and giving the other person confidence that you aren't just trying to make a sale by using some canned spiel that you present to everyone you talk to. Rather, you are trying to individualize what you are selling to his unique and specialized needs. This step heightens your credibility even further and is valuable as you progress further in the process of selling them.

Step 3: DETERMINE THE BUYER'S SELF-INTEREST

We keep coming back to the concept of self-interest. It is simply impossible for me to mention this concept too much in this book. So let me repeat: *Self-interest is the reason someone will do or give you what you want.* It is the surest way to be relevant, motivating, and compelling to anyone to whom you are trying to sell. And it will further your ability to establish a rapport with the person you are trying to sell to or persuade.

Ask yourself, "What does this person want? What's in it for him? What would make him feel that my idea, project, proposal, or product is valuable, worthwhile, or important? Most of all, what is his self-interest?" People's self-interest usually can be found in one or more of the following areas:

Money	Power	Popularity
Status	Promotion	Recognition
Security	Freedom	Creativity

You may discover that this person has other areas of self-interest besides the ones I have listed, or you may find an area that is a derivative of one of these areas. This is just a list of the more traditional areas that are of self-interest to people.

But to sell and persuade effectively, you must take his specific self-interest into account. If you are not sure what this person's self-interest is, ask questions about his goals. What's the most important benefit he expects to get out of what you are trying to sell? If you are still not sure, you may even propose a few of your best hunches and get him to validate whether you are correct in your perception of what his real self-interest is. Learn to trust your intuition and feelings. Sometimes we get so analytical and logical that we discount or minimize that special gift we all have of immediate cognitive knowing: our intuition.

Ineffective and unsuccessful selling is generally the result of not appealing to the other person's self-interest. And keep in mind that the person to whom you are selling may have several areas of self-interest. Consider the following sales scenario and the special role that appealing to the person's self-interest makes in sales success or failure.

SITUATION

Charles is trying to sell Alex a new piece of equipment. Let's call it the "super widget." It is a brand-new invention that has only recently come on the market, and it is expected to save Alex's company a lot of money and increase employee productivity.

Alex is a very cautious purchasing manager. He has been with this company for over 20 years. He is in his late fifties and seems to know his job well. Despite acknowledging the benefits of this new super widget, he seems skeptical and resistant to giving Charles an order for this equipment.

Charles can't understand why Alex hasn't jumped at the chance to bring a major innovation into his company. Charles has talked to Alex about the money his company will save and that once the equipment is in operation and improving productivity, Alex will receive a great deal of recognition for his wise purchase. "Who knows," Charles points out, "this new super widget may be your ticket to a big promotion."

However, Charles did not get the order—and he can't understand why. But the reason is apparent. Charles has not appealed to Alex's self-interest, which is his need for security. After more than 20 years with this company, Alex is approaching retirement. He can intellectually appreciate saving money and increasing productivity. And he has received enough recognition over the years; at this point in his career he isn't interested in the responsibilities that go with a new promotion. Further, in his company he knows that at his age it is unlikely anyway. Alex is not interested in pioneering a new piece of equipment. After all, it may still have bugs in it. What happens if there are major problems and the machine turns out to be a white elephant?

"No," Alex reasons, "I am not going to jeopardize my secure position here by making a major purchase in buying this new super widget. I don't want to take the risk of ruining the good name I have worked hard for so many years to establish. I just want to retire in peace. Let some young upstart take a chance with his career on this new invention."

You can see that Charles has not appealed to Alex's real self-interest, security. He has done a poor job of assessing Alex's self-interest. As a result, he didn't get the sale.

Charles's sales approach might have been perfect for a younger or newer purchasing manager who was trying to carve out a name for himself or for someone who was interested in recognition and promotional opportunities. This scenario typifies why so many people are frustrated when they think they have the best idea, for example, to save their customer lots of money and yet don't get the order.

You can maximize the chances of selling your idea, product, or service by discovering the other person's self-interest. Knowing this will make the difference between success and failure in any selling situation, whether it is in attempting to get the job you are interviewing for, getting a group to adopt your idea, or selling a customer your product.

Step 4: ANTICIPATE OBJECTIONS

Whatever the idea, proposal, or product you are selling—or even yourself—count on the fact that people will have certain considerations or concerns about it. Sometimes the considerations may have nothing to do with you or what you are selling. This was the case with Alex when Charles tried to sell to him: Even basic, bottom-line reasons (saving money, increasing productivity) were insufficient to overrule Alex's consideration about his security being threatened by the super widget's possible failure in some way.

Whereas a consideration is a thought or concern someone may have about you or what you are selling, an objection represents direct opposition to, disagreement with, or disapproval of what you are selling. Inherent in the process of selling anything is the fact that people will have objections. Some they will raise directly to you for discussion, others they may allow to fester inside, and still others they may not even be aware of. These last are of the greatest concern to you because you must be enough of a detective to ascertain what these objections might be.

This is one of the major reasons why you will want to anticipate objections that the other person may have, even to the point of anticipating and mentioning objections that he may not even have thought of. This will save you from many problems that occur for sales people who purposely or accidentally minimize, obscure, or avoid mentioning any negatives or objections that could be associated with whatever they are selling.

Why mention anything negative about what you are selling? Certain very short-sighted individuals think that they would be ruining their chances of making the sale if they mentioned anything negative about what they are selling. Their strategy is to mention only the positive points and leave out the negative points or objections. This is a grave mistake and one of the poorest ways of selling—and it is born out of very low integrity. It is known as "win-lose" selling.

The win-win strategy, where both parties' interests are looked after, occurs when you anticipate the other person's objections even before he has an opportunity to raise them to you.

Leaving out negative points and not openly discussing your product's limitations is bad selling. Doubts will still remain in the mind of the person to whom you are selling. This is true even if he does raise objections and you adroitly sidestep them. It is also bad selling because even if the person doesn't directly raise an objection to you, he may think about it after you have left—and then make a unilateral decision to say no when you aren't around to re-sell him.

Another problem can occur as a result of your not anticipating negatives and objections. You may find out later that the person you have "sold" will need to talk with his manager and will be unprepared to answer the considerations or objections that his manager may raise. This may result in your not getting the order or the acceptance you want. Part of effective selling is preparing the other person to sell and represent your interests to others who may be involved in the decision-making process.

By not anticipating objections or the "yes . . . but's" people may have about what you are selling them, you may find that their doubts, concerns, and reservations may begin to arise consciously or sometimes unconsciously. Even if someone is 95 percent sold, there is that gnawing 5 percent that represents objections or considerations which prevent that person from being completely sold.

When people are not completely sold, even if they say yes, you may end up with a shallow agreement that they may later decide not to live up to. We have all experienced making an agreement with someone that we thought was a fantastic deal for ourselves but not a very good agreement for the other person. What often happens is that the other person ends up breaking the agreement or doing a substandard job, even though he technically kept the agreement. Such is the fate of people who make "win-lose" agreements whereby only they benefit—usually at the expense of the other person.

As I mentioned, when objections have not been anticipated and openly discussed and resolved in the mind of the person to whom you are trying to sell, they tend to be magnified out of proportion. The person begins to feel real reservations about what he previously felt good about at the time you were selling him.

This is the experience Pamela had when she went into her favorite clothing store not meaning to do anything more than browse. However, a silver-tongued sales person urged her, "Just try it on." Besides, it was on sale! Pamela did, and she ended up buying the outfit.

When she arrived home, she had some regrets and real considerations about having made that purchase. This is called buyer's remorse. ("Why did I buy this? I'm not even sure the color looks good on me. And the discount off the regular price was only 15 percent. It will probably be marked down even more in a few weeks. And besides, I can't really afford it.")

Psychologists have another term for this state of mind. It's called "cognitive dissonance." This refers to the internal feelings of doubt and discord Pamela had—in this case, about buying something that she wasn't sure she really wanted. It is the incongruency of her actions (buying the outfit) with her real feelings ("I didn't really need that").

If someone has that feeling of disharmony or cognitive dissonance about something you have sold, you have done a poor job of selling.

In contrast, a sharp sales person would have handled Pamela (as a buyer who is just browsing and even reluctant to buy) in a manner whereby any objections she might later have would be addressed at the time of the sale. For example, such a sales person would have said to her in a sincere fashion, "The styling and color of this outfit are especially flattering to your figure and your skin tone. Also, I might point out that this is a very special sale on this designer's clothing, with a full fifteen-percent discount off the retail price. While this may not seem like a substantial discount, let me assure you that this is the largest discount we offer on this designer label. And once the sale is over in ten days, this outfit will be marked back up to its full retail price."

This sales presentation makes a strong appeal for the sale and yet anticipates at least several objections that Pamela might have or think about later on. Of course, there is no guarantee that she still won't bring back the outfit. But since several potential objections have been anticipated, our sales person has significantly reduced the odds of Pamela's returning the outfit. In the process, Pamela will feel more confident and secure in her purchase.

Also, by anticipating likely objections with people to whom you are trying to sell, you are further establishing rapport and credibility. In a magnanimous way, you are letting your buyer know that you have not only a great deal of overall knowledge about your product or idea but also that you have the savvy to consider all angles. And you are so confident of the overall value and worth of what you are selling that the positive attributes more than outweigh the negatives (or objections) you have mentioned.

By anticipating objections you are showing that you have big-picture thinking. This is the ability to examine all sides of an issue, problem, or question and not just confine your view to a limited part of the issue in a one-sided or self-serving way. This has the effect of building the buyer's confidence in you because of your willingness to anticipate objections and look at the product from the buyer's point of view, not just yours. And this shows that objections don't scare or intimidate you. This practice is bound to make the buyer ultimately satisfied with the idea, product, or service that you are selling.

Another good practice is, after having anticipated objections the buyer may have, to still ask him if he has any other considerations that might stop him from giving you the order or whatever you are seeking. Ask what criteria will be used in evaluating your request. Also ask what might be some of the considerations of other people who are involved in the decision-making process. If you need to gather more information to answer other objections, this will save you from gathering data that would not answer his objections or considerations.

Your homework: anticipate objections. Whenever you present an idea, conduct an interview, or sell a product or service, sit down to think of and write out every objection the buyer may have about what you are trying to sell. This way, you can be prepared to answer such objections or find out the appropriate answers from someone who knows how such objections are handled. Don't ever make a presentation cold, without having done some preliminary homework on what objections are likely to be made.

All of this is an important educational process for you because the better you know the pros and cons of your idea, product, or service, the more confident and in control you will feel at the time of your sales presentation. Also, this knowledge will aid you in the event you need to negotiate with the buyer. You will be better equipped to come up with a strategy that will satisfy an objection by knowing the "cons" or objections.

Let's go back to our example of Charles trying to sell to the security-minded purchasing manager, Alex. Since Alex has an objection about the reliability of the relatively new super widget and since security is a key self-interest point for him, Charles could answer that objection by offering a special service and warranty agreement for three years instead of the usual one year.

So keep in mind: Anticipating objections is important in establishing a win-win agreement with your prospective buyer. And it is necessary for you so that you are prepared and properly equipped with strategies to use in countering the objection.

Step 5: USE THE RIGHT APPEAL TO PERSUADE

To sell anything, it is extremely important that you use the right appeal to attract or interest a buyer in what you are selling. In effect, it is paying attention to the style as much as to the substance of what you are saying to the other person. By doing so, you will find your presentation much more likely to be well received.

For example, some individuals are much more likely to be persuaded by an idea that is presented in a very confident, self-assured manner. Others might find that same presentation manner to be cocky and arrogant and thus be turned off even to an otherwise excellent idea. Some individuals you sell to will be much more persuaded to buy what you are selling if you present what you have to say in a low-key, analytical, and objective manner.

Again, the whole purpose of considering the appeal you will use to persuade is to establish a rapport with the person to whom you are trying to sell. If, through no fault of your own, you happen to be a high-energy person who wants a quick decision now and you are selling to someone who is staid, conservative, and slow at decision making, you will quickly see how little rapport you have. You may have the right idea, but you presented it with the wrong appeal. In fact, what makes so many situations risky and uncertain is that a person's sales presentation does not take into account the appeal that will be used to persuade the other person. Consider the following example.

SITUATION

Ruth wants to sell one of the older, senior vice presidents on her new product idea. She is a statistical wizard and has assembled a number of graphs and charts showing figures and the mathematical ratios to back up her computations. She is very confident that her new product idea will be adopted. After all, the numbers look fantastic. This company is going to make a lot of money if her numerical projections are accurate.

As she makes her presentation to the senior vice president, Max, she notices that he seems to be uninterested in looking at the numbers. He's fidgeting and looking around the room as she talks to him. He's resistant and almost uncomfortable with her references to the charts and figures she has laid out. Finally, he says to her, "Ruth, why don't you leave this here, and I'll get back to you about it soon." She can't believe that he isn't as excited as she is about the money the product will make.

Unfortunately, Ruth did not take time to consider the proper appeal to use in presenting her idea. Instead, she used the appeal that would most impress and compel *her:* a full-blown quantitative approach with charts, graphs, and pages of statistics. This is one of the fundamental mistakes people make: projecting onto the sales target the appeal that they themselves would consider motivating.

Ruth should have considered the best appeal in selling to Max. She could have shown the same presentation to several other executives, asking them specifically what they believe Max's reaction might be. If she had considered the question of the best way to appeal to Max, she would have discovered that Max is not a statistically oriented or quantitatively inclined executive. In fact, since he joined the company many years ago, when he didn't need to have a strong statistical background, he has since gotten around his lack of knowledge in this area by hiring staff who have a strong mathematical background. He happens to be very uncomfortable with and intimidated by anyone who flashes ratios and pages of statistics at him. To him, that person is simply not speaking his language. He feels no rapport.

Here's how Ruth could have appealed to Max. Since Max is very qualitative and interested in the substantive ideas of her new product suggestion, she could have arranged a prior meeting with one of his quantitatively oriented staff assistants, whom she could presumably have excited with her numbers presentation. Once that was done, she could have assured Max that his own staff looked over her statistical presentation and was very impressed with her new product idea. Then she could have just talked over some of the specifics of the what, how, and why of her product idea. She could have eliminated her numerical presentation of graphs and charts, which only served to intimidate Max.

Here lies the answer for why there are literally thousands of great ideas that have never gotten heard or adopted—not because they weren't great ideas, but quite often because the wrong appeal was used to sell them. If you turn off, disenfranchise, make uncomfortable, or unwittingly offend your buyer with the wrong appeal, you will not close the sale. Worse yet, you will drive yourself crazy trying to figure out why the customer turned you down. Using the right appeal will help you produce sales results in whatever you are selling and, in the process, take much of the uncertainty out of selling.

Step 6: PAY ATTENTION TO FORM

Have you ever noticed that when you ask people for a small favor or minor request they usually say yes, but when you ask for something big, they usually say no? Perhaps you've also found that if you ask people to do two things for you, they will, but if you ask them to do three things, they will turn you down on the third thing. The way in which such requests are presented almost always affects the responses you will receive.

The essence of selling successfully is paying attention to the form you use. What form would the person you are trying to sell be most likely to say yes to? You must be aware of this component if you expect to be successful in selling others.

You can see how the principle of form works by noticing that in many organizations, the first ten items on a meeting agenda tend to get questioned and scrutinized thoroughly, while the last ten items (which may be presented just before lunch or quitting time) may get less attention and scrutiny and thus be passed with less discussion. This is an example of the part form can play in selling your ideas.

The reception certain people give your sales presentation can be affected by form, say, handwritten notes versus neatly typed reports.

Form can also relate more personally to the way people view themselves. For example, some people say yes only if the request is put in the form of being helpful to the image they want to project: "Susan, if you agree to adopt this policy, it will probably make you the most popular chief executive that XYZ Industries has ever had!" Some people say yes only if the form enhances their sense of power and status: "The nation and its citizens will be eternally grateful if you . . ."

Though form can relate somewhat to the use of appeal, the key point is that appropriate "packaging" is often necessary in gaining acceptance for what it is that you are trying to sell. Part of using form is making your presentation conform to the way a person is most likely to say yes. If a person tends to say yes only to requests that enhance his power, you will need to keep this in mind when you make your appeal. To distinguish form from other components of selling, remember the word *package*. What packaging form is most likely to help you convince the other person?

Although form is but a small part of the overall approach to successful selling, it can often spell the difference between success and failure.

Step 7: CLOSE THE SALE

Just about every time that you sell someone on yourself or an idea, product, or service, you will want to close or complete your sale. It is truly amazing how many people make an impressive and persuasive presentation and never ask for the order or a decision. Many people are so afraid of being rejected, they don't ask. Remember, *you* are not being rejected. Perhaps what you are asking for is being rejected. This is an important distinction to make, so that you remain positive about future attempts to present the same or other ideas.

Another reason why many people don't ask for the order is that they are afraid of being considered pushy. You may be pushing to get the order, but you are not being pushy by asking for it. Don't take responsibility for other people. If they do not want to make a decision on the spot, they can tell you so.

Quite often when I know that the person to whom I am selling will not be making a decision on the spot, I anticipate this and instead ask for a gut reaction. For example, I may say to Milt, the buyer, "Milt, I know that you will need to go over the facts and figures that I have presented to you in order to make a decision [anticipation]. However, I want to ask if you can give me an initial gut reaction as to whether you are favorably impressed enough to give me the order if you were making a decision today?"

Sometimes, just as you are about to close, you may want to summarize the benefits to the buyer as to why a favorable decision makes good sense. In so doing, you should mention again each self-interest point.

Step 8: FOLLOW UP, FOLLOW UP, FOLLOW UP

This is the last and probably the most important step in completing the process of effective selling. I have spoken of follow-up in earlier chapters. But it is impossible to say too much about the importance and need for following up. Until you get the order, you must be persistent and continue to follow up.

If you are not able to close and get the yes decision that you were looking for, you know that you will be following up until you do. Never leave a presentation with the other person saying, "Well, we'll get back to you on this." This is simply unacceptable. It leaves you totally out of control and much like some fool who may be waiting by the phone for eternity, hoping that the call will come in.

As a top-flight sales person, you always want to be in control of the sale. Here are some suggestions for how to do so.

Set Limits: When people say they will get back to me, I always say, "Great! Approximately on what date can I expect an answer from you?" I will literally take out my trusty calendar and write down a follow-up date. This lets the people know that while I will be happy to wait until they get back to me, I want them to know that if I don't hear from them by that date, I will call. Plus, psychologically, I feel better knowing that I have a specific time in which to wait. After that, I will follow up to make sure there is no problem.

When appropriate, I will often insist that since I am in and out of my office so much, I would appreciate calling them instead of having them call me on the agreed-upon date. If you haven't already noticed, people at work have a million excuses for why they didn't call you when they said they would. This is one of the classic reasons why I believe productivity has suffered so much in American business.

Also remember that if you aren't able to close on the spot, be sure to ask the other person if there are any remaining considerations or objections. This way you will know what specifics may still be standing in the way of your getting the order or request granted. Plus you will be able to strategize and do whatever homework is necessary to remove the considerations or objections.

If you aren't able to get exactly what you had wanted, you may have to discuss alternatives and compromises with the person to whom you are selling. All of these things should be considered if you don't get the order.

The Eight-Step Process in Selling

1. The art of listening

2. Interview and assess

3. Determine the buyer's self-interest

4. Anticipate objections

5. Use the right appeal to persuade

6. Pay attention to form

7. Close the sale

8. Follow up, follow up, follow up

These eight steps are simple, and the same steps are involved in any selling you will be called upon to do. If you need to sell yourself, for example, at an interview, when you sell your products or ideas to customers, or when you sell your ideas to your staff or upper management, go through each step as a way of preparing yourself and maximizing your chances for the successful outcome you would like to achieve.

Knowing and practicing these eight steps to selling will gain you the reputation of being a savvy, prepared professional and greatly increase your career opportunities and success in your dealings with others.

Exercise: SELLING AND PERSUADING OTHERS*

Directions: Here is your chance to sell someone something. You may want to sell someone on *you,* such as at a job interview; you may want to sell someone on a great idea you have; or you may want to practice selling someone a product or service.

1. Write down specifically what you want. People are often unclear about what they want from the other person. Sometimes they hope that the other person will help them to discover what they want. Or sometimes, when there is a lack of clarity, people can end up beating around the bush. Write down exactly what you want to sell.

2. Interview and assess. In preparation for your meeting, make a list of questions you will ask the other person. Also make a list of potential self-interest points that you may note or ask the individual about at your meeting.

3. Find out who has the power and authority to give you what you want. Sometimes you are literally talking to the wrong person, someone who will not be able to give you what you want. This person may lead you to the right person, but this is a very indirect way of selling. Worse yet, if you don't know who has the power to make decisions, you will end up spending a lot of energy talking with someone who has little power to assist you and who may end up stymieing your efforts for a decision.

4. List the self-interest reasons and benefits that will make the other person give you what you want. You already know what you want. But what are the actual self-interest reasons that would motivate and compel the other person? If you have had an opportunity to interview and assess your buyer, this will help you in coming up with personal self-interest benefits.

5. List and anticipate objections for why the other person may not want to give you what you want. Even if you haven't conducted a personal interview, consider the other person's most likely objections and ''yes . . . but's'' concerning your request. If you are having difficulty coming up with objections, discuss them informally with someone else. Get their suggestions. This should help you in preparing objections to discuss when you meet.

6. What would be the best appeal to use in persuading this person?

* Exercise and questions adapted from a model created by Elaina Zuker, sales trainer, New York.

If you aren't sure, try informally to interview people in the organization who might know or have dealt personally with this person. See if you can get some insight into how this person makes decisions. Ask others their opinion of what approaches are most appealing to the person, for example, cautious and reserved versus self-assured and confident.

7. What form would the other person be most likely to say yes to? Again, if you don't know or have no idea, ask others about how this person makes decisions.

8. How will you close and get what you want? You may just directly ask for it, or you may plan ahead of time to suggest that the buyer take time to study your proposal. This is especially effective if you already know [anticipation] that the individual will not be making the decision. One suggestion is that you role-play yourself as you imagine asking for the order. Hear yourself asking for the order out loud.

9. What follow-up or limit setting will you suggest? Your follow-up if you get the order might be just to make sure that the product arrives safely or that the paperwork on your idea is received. If you don't get the order, what would be a reasonable time in which to suggest following up?

USING A CALL REPORT TO ORGANIZE
AND FOLLOW UP

One of the keys to my many sales successes is the persistence and follow-up that I practice. People to whom I sell or with whom I work are constantly impressed not only with the follow-up but also with the fact that I *always* call on the exact date I promised. They know that I will not allow anything to fall between the cracks. Neither should you. So even if you aren't a sales person, begin using the Schwimmer Call Report and Calendar System. Feel free to adapt it in any way that works for you.

The system involves two components: your calendar and call report sheets. A call report is simply a written record of the steps and actions taken in completing a sale or project. Samples of the call reports I use are in Figures 12.1 and 12.2. They have general information, such as the organization or person to whom I am trying to sell, and any collateral information, such as the person who may have referred me, title, address, and phone number. Most frequently, I list the date and actions being taken as well as any comments pertaining to the sales presentation I am making. I make an entry on this call report every time I take an action toward my goal of completing the sale or project.

This sheet of paper gives me, at a glance, a status report on what is going on with any activity that I am involved in. So do not look at this as strictly for use by sales people who are selling products or services. While it is mandatory for that use, it is also excellent to use for any projects you are working on or as a follow-up sheet for the interview you had with a company you would like to work for.

A call report is especially important to have in the event that you leave your organization or die. This way, your successor will have a sheet of paper with a capsulized record of what has been going on with a customer or project you are working on.

Take a look at the two examples of filled-out call reports. The one on page 250 is for an account I am trying to sell my product to. The call report on page 251 is for a new project I am working on. Note that in both cases I have a working record of what is being done. The moment that I establish a new date that I will be following up on, I immediately enter it on my business calendar. That way I never forget when to follow up, because all I have to do is to look at my calendar each day and then pull out the particular call report for reference. Note: I only check off an item on my calendar *after* I have completed it.

Depending on how many call reports you have and what you are using them for (sales, projects, people, etc.), you should alphabetize them for easy access. When I was using this system strictly for selling, I also put the call reports in a priority system. (Notice the reference on each report to A, B, C, and D.) I then decided that my A accounts I would call on every 30 days, B accounts every three months, and C accounts every six months (perhaps because they were less likely prospects). My D accounts were people I had called on who were not bona fide sales prospects.

You will feel very much in charge of your sales efforts if you use this system, and you will be organized in a very efficient manner to produce results. The fun part is developing and adapting a call report form that fits the use you have intended and works in your own organizational setting.

REFERENCE AREA: *Selling Super Widgets*   PRIORITY: A B C D

Schwimmer & Associates
San Francisco, CA

CALL REPORT

DATE *4/2/84*

COMPANY NAME *R. Q. Industries*   PHONE *(415) 421-8011*

ADDRESS *123 Success Street*

TYPE OF BUSINESS *Manufacturing*   REF. BY *Art Smith, buyer*

at R.Q. Industries

INDIVIDUAL SPOKEN TO *Harvey Phillips*   TITLE *VP Marketing*

DATE	ACTION BEING TAKEN/COMMENTS
4/9/84	*Met with Harvey; presented Super Widget; left literature. He was impressed and will look it over and consider giving me an order. Next follow up 4/19/84.*
4/19/84	*Called Harvey. He's still impressed but needs to show product to several staff for their input. Follow up on 4/26/84.*
4/26/84	*Harvey asked me if I could get him extended service warranty on the first order—must check. Follow up on 5/1/84.*

Continued

Continued

4/28/84   *Received approval for extended warranty from my*

            manager.

5/1/84   *Offered Harvey extended warranty. Harvey and I will*

            meet to sign agreement for first order on 5/7/84.

5/7/84   *Received signed order. Will follow up in 1 month (6/*

            7/84) to make sure merchandise has arrived in perfect

            condition.

REFERENCE AREA: *New Product Introduction*   PRIORITY: **A B C D**

Schwimmer & Associates
123 Promotion Street
San Francisco, CA
(415) 686-4500

CALL REPORT

                           DATE   *4/2/84*

OBJECTIVE: *Gain cooperation and support for*
                new product introduction.

INDIVIDUALS SPOKEN TO   *Harvey Phillips*   TITLE   *VP Marketing*

DATE   ACTION BEING TAKEN/COMMENTS

4/2/84   *Meeting set up on 4/9/84 to go over new product*

            introduction with Harvey

                                      Continued

Continued

DATE	ACTION BEING TAKEN/COMMENTS
——	———————————————————
——	———————————————————
——	———————————————————
——	———————————————————
——	———————————————————
——	———————————————————

I also recommend, especially if you are a manager, that you have all your staff keep call reports. The system makes it easy to review and monitor work that is being done, time spent, and any problems that should be discussed. It organizes and gives structure to the efforts of others. Best of all, it allows you to manage and empower others by letting them do their jobs instead of needing to ask questions all the time. I know one manager who asks no questions about the results being achieved. Instead, he asks his people to send him all their call reports on a monthly basis. He reads them and then discusses with his people any reports he has questions on.

Learning and applying these basic selling skills will make you much more effective in accomplishing your job. It will help you produce results far beyond your expectations. Best of all, it will truly lead you to winning more promotions.

chapter 13

Mentors:
Getting
the Pros to
Advise You

So often it seems that you are all alone in facing problems in your job or career. Yet there are many ways to get help and support so that you will maximize your likelihood of handling a difficult work situation successfully, asking for a raise or a new title, or making a major career decision.

One way to do this is by getting coaching or guidance from someone who is sincerely interested in your achieving your career aspirations. This is exactly the role that a mentor can play in your professional life.

WHAT IS A MENTOR, REALLY?

By definition, a mentor is a "nonparental career role model." Usually, this is someone who is older and wiser, often with direct successful experience in the industry or field you are in or want to be in. A mentor is dedicated to helping you achieve your career hopes and wishes.

In recent years, there has been an enormous amount of interest in the concept of mentors. Newcomers to the corporate world seem to believe that a mentor is a prerequisite to upward mobility. Young management trainees speak of "getting a mentor" as though one could be found by advertising in the company newsletter. "Wanted:

one mentor." Indeed, it almost seems as though having a mentor has become one of the corporate status symbols of the 1980s. I have spoken to hundreds of professionals who feel some sort of inadequacy because they haven't found a mentor and have some gnawing concern that not having one could undermine their chances of being successful in their organization or winning future promotions or that they will be at a disadvantage with others who do have a mentor.

Most people who talk about having a mentor don't really have one. They aren't even clear on what a mentor could do for them in their career. You see, in the true classic mentorship relationship, the mentor is totally involved in the person's career over a long period, perhaps years.

Many people call a person with whom they have a short-term, occasional relationship a mentor. That person might be a nice individual who seems to offer reasonably good advice, but such an individual might much more logically be called an interested friend, not a mentor.

In truth, it is very difficult to establish a genuine mentor-protégé relationship. It takes years, plus a certain mental and emotional chemistry that creates a bond not unlike that between parent and child. The classic mentor is someone older and more experienced who for a number of reasons is willing to pass on his expertise, go to bat for you, and generally show you the ropes. It is possible through your own initiative to seek out a mentor. However, despite all that has been written about mentor relationships, I believe an obvious point has been overlooked—that the quest for a mentor implies that one actively pursues or seeks such a counselor or adviser, when in reality mentors (or more appropriately, sponsors) themselves usually seek out protégés.

In other words, just like a baseball scout, or perhaps a coach who looks for talented ball players to develop, upper management types are sensitive to real "comers." To a great extent, it is out of their own self-interest that they decide to cultivate a particularly talented individual in the organization for a higher leadership position.

So I think it is a bit illusory to conduct a mad quest to find a mentor. Yet popular writing on the topic of mentors suggests strongly that not only do you need a mentor to succeed and reach your career potential but that you are in charge of finding one.

Worse yet, very few people consider that having a mentor can present dangers to their career. Chapter 6 spoke about "guilt by association" as one of the ways that your charismatic leadership style can be undermined. If the one person who is your acknowledged mentor falls out of grace with upper management, consider what the liability to you would be. You could be out of a job or relegated to a position of diminished respect and responsibility. The point is, getting a mentor is risky business. Even if you *could* find one, you might later regret it.

BE REALISTIC

Of course, it is naive to think you can pick up a mentor as if one were available in your grocery store. Individuals with the competence, experience, and interest to be your mentor are few and far between. And generally, mentor candidates are very busy, successful people with little motivation to dole out large amounts of time and energy to guide and direct your career.

If someone does volunteer to act as your mentor, be sure you are aware of his true motivation. I have known many naive and overly trusting junior executives and young professionals who were easy prey for a "mentor masquerade." In reality the mentor was using them for some personal gain or was jockeying politically for his own benefit.

However, let's examine some of the real-world reasons that cause mentor types to be interested in fast-track, upwardly mobile types like you.

SELF-INTEREST

Many savvy executives assume a mentorship role of counseling bright, promising executives or employees who they believe will do a great job and make them look good. Remember our definition of self-interest: the reason why someone will do or give you what you want. This concept is the motivation for many mentors who are actively assisting and directing the careers of their protégés.

I knew one executive who would recruit the sharpest and most gifted people who he knew would make him look good. In return for their high performance and loyalty, he would review their career goals and help them plan their next moves. The moment any of his people slipped in their performance or showed any disloyalty, he became "very busy" and unavailable to meet with them for lunch or after-work discussions.

STAR DEVELOPMENT

It is a real feather in the cap of upwardly striving executives to be able to spot, identify, and develop talent for the organization. It shows their ability to be a leader who can put together a winning team. In fact, mentors with a "star development" motivation have almost a coachlike mindset where they want to develop their "ball club" (department or organization). By developing promising rookies or whiz kids, they are casting a direct reflection on their own ability to pick and attract the very best talent.

Upper management often expects its more senior executives to seek out new talent to groom for positions that will be opening down the road. This is certainly in contrast with any image you might have of a bunch of dullard executives waiting to be approached by young superstars begging for mentorship.

ALTRUISM

Almost like a parent wanting to develop the natural talents and abilities of a son or daughter, the altruistic mentor sincerely cares about people in general and about you in particular. Make no mistake, such a relationship comes out of the intangible chemistry we spoke about before. It could be based on you reminding the mentor of himself when he was young and filled with "piss and vinegar." It could be that you are the child he never had. It could be the mentor's strong feeling that you are someone whom he feels a responsibility to look after and develop.

This type of mentor sincerely has the desire to help you along the way and up the ladder, with little regard for what he may get out of it or without concern for what upper management thinks. But such a mentor is as rare as a unicorn.

THE BENEFITS OF A
MENTORSHIP RELATIONSHIP

COUNSELOR

Mentors can act as counselors from whom you can learn and who
have years of successful experience and savvy. They can assess your
strengths and weaknesses and help you devise strategies to achieve
your career goals and ambitions. They can point out career opportunities and anticipate pitfalls.

CONTACTS

Mentors usually have numerous contacts and connections, both within
and outside the organization. Most important, they are willing to
share them with you and make the appropriate introductions. If your
mentor is possessive about you and very protective of his contacts,
it should be a warning sign to you about his limitations as a bona fide
mentor.

CREDIBILITY

Mentors are often acknowledged high performers and successful in
their companies and in their field. Generally, mentors are respected
by friends and foes alike and judged to have high standards of integrity.
Their name, quite often, carries a great deal of influence. So if you
establish a mentor relationship with such a person, people will take
note of you. They will accord you a form of "reflected power" whereby
your association with the mentor credits you with some power based
solely on your relationship with the mentor.

PROTECTION

Often out of your relationship with a mentor you will be protected
from much of the politics and infighting that can end the most promising fast-track careers. One of my favorite organizational rules to
live by is *never underestimate the illogical and irrational behavior
and subsequent actions that follow a battle of executive egos.* Having
a true mentorship relationship is like going into battle with a bullet-
proof vest. You could get hurt, but you are superbly protected. The
odds are drastically in your favor. Thus your mentorship protection

signals to others that you are to be left alone and that more powerful resources (those of your mentor) are there to protect you from harm. In many ways, it is like having your own personal Godfather.

SPONSORSHIP

Mentors not only have contacts and connections that can be useful if you need to get an audience to present an idea or find out special information or to investigate a promising career opportunity. Mentors also have clout—the ability to influence and persuade people, especially people at high levels, to do, act on, or at least give serious consideration to their suggestions. In fact, the mentors' credibility, influence, and power allow them to sponsor you for assignment to key responsibilities, high-exposure projects, and upcoming promotional opportunities. The fact that mentors have confidence and faith in you is often enough for their recommendation alone to secure you a special opportunity or promotion. Your association with them may save you the standard interviewing process where you will have to compete with many other applicants. As your sponsor, they can vouch for you. Their sponsorship is one of the most valuable benefits of your mentor relationship.

APPRENTICESHIP

Many mentors are legendary experts or masters in their field. They can be like elder statesmen who have been through all the wars and political fighting. They have been through countless business cycles and have survived the administration of many of the organization's presidents. They have accumulated a bank of experience and know-how that makes it an honor for you to be their protégé. In some cases, such a relationship can destine the protégé to a special position of responsibility, perhaps even heir apparent, if the mentor is grooming him for this future position.

FIND A CAREER CONSULTANT TO BE YOUR MENTOR

As I have already said, it doesn't make sense to put too much energy into finding a mentor. Such a relationship is generally not available for the asking. A better tactic is to find a career consultant who can help you plot strategy to achieve your career goals and ambitions. See this counselor periodically, especially when promotional opportunities are around the corner or before a big salary review.

People go to a doctor when they have a medical problem, they go to a tennis pro when their backhand isn't working, and they go to an attorney when they need legal advice. Yet it amazes me that many of these same professionals do not seek out competent career consultants when preparing for a big job interview, salary review, or promotional opportunity. The right career consultant can act as a mentor and more than cost-justify the fees.

I have personally counseled and prepared hundreds of people for their salary reviews, with the result that they negotiated salary increases and perks (special employee benefits) worth thousands more than if they had had no guidance or direction on strategy and implementation. My own prediction is that the upwardly mobile executives of the 1980s will have their own mentor–career consultant to help direct them in resolving on-the-job problems and seizing promotional opportunities.

ESTABLISH A NETWORK OF MINIMENTORS

In addition to using a career consultant as a mentor, consider what I term a "minimentor." This is usually a person who likes you and with whom you have a good rapport. He recognizes you as having integrity and talent. And out of this positive relationship with you, though not committed to you or devoted to you as a mentor, this person is nevertheless willing to help you succeed and move up in the organization. A minimentor is a person who, while not making a long-term commitment to your career success, is willing to help you in the here and now.

Full-fledged mentors offer you the many benefits of advice, contacts, credibility, protection, and apprenticeship. By contrast, minimentors are often strong in only one or several of these areas. They have a special expertise in an area that may help you in resolving a particular career problem or dilemma that you are facing at a specific point in time.

For example, at one company I worked for, I heard rumors that budgets were tight and thus salary increases would be very modest.

I went to my minimentor, Pete, who was reputed to be one of the best salary negotiators in the company. He was well respected and knew exactly how to read upper-echelon pronouncements. In other words, Pete could read between the lines and knew what perks a person could negotiate for and get in any given calendar quarter. He had numerous contacts at headquarters, so he knew the prevalent attitudes toward giving out raises and benefits. He also had such great access to the grapevine that he knew what upper management thought of each executive's future. Pete knew whom they had plans for and which executives they would not feel bad about losing over differences in salary negotiations.

So I made plans to take Pete out to lunch to ask his help in counseling me on how to get the most money and benefits, based on his information and contacts. After obtaining his sagelike advice, I walked into my salary negotiation with a great deal of confidence. The result was that my salary increase was much higher than what I had heard other executives grumbling they had received. And I was able to obtain a few extra fringe benefits and get the company to cover some expenses they had not been willing to cover before, as a trade-off for not receiving as much of a salary increase as I had wanted.

Make no mistake: I was a high performer in this company and well regarded; otherwise, counsel from a minimentor would have had only a minimal effect. But Pete's counsel was a fantastic resource to me. It was the decisive factor in my successful salary negotiation.

Minimentors share some of the characteristics of full-fledged mentors, but in a much more superficial way. They may be fair-weather friends; they may be political opportunists; they may want an exchange of favors in return for their help. But they are a network of supporters who like you and are willing to support your success out of their positive relationship with you. If you are someone of high integrity and talent, they will be willing to ally with you, identify with you, and in some cases even stand up for you.

Using minimentors also protects you from putting all your eggs in the basket of *one* mentor, who could fall from grace and take you down as well. You should attempt to form a network or support system of minimentors that offers you assistance and expertise in every area in which you may need it.

I refined my network when I worked for one large organization so that I had people to go to for advice not only in general categories but also on specific matters. I had several minimentors whom I could consult about raises, promotional strategies, and political conflicts.

For example, as a marketing executive, when I needed to make a presentation before the executives in the finance department to get their support, I would go to see Janet. She was well respected and always willing to give me counsel on how to tailor my presentation in a manner that would pique the self-interest of her colleagues. Sometimes Janet would even talk individually to key financial executives about a pet project of mine and point out ways in which their support would benefit not only me but everyone in the department. My association with her gave me credibility and the accompanying support I could never have gotten if she weren't a minimentor to me. Our relationship helped me to cut through lots of red tape and become successful in the process.

TIPS ON ESTABLISHING
A MINIMENTOR RELATIONSHIP

1. Be willing to ask for help. It may sound simple to say, but I have known many people who needed help but didn't want to ask for it. They had already psyched themselves into the belief, "Why would anyone want to help me?" You'll find that if you aren't willing to initiate a relationship, potential minimentors will be less likely to extend themselves. However, for many people, just the opportunity to help you makes them feel good. If you are indirect about asking for help, minimentors may not appreciate the importance of helping you or may misunderstand your intention. You may have noticed someone who appeared to be fishing for information when in reality he just wasn't comfortable asking you directly for assistance. Don't make this mistake. People like to help you and be acknowledged for doing so.

2. Use self-interest in establishing minimentor relationships. There is nothing wrong in appealing to someone else's self-interest as the reason why they should take time out to assist you. Sometimes the smallest self-interest registers in the form of appreciation. When Pete counseled me about negotiating for raises and benefits, I jokingly told him if his suggestions worked, I would take him out for a night on the town. We both laughed as I said this—but we both know I meant it. His self-interest was that he just wanted some tangible token of my appreciation.

In the case of Janet, the financial executive, I reminded her that I hoped she would seek my counsel if she had any matters relating to marketing that I could advise her on.

3. *Initiate and persist in establishing minimentor relationships.* It is vital and mandatory that you be willing to initiate get-togethers, particularly at the beginning of your relationship. Your minimentors need to get to know you personally and trust you in order to feel comfortable about being a resource to you.

Madeline is in sales and is trying to establish a minimentor relationship with Danielle because Danielle has lots of contacts from her previous position in sales with a competing firm. Madeline has called Danielle a few times to go out to lunch, but Danielle was always busy. Madeline now feels discouraged and thinks that Danielle ought to start calling her for lunch.

This is the *wrong* way to establish a minimentor relationship. Initiating and being persistent means that Madeline will call Danielle every week if necessary and, ideally, be patient and understanding, even if it takes forever to begin their relationship. In Madeline's case, a relationship with Danielle is sure to yield some new sources of sales that will aid her in surpassing her sales quota. That benefit is worth being persistent about. Once she has a relationship with Danielle, future get-togethers will be much easier and more mutual.

4. *Do favors.* I call this the "Don Vito" approach, which I coined after seeing the movie *The Godfather.* Don Vito Corleone, the Godfather, went out of his way to do favors and help people in his network of associates. When people thanked him profusely and asked how they might repay him, he would say, "Some day, I am going to come to you and ask you a favor and you'll help me."

This may seem like a simple idea: Do favors. But many people are stingy with favors, or they look for an immediate return favor as their justification for doing a favor. Now, I am not talking about keeping a tally sheet on how many favors you have done for everyone. But I am talking about a strategy of how you will behave. And I am talking about a positive mindset that should be in everyone's best interest: that you help people achieve results whenever you can. This is the mindset of an effective leader who can establish not only minimentor relationships but also gain the cooperation and support of people in an organization. Doing favors is a clever way of not only establishing minimentor relationships but also becoming a power broker in your organization. And it is another way to position yourself to win future promotions.

Finally, remember that doing favors must proceed out of faith and the belief that somehow, some way, someday they will be returned. Otherwise, you will be angry and resentful, like the person who walks around with a frown saying, "I do so many favors for everyone and no one does any for me." That is the exclamation of a powerless person who hasn't used favors to establish relationships. This person acts like a broken vending machine where people don't put any money in and yet continue to take out the vended item.

When I use favors to establish minimentor relationships, I try to make a point of replying to the inevitable "Thanks for the help, Larry." I respond, "It's my pleasure to be of help. Would you mind if I called on you sometime to get your good counsel in return?" You'd be amazed at how happy people are to return a favor.

A NEW CONCEPT: PEER MENTORING

Here's a very innovative approach to mentoring—and one that will be much easier to achieve and much more workable than trying to find a full-fledged mentor. It is called peer mentoring. Note that the individuals in this process are not mentor and protégé but peers.

The peer mentor model was originated by two New York consultants, Joan Alveras and Elaina Zuker. I have adapted their original model for easier application to the organizational setting.

THE PEER MENTOR MODEL

The process involves peers with complementary skills and needs who agree to help each other. The two peers meet to discuss the specific ways in which they can assist each other, based on their own individual skills, strengths, resources, and contacts. I call these *haves*. The two peers also discuss their own individual areas of weakness, deficiencies, and lacks of expertise or contacts. I call these *needs*.

Based on these haves and needs and their common interest in

wanting to assist each other, they arrive at a contractual agreement. In this agreement, the partners agree to help each other in specific ways, using a mutually agreed-upon strategy to produce the desired results. And they agree to do so in a specific time period.

Key to the effectiveness of the peer mentor concept is that the two self-selected peers arrive at a structured written contract that specifies in detail the goals each person has, the strategies each will use to achieve them, and the targets, times, and measurements they will use to evaluate the achievement of a goal. Make no mistake: This is not a relationship of good friends who in some vague manner agree to help each other. This is a firm agreement between two peers to help each other in very specific ways.

Establishing a peer mentor relationship gives you most of the benefits of counseling, contacts, teaching, and advising that a true mentor relationship might offer you. Rather than searching for the usually unobtainable, already successful mentor, you have a new option. The peer mentor can be a role model for you. Such people have valuable skills, resources, and contacts that are often overlooked in favor of the quest for a more senior mentor.

BENEFITS OF PEER MENTOR
RELATIONSHIPS TO YOUR ORGANIZATION

Using the peer mentor model encourages the professional development of individuals in the organization. It economizes and uses wisely the existing human resources of the organization. And it promotes esprit de corps, based on the mutual-support aspect of the concept. It moves people from the attitude "I don't need help, I'll do it myself" to the attitude of "I have a large bank of people I can turn to for assistance."

Peer mentoring is an excellent way for managers to use staff with strengths in one area to improve the abilities of staff who are weak in that same area. This is a big departure from managers who don't want to invest the time to improve an employee who shows weakness in a given area. For such managers, it becomes much easier instead to use people only in the areas of their greatest talent. This ends up leaving staff relatively undeveloped in areas that may not require high competence in the short run but will in the long run.

This superspecialization can have the negative effect of leaving the organization overly vulnerable and reliant on too few key people. It is bad business to have employees who do one or two things well but perform only marginally in other important areas. In fact, there is a growing trend toward developing people more as generalists— not only to give them the much needed versatility to be effective in the organization but also to prevent the job burnout that can often come from doing the same activities, projects, or routine work.

HOW TO ESTABLISH A PEER
MENTOR RELATIONSHIP

First of all, be on the lookout for bright people who have talents that may complement your weaknesses (areas and abilities within yourself that need developing). People with great expertise, well-developed skills, or unusual talent are everywhere, not just in your immediate department or organization. Often they are professionals you meet at trade associations and networking groups.

However, even if you meet a talented executive who seems to have just the background and experience you require for a particular project or upcoming assignment, how can you approach this person? After all, it can be a bit unnerving to say, "You know, you are the perfect person to review and evaluate the five-year budget plan I have to prepare for my department. It would take you only about three weeks!"

Of course, you know very well that it is highly unlikely that someone you have just met (let alone someone you know fairly well) would be willing to spend several weeks working with you on your plan. After all, this person doesn't even know you and has little incentive to help you.

Here's another situation that demonstrates the need for a more formal way to ask for assistance. You develop great rapport after meeting and talking with someone. He seems very talented and likely to be a great resource to you in several areas where you could use counsel and advice. So you say to him, "You have some pretty impressive work experience. We ought to get together and get to know each other better." And he says, "Sure, we'll have to get together sometime." This is equivalent to "Whenever you're in the neighborhood, drop by." It rarely happens.

Offering someone a peer mentor relationship is the perfect way to *make* it happen, whether you want to enroll someone to assist you with a five-year plan or whether you want to cultivate a relationship with someone who has some talent and expertise that could benefit you.

You can develop a peer mentor relationship by having talents, skills, resources, and contacts to barter with whoever you believe has talents, skills, resources, and contacts that would benefit you. Here's how Doug and Angie formed a peer mentor relationship.

First, they made a list of haves and a list of needs. What do I have to offer the world? What are my strengths? What are my talents? Where am I expert? Where do I have knowledge, information, contacts, and resources?

Doug thought of five strengths he has to offer. First of all, he's very creative; he has good knowledge of new product development. Second, he has good financial investment knowledge. He knows how to cost-justify equipment, for example. Third, he has a very strong sales management background from years out in the field. Fourth, he has good contacts with the marketing and sales staff executives. Fifth, he has an excellent understanding of public relations. He knows how to gain visibility in the community.

Doug also has five areas where he feels he's deficient. First, he's deficient in statistical math. He can look at a five-year budget plan and understand how they got to the bottom line, but when he tries to figure out those simple financial ratios, he starts getting confused. He needs somebody who can take him through the mathematical process by literally using a calculator to show him how to reach those numbers.

Second, he's weak in writing skills. He needs someone who can help him with editing and formatting some of the executive reports he prepares. He needs someone with a certain amount of intellectual savvy to understand what he's written.

Third, he needs someone to network him into the grapevine for information about the new division vice president.

Fourth, he has no contacts in the research and development and accounting departments. To him, those folks are from a different planet. He doesn't communicate with them and doesn't know what's going on in their areas. He knows that in his next position, he will have to start interfacing with them.

Fifth, he recently moved to this city, so he doesn't know what networks, trade associations, or clubs he should join.

Here is how Doug's haves/needs list looks:

Doug's Haves/Needs List

MY HAVES: (*strengths, talents, expertise, knowledge, skills, information, contacts, resources*)

1. Creativity in new product development

2. Financial investment knowledge (equipment)

3. Strong sales, marketing background

4. Contacts with marketing and sales staff executives

5. Publicity knowledge, visibility, community

MY NEEDS: (*weaknesses, knowledge, depth, deficiencies, development and growth areas, contacts, resources*)

1. Deficiencies in statistics, math

2. Grammar/editing and review of executive reports

3. Need grapevine information: new division VP

4. No contacts in R & D and accounting departments

5. Need to know what networks and trade associations to join

TIME COMMITMENT POSSIBILITIES:

1. Phone calls

2. Face-to-face meetings (days, weekends)

3. Meal get-togethers (breakfast, lunch, dinner)

4. Working sessions (one hour, half day, full day)

5. Informal/social get-togethers (drinks, sports, social events)

Angie has also prepared a haves and needs list. Among the haves and needs of both Angie and Doug they found three areas in which they could assist each other. Remember, this is a fair exchange of effort on both their parts. There is no expectation that one should do more than the other. This way, no one feels taken advantage of.

Angie and Doug have discussed the time commitment possibilities that they will commit to in order to help each other produce a desired result. For example, their time together will include phone calls, face-to-face meetings in the evenings or on weekends, meal meetings (breakfast, lunch, or dinner), and informal social get-togethers.

They have filled out a Resource Sharing Agreement (see page 270) that simply states the specific areas of assistance that each will provide the other. The agreement also states the strategy or method with which they believe that the desired goal can best be achieved. And they have been specific about the time involved and the actual dates on which help will be given to accomplish this goal.

Note in the following example that the Resource Sharing Agreement requires a signature by Angie stating that she will honor her agreement and time commitments to the best of her ability. Doug, too, will sign a similar agreement to assist Angie.

Let's take a closer look at the three things Angie has agreed to do to help Doug.

1. Angie agreed to review the five-year budget plan with Doug and go over the ratios. The strategy will be to take a calculator and actually punch out the numbers so that Doug can readily see how she arrives at her figures. The time required will be one to two hours. The date will be after work between 5:00 and 7:00 P.M. on August 7.

2. Angie knows people in R & D and accounting. She agreed to introduce Doug to them, and the strategy will be to arrange two lunches. One will be during the week of August 12 and one during the week of August 20.

3. Angie agreed to discuss with Doug the new divisional vice president, a woman who is going to be coming in and taking over Doug's department. Doug doesn't know her, but Angie worked with her and other influentials at headquarters. The strategy is that Angie and Doug will compare information, sources, and rumors. Since the new VP is starting on September 1, Angie agreed to have four conversations with Doug, one each Friday in August. For 5 to 15 minutes she will talk with Doug specifically about any new information she's heard about the VP.

In like manner, Doug and Angie agreed on the areas where Doug would assist Angie and the strategies they would use. They each had a copy of the agreement and signed them.

It is necessary to put this all into contractual form so that both parties are totally clear on what they have committed to do for each other. This is not a friendship relationship; it is a professional colleague relationship, and it deserves to be in writing. It gets people to feel committed; thus, both parties know exactly what they promised and what they expect in return. There is no way Angie is going to spend a couple of weeks helping Doug with his five-year plan in the hope that he might help her. Not unless Doug is serious enough to say, "Look, let's talk about how I can help you, too. I really want to get your help, and whatever it takes to get it, I'd be happy to do."

Developing peer mentor relationships is an integral part of your own support system. And in the process of being a peer mentor to others, you develop useful relationships and leadership skills and, most important, a resource bank of counselors and contacts that will be especially valuable to your career advancement.

Exercise: ESTABLISHING A PEER MENTOR RELATIONSHIP*

Directions: Fill out the haves and needs lists. Be honest with yourself about your true strengths and weaknesses. It is important for you to know both of these so that you can quickly identify where someone else's talents can benefit you and where you can benefit the other person.

MY HAVES: (strengths, talents, expertise, knowledge, skills, information, contacts, and resources)

1. _____

2. _____

3. _____

* Exercise concept developed from "Peer/Mentor Model," by Joan Alveras and Elaina Zuker.

4. _____

5. _____

MY NEEDS: (weaknesses, areas that need developing, deficiencies)

1. _____

2. _____

3. _____

4. _____

5. _____

RESOURCE SHARING AGREEMENT (Sample)

Angie Patterson agrees to help *Doug Jackson* in the following areas:

AREA OF ASSISTANCE	STRATEGY TO BE USED	TIME INVOLVED	DATE TO OCCUR
1. Review budget ratios, 5-year plan	Discuss, analyze using calculator	One 2-hour meeting	5–7 PM August 7
2. Introduce to R&D and acctng. staff	Set up lunches with them	2 lunches	August 12, 20
3. Discuss new VP/ organization changes	Compare info, sources, rumors	4 weekly phone conversations	August 3, 10, 17, 24
4.			
5.			

I agree to help and be a resource to *Doug Jackson* as noted in the above areas of assistance, using the appropriate strategies to accomplish this. I further agree to honor the time commitments involved on the dates listed to the best of my ability.

Date: *August 1, 1986*   Signed: *Angie Patterson*

Exercise: RESOURCE SHARING AGREEMENT

Directions: Choose a peer to establish a peer mentor relationship with. You may want to discuss each other's haves and needs list. Then begin negotiating the areas, strategies, time, and dates for assisting each other. Sign your respective agreements. Each person should have a copy of each agreement.

RESOURCE SHARING AGREEMENT

AREA OF ASSISTANCE	STRATEGY TO BE USED	TIME INVOLVED	DATE TO OCCUR

1.

2.

3.

4.

5.

TIME COMMITMENT POSSIBILITIES:

a. Phone calls

b. Face-to-face meetings (evenings or weekends)

c. Meal get-togethers (breakfast, lunch, dinner)

d. Working sessions (1 hour, ½ day, full day)

e. Informal social get-togethers (drinks, sports, social events)

I agree to help and be a resource to _____
as noted in the above areas of assistance, using the appropriate strategies to accomplish this. I further agree to honor the time commitments involved on the dates listed, to the best of my ability.

Signed: _____   Date: ___

Networks: Finding and Using Them to Help You Get Ahead

- "Should I accept a new position that is a lateral move in order to get some marketing experience?"
- "I wonder if this company is really a dinosaur in the industry."
- "I just moved here and don't know anyone—and I'm lonely."
- "I wish I knew what part of town would be the best place for me to live."
- "Where can I find some talented people to hire without spending all my time running employment ads?"
- "It's always so risky hiring a new executive. Where can I find someone with a proven track record?"
- "I've heard rumors about our company merging with another company. There must be some way to find out what's going on."

These are just a few problematic situations that you'll confront more confidently if you are a member of a business or professional networking organization.

Networking has become the catchword of the 1980s: Indeed, as a term, it is so overused that it's often the butt of jokes. Do not, however, make the mistake of underestimating the importance of networks. For many years, men have relied on the "old boy" network in its many incarnations to provide jobs, contacts, leads, introductions, information, and so forth. Bear in mind, too, that according to the

Bureau of Labor Statistics, 48 percent—almost half—of all jobs are found through personal contacts. And contacts are what networks are all about.

The term *network* refers to an informal association of individuals who share common goals and interests. A network's purpose is the exchange of information, ideas, and favors. Network members do not, however, help one another in the classic sense of the strong and successful aiding the weak and inexperienced. If that were the case, networks would be composed entirely of low-level or inexperienced people, and there would be little incentive for anyone else to participate. The operative word is *use*. You join a network to *use* other people's information and contacts, and you offer the use of yours in return. It is an arrangement based on mutual need and benefit.

The benefits of joining a networking group or trade association are many. Yet I am convinced that most people do not fully comprehend how important a network is to the success and upward mobility they achieve in their careers. And since you face enough risks daily, why not have an entity that supports you and brings more certainty to the likelihood that you will be successful and promotable?

At the seminars I conduct for business and professional people, I ask a standard question: "How many of you belong to a network group or trade association?" The number of hands that go up at each seminar is consistently no more than 25 percent of the group. The remaining 75 percent are missing out on some fabulous benefits. To appreciate the full importance of being a member of at least one network or trade association group, let's examine the many benefits your membership will provide.

JOB OPPORTUNITIES

As I already mentioned, almost half of all jobs are found through personal contacts. There is no better place to make those contacts than through membership in a network organization. In many groups, there are members who may be able to refer you to a company that is looking for someone to fill a position that you may be superbly qualified for. If you can get a personal reference ("Here's Arthur's phone number; call him and tell him we met and that you are interested in being considered for . . ."), you have an inside track that may put you ahead of the pack.

SCOUTING TALENT FOR YOUR ORGANIZATION

Not only can you get leads for upcoming jobs you might be interested in, but you can also scout talent for your company. Quite often, you will meet someone at a network gathering and be very impressed because this person "would be perfect for the new position that will be opening up in the finance department." Such scouting can be of immense value to your personnel department or the manager of the department looking for talent. And in the process, you may be saving your company thousands of dollars in executive search fees. (By the way, bringing in a talented star can be a great source of publicity for you.)

INDUSTRY INFORMATION

Working in only one organization can result in your getting stale and losing a sense of objectivity about what is really going on in your industry or even in your own company. I have known a number of executives who were so close to their company that they were amazed at the knowledge (both accurate and inaccurate) that company outsiders in their industry shared with them about their company and others. You can quite often get an objective evaluation from executives who are in competition with your organization.

You can also hear important industry information relating to other companies. It is not unusual to hear about buy-outs, reorganizations, or impending merger talks at a networking gathering. This kind of information could be worth its weight in gold. In fact, I know one executive who heard about a competitor putting out feelers indicating the company's interest in being bought out. This executive went directly to the VP of acquisitions in his company with this information. The VP was so pleased at the tip that when his company eventually bought the other company, the networker was given a fat bonus for his "above and beyond the call of duty" information.

CLIENT CONTACTS AND LEADS

Most networks are a haven for sales leads and contacts. If you join the right organization, you may find that a majority of the members are customers or potential customers for your products or services. In fact, I used to ask my clients and customers the names of organizations in which they were members so that I could consider joining those organizations, too. Not only did I get valuable leads, but I also strengthened many of the relationships I had with preexisting customers.

Many people you meet will also know other potential customers that they can refer you to. I have asked people I had a great rapport with if they would be willing to call up the potential customers and do an advance introduction for me. This made my selling much easier and more successful.

BUYING PRODUCTS AND SERVICES

One of the handiest benefits of being a member of a network occurs when you want to buy a product for yourself or for your company. Many networking groups will attract a membership that includes the major competitors of a particular product. This makes comparison shopping a buyer's dream, because everyone would like your business.

This happened to me when I was looking into buying a personal computer for myself. I went to a particular network gathering where I met representatives from several computer companies. I subsequently got the kind of personal attention, explanation, and price quotations that would have taken me weeks of research to accumulate. In the process, I created goodwill as a result of buying from network members as well as the possibility of their using my services in the future.

MENTORSHIP COUNSELING

People at network gatherings can often act as mentors to you by taking an interest in you and giving you very wise counsel. Here's how it can work. Often at network gatherings you can talk shop with peers and more senior executives who have (or have had) your current position or have some knowledge you can use in your position to climb the ladder in your company. They can often relate their own personal experiences and strategies that, used effectively, can make you more promotable. At one network meeting, I heard an executive counsel another more junior executive (from another company in the industry) to consider making a lateral move into marketing because "no one in our industry ever makes it to the top without at least a couple good solid years of marketing under their belt."

You can find relevant and useful information about handling certain management or product problems just from talking to executives from other companies. And you can learn which are the fast-track companies as well as which companies are experiencing employee turnover and why. You can find out which moves will advance your career most quickly in the short and long run.

PEER MENTORING RELATIONSHIPS

You are already aware of the benefits of a peer mentor relationship. There is no better place in which to form one than your network association. You will often meet skilled people who have had the experience in doing the particular report or project you are currently working on. These people can be a valuable resource to you. You, in turn, will have to find out how you can be a resource to them so that they have a reason to help you. This is especially true if you want help with a long-term project that may involve conferring with them over a period of months.

The key is that in a network organization, you have a tremendous brain trust of professionals who can assist you, sometimes in even a more impressive and sophisticated way than some of your current company's most senior executives. Also, by working with peers in other organizations, you can enjoy a certain confidence and privacy in seeking assistance that might not be available to you in your current organization. And great satisfaction can come from developing a peer mentor relationship in which you support each other's success and serve as a resource at the same time.

STATE-OF-THE-ART INFORMATION

One of the greatest benefits of most networking groups is the excellent guests and experts who come to speak to the membership and provide continuing education and learning. These speakers address topics that are directly or indirectly relevant to your job or career. Usually, the group's membership decides on the focus or theme that they want guest speakers to talk about—dressing for success, this year's new tax laws, management practices for a high-productivity environment, and the like. You will also find that some of the speakers talk on the most technical or esoteric topics you can imagine. But since these meetings are usually after working hours, there is an effort to make sure that speakers are not only informative but also entertaining.

I have personally learned a great deal from many of these experts and in the process have gotten some great ideas that I have applied to advance my career. Sometimes I have been so impressed that I arranged for a speaker to talk to my department or my company.

LEADERSHIP OPPORTUNITIES

One of the easiest and best ways to get some leadership experience is to be an executive or officer in a network or trade organization. Whether as a membership chairperson (which can provide you with great sales experience) or as a program chairperson (which can give you direct exposure to some of the leading experts, authors, and executives in the country) or even as president, you will have an opportunity to manage people and produce results in your network position. If you attain the position of president of your network, it can be especially prestigious and useful in gaining visibility in your own organization (see Chapter 9 on publicizing yourself). But most important of all, a leadership position in a networking organization will give you an opportunity to experience many of the same problems you would experience in a high-level management position with a company. It is a great way to practice your skills and gain valuable experience.

PROFESSIONAL SERVICES REFERRAL

When I relocated from Chicago to the San Francisco area, I didn't know any professionals such as lawyers, doctors, insurance agents, real estate brokers, accountants, or even a hair stylist. Using a network group is one of the quickest and best ways to get recommendations and referrals. This is a great benefit to anyone who relocates and good for anyone who wants to shop around for professional services.

LIFESTYLE AND LOGISTICS

When you are new to an area (as was the case for me) or if you are wondering where to move, networking organizations can be a great source of information about neighborhoods. "You might consider Winston Valley because that's where many of the young, upwardly mobile executives live." Or you might be the type that hates a long commute or wants to live near a tennis court or a golf course. These lifestyle and logistic choices can be made very quickly and accurately when you have a large number of people to talk with about your particular needs and interests. Again, most networking groups usually have a broad cross section of members from a large area who can direct you to a multitude of people who have had the same lifestyle concerns that you have.

SOCIALIZING

Whether you are new to a city or not, you are sometimes unaware of the fact that there are some great opportunities to socialize that you aren't taking advantage of. Either you don't know about them or you don't have the contacts to get into certain social settings. For example, I knew one executive who wanted to join a country club that some of the more senior executives belonged to. Through the network group he was a part of, he established some relationships with people who helped him get into this club.

If you are married and are looking for new couples to socialize with, or if you are just looking for new friends or a romance, many network organizations have informal cocktail parties before or after their actual meeting. This is a fabulous way to meet new people and establish social relationships.

You can also learn of the "in" clubs to connect with other influentials or contacts you would like to meet—through a networking organization. You can find out which is the best athletic club for you to join to be with people who have similar interests and backgrounds. All this information is readily obtainable through your networking organization.

FUN

This might be one of the most important reasons to join a networking organization. Most of them have fun, whether it is planning a ski weekend, a wine and cheese party, or a Christmas celebration event. Often we take ourselves so seriously in our work that we forget how much fun it can be to be among new people, hear the latest joke, or discuss a good movie. This kind of enjoyment is a big part of what your membership and involvement in a networking organization can bring you.

WHICH NETWORK ORGANIZATION
DO I JOIN?

My own recommendation is to join at least two organizations. One should be an organization that represents individuals involved in the same activity or function that you perform at work. For example, if you are in sales, you may want to join a sales networking organization. Such a group will have professionals from your industry as well as others. Many of the educational topics discussed by guest speakers will be relevant to you. It will also give you an objective opportunity to discuss the sales profession with peers as well as high-ranking sales executives. And this is the perfect organization in which to hear about sales positions that will become available.

There is also real value in joining an organization that represents an industry. For example, if you have a marketing position in a bank, you may want to join the American Institute of Banking. If you do some public speaking in your company, you may want to join the National Speakers Association. If you have a small firm, you may want to join a networking group of entrepreneurs. You may wish to join an organization that represents an area that you would like to know more about. For example, you may currently be in customer service but are very interested in pursuing a career in marketing. You might join the American Marketing Association chapter in your city.

If you are reentering the job market or are civic-minded, you may want to join a group that represents many business interests, such as your local Chamber of Commerce. If you know nothing about an occupation or field, joining an organization that represents that group can be an excellent way of getting information and developing contacts that will enlighten you to opportunities that may be of interest to you.

There is a networking organization for just about every business and professional area of interest you can imagine. Best of all, almost every organization will allow you to attend one of their meetings to meet their members and find out more about their network. In fact, if I hear that a particular organization is sponsoring a guest speaker that I want to hear, I will go just to that particular meeting.

The Chamber of Commerce in many cities has organizational

directories that are available to you. They list every organization and trade association in your area. It is ideal to skim through and decide which organizations you might consider looking into or joining.

SPECIAL TIPS ON WHICH ORGANIZATIONS TO JOIN

Find out which organizations high-ranking executives in your company belong to or support. Ask influentials and people who appear to be on the move in your company which organizations they respect and belong to. See if you can be sponsored by them (which isn't usually necessary but is nice), or at least see if you can attend a particular meeting with them so that they can take you around and introduce you. If you can't find someone to take you to a meeting, do not use this as a cop-out for not going on your own. Part of the fun and adventure is to extend yourself and meet people on your own.

Another source to help you decide which organizations to check out or to join is to ask customers and suppliers which organizations they belong to. This is a great idea, especially if you are in sales, but it is an equally excellent idea to find out what people outside your organization view as good groups to join. Ultimately, you will make the final decision.

Joining an organization is a low-risk undertaking with fantastic potential benefits to you, your company, and your career. It is a very special and unique support system, filled with professionals like you who want to be successful and who have the winning attitude of wanting to develop and improve themselves. That's the right company to keep.

chapter 15

Creating
the Perfect
Job

Few prospects are more difficult than trying to figure out what career moves will maximize your chances of being successful and more promotable. There are so many questions to consider in making important career decisions—and the right decisions can make the difference between career stagnation and career momentum.

In my workshops and seminars, I ask the question, "Where do you want to be in five or ten years?" Most people are either vague ("a supervisory role," "a responsible position") or unambitious ("assistant manager," "middle management").

The truth of the matter is that most people don't really give serious thought to their career path beyond the next position they are hoping for. They also have no specific plan for getting where they *say* they want to go. Is it any wonder that so many people feel frustrated or stagnating in their careers? Winning promotions in your career is tough enough, let alone without a well-thought-out plan.

Yet, ironically, if you were driving through unfamiliar territory, you would want to have a map in hand. Why then do you feel you can function without a career map? The business terrain has just as many roads that initially appear interesting but eventually lead only to detours or dead ends. Hard as it may be to visualize what you want in ten years, mapping out your path is vital. How can you be sure where you're headed unless you know where you are and where you came from? A career map is a way of both checking your progress and ensuring that you're still on the main road toward your destination.

I cannot tell you what your short- and long-term goals should be. Only you can make those determinations. I can, however, help you evaluate some of the pros and cons of the various possible routes open to you. Should you, for example, make a lateral move within your company, from a staff to a line job? Should you accept a high-level staff position if your ultimate goal is top management? If you are just starting out, what kind of entry-level position might put you in the best position to move up quickly? Of what value is further education? Would it be a good idea, in terms of your goals, to take a year or two off to get an MBA or other advanced degree?

These are all-important questions to consider before making any career decisions. Let's begin examining these questions and the process of diagramming your future. But first, since all your efforts are based on trying to be successful, it would make sense to look at what success really means.

WHAT IS SUCCESS?

Probably a whole book could be written on what success really means, because it is unique to each individual. To me, a successful career contains several important ingredients. First and foremost, it means that you are happy and fulfilled in doing the work you do. It also means that the relationships you have with people on the job are, for the most part, supportive and nurturing. Face it, you spend half your waking hours working. If your work life is unhappy or unfulfilling, it will affect all the other aspects of your life as well. Working for a paycheck may be possible in the short run but terminally frustrating in the long run.

I believe that people are successful when they are happy, fulfilled, and nurtured in their work environment, are paid for their high performance, and are doing the kind of challenging work that uses their talents and abilities to the fullest.

IS YOUR ORGANIZATION NURTURING?

I used the word *nurturing* in describing the work environment and people you will want to work with. In a very political and supercompetitive work environment, there is back stabbing and a "survival of the fittest" mentality. Real talent and competence are subordinated to power plays and contests of egos. As a career consultant who has heard just about every horror story imaginable about mistreatment, unfairness, and political firings, I can tell you that no amount of money or position is worth having if it is contingent on surviving in such an environment.

By contrast, when you are in a nurturing environment, the people you work with and the management in power tend to provide you with an encouraging and supportive atmosphere in which to produce results. Playing politics is held to a minimum, and a high value is put on esprit de corps among employees. In a nurturing environment, management is sincerely interested in improving the quality of work life for everyone, not just for a few executives in the ivory tower. In such environments, management cares about training and educating the staff—as opposed to the more archaic management philosophy, which views time away from the job, such as attending a professional development seminar, as a waste of time or loss of productivity.

Organizations that provide a nurturing environment demonstrate it through policies and actions. Often they have recreational facilities available. They may offer day-care assistance to employees with children. They encourage participation in continuing education, whether through seminars or classes, and provide tuition reimbursement programs. They even provide opportunities for sabbaticals and other leaves. Many companies provide psychological counseling services. I know of one very progressive corporation that has physical therapists on the staff to offer employees free massages as a means of reducing stress, encouraging relaxation, and increasing productivity.

The point is not the particular *way* that the organization exhibits its interest in providing a nurturing environment. The point is that you will want to work for an organization that has upper management leadership with an attitude of wanting to improve the quality of work life for all its employees. To do so is just plain good business. A lot of research has been published confirming what many of us have known for a long time: If you treat people well, as if they were part of a large family, you will get the highest productivity, the lowest turnover, and the greatest loyalty and commitment to excellence any organization could want.

YOUR SELF-IMAGE AND ATTITUDE TOWARD "CLIMBING THE LADDER"

Before we get into answering specific and important questions about your future career plans, it is vital that you do some self-assessing about your attitude toward climbing the organizational ladder. In our culture, particularly for men, it is assumed that they naturally want to be important, high-ranking executives, perhaps presidents of organizations. Yet in reality, most men are scared to death at the thought of such responsibility. They assume it is something that only super-ambitious, gifted, or well-connected types have a shot at. Nonsense! Women also have not been encouraged to strive for high leadership positions. Happily, that, too, is changing.

A few years ago, I did an informal survey with a number of individuals who were presidents of their own companies. Most of them (with the exception of some entrepreneurs who were self-appointed presidents) really hadn't thought in terms of "becoming a president." Instead, it was an idea that, over a period of years and a series of promotional moves, as well as observation of others in presidential positions, made them consider themselves in that role. In many cases, these people became presidents not because they were really "going for it" but because other higher-ups recognized their potential and their successful track records (perhaps while they were in vice presidential positions) and recommended them for promotion.

So don't assume that people who are presidents have been planning it since they were 10 years old. It just isn't so. Yet many people don't even envision themselves as vice presidents or directors. Just like the people I mentioned earlier who were unambitious, there are many people who are afraid to declare their intention or desire to attain a much higher position than they currently have. Or they say it with such little conviction that you get the idea that they must be saying it for the benefit of people who have told them what they *should* want. They are only mimicking.

I am convinced that at least half the process of being a high-level executive is personally believing that you have what it takes. Once you begin to interface with powerful executives, you will begin to realize that they put their coats on the same way you do, one sleeve at a time. They don't come down from Mt. Olympus or walk on water.

Begin to develop a mindset that you are truly destined for a responsible, high-level, high-paying position. If you don't want to do this, that's fine, too. Just remember that attaining a high-level position is to a large degree based on your truly believing that such a position is appropriate for you, no matter what your parents did or didn't do for a living, no matter what your grades were in school, and no matter what kind of jobs the other kids from your block are in.

Remember, just about everyone has access to the same information you do on how to become successful or how to become whatever. So there has to be a difference between the masses and the few who break out of the pack. That difference is based on having high self-esteem and a belief that an upper-level position is not only appropriate but very possible for you. The right attitude of confidence will help you meet the necessary challenges and thus produce the results that will ensure that you do climb the ladder—even to the presidency.

WHAT WOULD BE THE PERFECT JOB FOR YOU?

You may be saying to yourself, "Gee, Larry is talking about having a mindset to be president, and I don't even know what kind of job I really would be happy doing." Well, welcome to a very large club, filled with millions of people who are in your situation. Sure, they may be in jobs they have had for years, but they ask themselves the same questions that novices do: "Is this the kind of job I want to do—let alone be in—for the rest of my life?"

Most people simply do not sit down and rationally ask themselves what they want out of their jobs. You wouldn't want to go into a hospital to have your appendix removed by a surgeon who only has a "general idea" of where your appendix is, would you? You want the surgeon to know *specifically!*

Why should it be different with a job that you will work hard at, perhaps for years? So forget about your job being generally what you want. Let's talk specifically about the perfect job for you.

Creating the perfect job is not easy. In fact, it is probably impossible, because in life nothing is perfect. Yet if you strive for excellence, you may come closer than you ever imagined. To do so, it is necessary that you take into account the psychological, personal, and material factors that are a part of every job you accept and every working environment you are in. These factors need to be examined, considered, weighed, and then consciously chosen.

This is not to suggest that everything that you want must be in your job. Compromise is almost always necessary. However, know what you are compromising, specifically. Then you can devise a strategy to live with, instead of letting it gnaw at you when you finally realize you can't live with it or you can't change it. By your being aware of the important elements in the perfect job, you can make your best choices, compromise, and take total responsibility, instead of blaming others for why you are unhappy with your job or your work environment. With this general overview in mind, let's look at each of the three prime factors—psychological, personal, and material—involved in creating a perfect job for you.

PSYCHOLOGICAL FACTORS

Many people like a high-energy environment where work is done at an almost frenetic pace and where there is constant pressure and deadlines. You might even know people who have jobs in such work environments. And for all their complaining, just try to put them in a job where they are working at a slow, relaxed, comfortable pace and watch them fall asleep or lose their enthusiasm, motivation, and even productivity.

For other people, to be happy and produce great results, they need psychologically to be in an unstructured job with little supervision. This is quite often the case for people in sales. Frequently, when managers promote one of their best sales producers to an inside position, they find that that individual is not as happy and certainly not as productive.

Other people will work in a low-paying job if they have management that openly acknowledges, compliments, and recognizes their achievements. And these same people will not complain about wanting to make more money because their need for recognition and acknowledgment is so well satisfied.

I had a college buddy named Allen who had very high standards and ethics. He thrived on associating with causes, organizations, and people that had high morals and integrity. It was almost a psychological requirement for him to feel good about an organization and the people in it. He subsequently became very unhappy when his first job out of college was with a real estate firm that engaged in some questionable practices. Allen became very nervous, uncomfortable, and tense in this job. Within six months, he left the firm. Psychologically, there was a values incompatibility between him and his firm.

If you are going to be happy in any job, it is vitally important that you be psychologically suited to the people and your working environment. Important factors are high-energy versus low-key, relaxed atmosphere; high versus low supervision; structured versus unstructured positions; and compatibility of values. These can make the difference as to whether you are in a position in which you will thrive and advance quickly or whether you are only marking time until you finally figure out why you are unhappy and unproductive.

You may be thinking, "Well, how do I find out whether the psychological factors are supportive and positive for me?" First of all, be aware of what psychological factors are important to you. (An exercise at the end of this chapter will help you identify those factors.) Second, ask others about these factors and whether or not they exist in the position and environment you are considering working in. Also interview at least three people who already have the position you are considering. Ask each of them the same questions in order to get some sort of consensus. Don't make the foolish mistake of figuring that you can live with it or that you can change it. You probably can't live with it and you probably will not be able to change it.

PERSONAL FACTORS

There are obviously psychological aspects to some of the factors I am listing as personal. I consider them personal factors because they can directly affect your lifestyle—the hours you work, the type of customers you sell to, and the amount of traveling you do, for example. Consider the people in the following situations.

Kathy is a very bright, competent manager, and her company is impressed with her performance over her first six months of employment. Unfortunately, she is not as impressed with her company. In her previous job, she liked the idea of coming to work at 9:00 A.M. and leaving at 5:00 or 6:00 P.M. This working schedule was quite adequate to produce superior results. She had planned on keeping similar working hours in her new job.

However, within one month of her arriving on the job, she heard subtle hints and joking comments from her peers, such as, "Kathy, where do you think you're working, at a bank? You're coming in at nine and we've been here since seven-thirty." She practically felt like a criminal sneaking out of jail as she left her office at 5:30, knowing that most of the other executives would be there until after 7:00.

Kathy eventually made the decision to bow to peer pressure, but over the next six months she became increasingly resentful about her organization and the people in it. She was also upset about her social life—because she had none. By the time she got home, exercised, and ate, it was time for bed. Her life seemed to exist only for the sole purpose of working!

Jonathan came from an Ivy League school and an affluent family that raised horses and belonged to the country club set. He had certainly known the finer things in life. When he took a sales position in an insurance firm, he was excited about calling on young, upscale professionals like himself. Unfortunately, the insurance firm felt that Jonathan would do well to acquire some more grass-roots experience. So they gave him a territory filled with blue-collar, ethnic types in the urban renewal section of town. Jonathan is miserable and looking for another job. Calling on and selling to these kinds of insurance prospects is not what he had in mind.

Now, some people might argue that Jonathan needs this experience and it's good for him. But he could be learning and gaining equally valuable experience calling on upscale professionals and perhaps producing even greater results—and loving the experience.

Bill had done some traveling and liked doing it, as long as it was a minimal amount. His job called for "25 to 50 percent" travel. At his original interview, after hearing his boss tell him this fact, he passed it off, figuring that he could tolerate a 25 percent level of travel, and said no more about the issue. Now, after almost a year of travel consistently at the 50 percent level, he is upset at having a job that permits him so little time with his wife and children.

In all three instances, personal factors strongly affected the happiness and productivity of the people involved. In Kathy's case, while she is hoping for a bright career, she is not interested in a position that requires a consistent 12-hour-a-day commitment. She wants to have a personal life, too. And Jonathan really did have a preference for the kind of clientele he wanted to call on and sell to. There's nothing wrong with his preference. And for Bill, traveling was definitely something that he had a strong personal preference not to overdo. Yet he hadn't been honest with his prospective boss about his real feelings toward traveling.

These people undermined their chances of being successful because they were not assertive: They did not tell their managers honestly and directly what they wanted and didn't want in a job. At least by discussing it assertively, there would have been some possibility for a compromise or a way to make the conflicting personal factors somewhat more tolerable.

The worst mistake you can make is to get the job in the manner that salesmen from the "old school" advocate: "First, get the order. Worry about any problems later." Under that philosophy, they didn't bring up any objections or concerns until it was too late for the customer to object.

If you apply that same philosophy with your new employer, you will most likely live to regret it, like Kathy, Jonathan, and Bill, who all kept their concerns to themselves. After all, if your new company is not willing to work out any personal or psychological considerations, in the long run it will be much better for all concerned that you not accept the position they are offering. By the time you have a serious dialogue about the imminent possibilities of being offered a job, your prospective employer is very interested in you and probably very willing to find ways to accommodate you or at least compromise. By not mentioning your concerns, your employer will eventually realize that you were either too immature, irresponsible, or even dishonest to express up front how you really felt.

MATERIAL FACTORS

We all have ideas and pictures of the tangible or material rewards we hope to obtain by working for ourselves or for an organization. And in many cases such material factors can even outweigh the psychological or personal factors. If money is important to you, you will want to let your prospective employer know this without being concerned that you will be thought of as being greedy or avaricious.

Sandra, from her upbringing, had always felt uncomfortable talking about money with prospective employers. She had reservations that this issue wasn't feminine and that there were other things in life besides money. Yet she liked nice clothes and driving an expensive, new sports car. She had a real conflict about the fact that in her gut she wanted to make big money. Publicly she played down this desire. She rationalized that if she did a great job, her manager would recommend her for merit increases without her needing to discuss the money issue.

After her first review, Sandra got a modest salary increase, even though her manager told her she was doing a great job. She was very upset by this, but she said nothing. Six months later she came into her manager's office to announce that she had accepted a position with another company with a 20 percent salary increase.

Her manager was livid when she told him this. He confronted her further and said he thought that she loved her job. Sandra said that was absolutely true, but that she liked making big money and was dissatisfied with her previous salary increase and her future prospects for getting the big raises she had hoped for. Her manager rebuked her for not telling him that making big money was such an important priority of hers. The manager went on to say that he was a very traditional man and unused to women being so concerned about money. If he had known this before, he would have been happy to go to bat for her and talk to upper management about the kind of raise that would keep her happy, especially since she was so well thought of in the organization.

The game of the raise is a large psychological bluff.* You see, getting raises, especially on the executive level, is very subjective.

---

* Lawrence D. Schwimmer, *How to Ask for a Raise Without Getting Fired* (New York: Harper & Row, 1980).

For example, when a salary range of $28,000 to $34,000 is offered for a position, the manager who is doing the hiring has a good deal of latitude in deciding the ultimate salary to be offered.

As a quick aside, I must point out that when I prepare my clients for their job interviews, or even a salary negotiation in their current position, I find out "what the pie looks like." If I hear that there is a $6,000 range (as in the case of a $28,000 to $34,000 spread), you can be sure that I will help my clients devise a strategy to assure that they get a salary somewhere between the midpoint of $31,000 and the high point of $34,000.

This is accomplished by using several techniques. One technique is to set a limit with the prospective employer at the time that he literally says, "We'd like to offer you this position." Once those immortal words are uttered, you can negotiate by saying, "I am very excited about this opportunity, and I want to accept. However, for me to feel good about this offer, I will require a starting salary of $32,000" (or even the full $34,000, if you believe you are a strong candidate). "I want to be honest with you and let you know that making an excellent salary is very important to me, and I fully plan to give this company the kind of high performance that justifies that salary."

Unlike Sandra, who masked her strong desire for money, you can honestly and assertively put your manager on notice about how you really feel. No one need ever feel bad about telling an employer that they really like making big bucks!

In this discussion, and specifically in Sandra's situation of having a manager who didn't appreciate her interest in making money, I want to point out that this is not a dilemma that is confined to unenlightened, chauvinistic males who think that women only work for pin money (although some, unfortunately, do). In contrast, I have known male managers who personally weren't motivated by money, so they projected their lack of concern about money on their staff by giving them minimal increases and a very few merit increases. At the same time, they were oblivious to the notion that their staff members were very money-motivated.

I have also worked for managers who were very stingy with the company's money, as if they were being asked to take it out of their own pocket. Such managers have to be reminded, through self-interest, that it will cost a great deal more to replace you in training time and money. I found this logic to be very compelling, even to a stingy manager.

When it comes down to the material factor of money and discussing salary with people you work for, *don't ever take it for granted that everyone else feels the way you do or wants to make the big money you do.* You have to ask assertively for what you want and even set limits so that others will know what your expectations are. They can always discuss them further with you if they disagree or want to compromise.

There are other material factors that should be considered in creating the perfect job: for example, getting a great office with a view and lots of sunlight. Such was the case for Denny. He had lots of friends in town, and he wanted to impress them as well as prospective clients he was going to bring to the firm.

When he came down to the final stages of his interviewing, he showed his savvyness and his willingness to ask for a material item that he felt was an important factor to his job acceptance: a fancy office with a great view. He had heard that newer executives were often given whatever office was available during the first six months of their employment. And he was told that such offices usually were in the back, with no view and quite often with no windows.

So at the time he was offered his job, he was very assertive and said to his employer, Gil: "Gil, I must be honest and tell you that the salary and benefits sound great. However, I have one requirement that is extremely important to me. I would like one of the offices on the south side of the building that has a panoramic view and is sunny. I look at my office as my home away from home, and [self-interest] I can be much more productive, as well as impress some of the new clients I plan to bring into the firm, if I have an office I can be proud of. Would you be willing to assure me of one of those offices?"

I happened to have counseled Denny in this matter. He told me that he was a bit afraid that he would be turned down; he was ecstatic when Gil told him that he understood, had similar feelings, and would arrange for one of those offices.

Keep in mind that even if Gil's assertive approach hadn't gotten him the office (i.e., material factor) he wanted, there was no harm in asking and letting his new manager know how strongly he felt about that one factor.

Other material factors include such items as company cars, use of the company recreational facilities, and a whole host of perks (special employee benefits). If perks are important to you, ask for them directly and make them part of your negotiations. Try to use the limit-setting technique discussed in Chapter 3 to assure that promises will be kept. Whatever you do, don't leave any of these factors up in the air in the hope that they will be magically resolved to your satisfaction. And the time to ask about them is not *after* you have accepted the position. Your strongest negotiating position is *before* you accept, when you have the most leverage. It is also much fairer to your prospective employer.

A CAUTIONARY NOTE ON CREATING THE PERFECT JOB

Most people have an automatic tendency to look for the middle of the road between two extreme factors, such as structured versus unstructured or high versus low supervision. Looking for the best of both worlds can be both naive and unrealistic. For example, in a session with me, Ellen said she'd like to find a job where "there is some structure, but they pretty much leave you alone." Hank said to me, "I'd like to find a job where you can work inside part of the time and outside part of the time." Bea was looking for an organization where the environment was high-energy, but in a relaxed atmosphere.

My point in recounting these people's wants is that while you can look for the perfect in-between, be careful not to be unrealistic. After all, in most environments where there is structure, they don't leave you alone. They usually insist on close supervision. In Hank's case, while there undoubtedly are jobs that might call for his dividing his time half in the field and half in the office, they are not that common or that balanced. So Hank may have to compromise and be more realistic about his expectations.

Also keep in mind that sometimes people look for favorable factors that are incongruent (i.e., that don't agree). For example, Bea is not likely to find an environment where people are both high-energy and relaxed. The two styles are generally incompatible and rarely found in the same organizational environment.

None of this is to say that you *can't* find exactly what you want in creating your perfect job. Of course, you may end up spending many years searching for it. So it will be up to you to prioritize what is most important and to recognize whether you are being realistic or not and whether you are looking for factors that are generally incompatible with each other.

The key is to be consciously *aware* of these different factors, psychological, personal, and material. Pick out the ones that are most important to you in having the kind of job environment that you will really like and can thrive in, where you can produce fantastic results and be promoted.

MORE ON CREATING YOUR PERFECT JOB

The exercise that follows lists all three factor categories we have discussed: psychological, personal, and material. You will undoubtedly think of additional factors under each of the three main categories. Just add them to the list.

Pick out at least three factors in each category that are high-priority for you. Ask yourself if they are present in your current position. If not, are they a partial reason to account for why you aren't as happy and productive as you could be? Can you do anything to get them to be part of your current job?

Also note that there are ten more questions that ask you to list the main responsibilities you would like as part of your perfect job. Don't be afraid to use your imagination and ability to fantasize. Actually write out the title of the position you would like and the salary you would expect to be making. Answer the other questions about your staff requirements and what you see yourself liking *most* and *least* about your perfect job.

If you do this, you will begin to get a very good sense about the ingredients you need for a position to be the perfect job for you. You will begin to understand what is truly important to you in your present job. And you will be in an excellent position to apply this knowledge to your current position and especially to your next job, which you may be able to make your perfect job!

Exercise: CREATING THE PERFECT JOB FOR YOURSELF

Directions: Consider the following factors in trying to imagine what would be the perfect job for you. Answer each of the questions; be creative, ambitious, and honest with yourself. Rank the three most important in each category.

PSYCHOLOGICAL

___ pressure

___ low-key

___ relaxed atmosphere

___ low supervision

___ high supervision

___ unstructured environment

___ structured environment

___ power

___ acknowledgment

___ values compatibility

___ light responsibilities

___ heavy responsiblities

___ _____

MATERIAL

___ commission

___ bonus

___ office

___ company car

___ status

___ flexible time

___ outside seminars

___ stock option

___ pension plan

___ expense account

___ country club membership

___ vacation time

___ _____

PERSONAL

___ your boss

___ your staff

___ your peers

___ your clients

___ time commitment for job

___ working inside

___ _____

___ working in the field

___ travel

___ distance from home

___ transportation to work

___ commuting time to work

___ salary

___ _____

1. List the three main responsibilities that are part of your perfect job.

2. What is the title of this position?

3. What industry is it in?

4. What is your salary (commission, bonus, etc.)?

5. How many people report to you?

6. Briefly describe the main responsibilities of two members of your staff.

7. What would your staff or coworkers say are the three best qualities you bring to your job?

8. List the three most important qualities you'd like to have in your manager.

9. List the three parts of the job you like most.

10. List the three parts of the job you like least.

chapter 16

Having a Presidential Mindset: Ten Years to the Top

You now have some insights into the perfect job for you and the factors that are conducive to your being a high performer. And in creating the perfect job, you have given yourself an excellent launching pad from which to win your next promotion. It is now time to see whether or not that perfect job is really on a track to the top or whether it detours and goes nowhere. If you want to stay in one place forever, that is up to you.

But either way, make sure you know where the train is going and whether it is going in the direction you think it is. We all have had the experience at some time or other of being on a train and finding out just before we hit the end of the line either that we missed our stop or that the train was never going to stop where we thought it was going to stop. This is an unforgivable miscalculation to anyone who sincerely wants to win promotions and rapidly advance in a career.

To prevent such a big mistake from occurring, all you have to do is to make what I call a "track to the top" chart. This chart lists the typical progression of both experiences and positions that you must have in order to become president of your organization. If you are not aiming for the presidency, you can use this same chart to lay out a track for whatever position you are aspiring to.

Also, while there can be more than one track that will qualify you for consideration for a presidential opportunity (or an opportunity for another high-ranking position), most companies establish some basic criteria: experience, responsibilities, and positions that they believe their presidents need to have in order to govern the company properly. For example, in a sales-oriented company, it is unlikely that someone who has a great deal of experience in running the personnel department but no actual sales or sales management experience will be chosen to be president.

My point is, don't take comfort in the naive belief that you will be the company's first president without sales experience, even if you have been successful as a personnel executive. Your track-to-the-top chart is not perfect, but it is an excellent map to use in prudently directing your career. Best of all, even if you elect to take a detour from the experience traditionally expected of presidents-to-be, at least you will know you are doing so by choice! This is in contrast to people who operate their careers in the blind. Only after it's too late do they discover that there was no way they would be deemed qualified for higher-level positions, considering the positions and experience they had accumulated in their careers.

This chart is also excellent for you to plan out whether or not you want to be in an organization where, if you want to become president, you'll have to gather experience in areas in which you have absolutely no interest, such as a field position with the sales force, or have to change your lifestyle because being president would obligate you to accept relocation to a city where you have no desire to live. Doing a track-to-the-top chart is of great strategic importance in planning out your career and making necessary decisions. It will show you the kind of career moves you will need to make in order to be in the running for a high-level or presidential position.

Again, the objective of this exercise is not to force you to make a plan to be president if you don't want to. It is merely to help you make a map for your career so that you can see what the path looks like to the top, should you choose to go in that direction. Today you may not want such a lofty position, but tomorrow you may discover that such a position is exactly what you want. Either way, you'll be in the know!

PREPARING YOUR TRACK-TO-THE-TOP CHART

You may be thinking to yourself, "How am I going to find out the traditional track to the top in this organization?" First of all, begin by interviewing high-ranking individuals in the organization and asking them about their background and how it qualifies them for a higher leadership position, even the presidency. By the way, when I say interview them, I am not implying that you set up a "Meet the Press" conference. Ask to speak to each person for 15 minutes about your career or go to lunch together to ask questions and discuss your career.

During these brief meetings, make a few notes and ask these people if they have studied what track is most likely to qualify them for their next leadership position. Ask how they verified that they were on the right track.

The interviewing that you do should also include old-timers or historians in the organization, who have seen presidents come and go. They can often tell you the hidden agendas that one must observe in order to move up the ladder. Often your personnel department can give you some case histories of high-level executives' backgrounds.

You might also contact local executive search firms or personnel agencies that may be familiar with your company or industry. They may also give you insights on what career experience is necessary to qualify for the ultimate position you are seeking.

I did that at one company I worked for, where I had a position as a *product manager* in the marketing department. My assessments and interviews indicated that this company was highly marketing-oriented. Yet they wanted candidates for higher leadership positions to have at least one year as a *sales person* in a territory. This would most likely mean relocation for at least one year, maybe two. And to progress further, I would require sponsorship for a marketing position to a higher level, such as *group product manager* or *director of marketing*. Otherwise, I might find myself "left out in the field" (that is, the sales force). A hidden agenda was that if I were not considered upper management material, I would indeed be left out in the field with the excuse that there were no headquarters positions available.

Assuming that I was being considered for a higher leadership position, I might then be promoted to *group product manager* or *director of marketing*. I was then someone who could be considered for the *vice president of operations* position, where I could use my marketing and sales background to direct other functions within the organization, such as manufacturing and finance. This position was the pool from which the organization got its supply of potential presidents. Sometimes the organization had to go outside to find presidents. But when it did, most of the presidents seemed to have had similar backgrounds and responsibilities in their former positions.

MY TRADITIONAL TRACK TO THE TOP

7. President

6. VP general operations

5. Director of marketing

4. Group product manager

3. Field sales representative

2. Product manager

1. Assistant product manager

This chart shows each position following in sequence to the next. Your previous experience in other organizations might result in your not needing to serve time formally in each position. In my case, I had enough marketing experience to qualify me directly for a product manager position. Thus I bypassed the entry-level marketing position of assistant product manager. I also had field sales experience, so I was a candidate for the more senior marketing position of group product manager, to which I was eventually promoted. I was then eligible to be considered for the director of marketing position. If I had enough impressive achievements as group product manager, I might in some cases be considered for a VP of operations position or for another VP position.

Again, the track-to-the-top chart is not cast in concrete. It is just an excellent guideline for the kind of experience and positions you should expect to have in order to be considered for future higher-level positions in your organization.

Knowing the various track-to-the-top positions will spell the difference for you between career momentum and career stagnation. Even if you don't care about being president, use this chart to help you plan out the experience and positions you'll require to be qualified, for example, for being a department head. The key is in using the chart to develop a career plan, not necessarily to get you to plan on being president.

HIDDEN AGENDAS AND YOUR FUTURE RISKS

In Chapter 2 you did an exercise where you created an organizational personality profile. You looked at upwardly mobile people at your level, below your level, and above your level. And you asked yourself some basic questions about their backgrounds, lifestyles, and affiliations. These made up the basis for the many hidden rules and agendas that you discovered were operative in your organization. As you plan your career strategy, ask yourself such questions as "Do I have a future here?" and "Do I have the right qualifications?" You will want to consider the organizational profile you have assembled. It will help you in plotting your own career strategy within the organization you are working for.

For example, suppose you see from your track-to-the-top chart that you have had the necessary experience and positions to qualify for several higher leadership positions. However, you discover that one of your organization's hidden rules is that you must have a master's degree in business administration (MBA) to be considered seriously. This may mean that you will have to enroll in a special night school program to get your MBA. Or, another hidden agenda might be that this organization has never promoted women and minority groups past a certain level, even if they have the right experience. You had better be savvy to that before you set yourself up for expectations that are unlikely to be realized. Then you can decide if you want to try to become the organization's first female or minority president. If you don't, go to another organization.

LINE (DECISION-MAKING) VERSUS STAFF (SUPPORT) POSITIONS

One of the classic detours that blocks the progress of many ambitious men and women who want to be on a track to the top is the staff position. A staff (support) job is basically service-oriented. Staff departments are generally not profit centers; rather, they perform the vital functions that support an organization's money-making operations, for example, research and development, personnel, advertising, publicity, customer relations, data processing. Of course, if the company's business is advertising (such as an advertising agency), that would be its profit center and would not be considered a staff function. It would then be a line (decision-making) function, because advertising services are the way the organization makes money.

Line departments, on the other hand, are specifically the profit centers of the organization. These are the operations that have direct responsibility for making money for the company, such as management, sales, production, or marketing. Line positions are where the power is in the organization because line executives are charged specifically with the responsibility of making the decisions that directly affect the organization's profitability. In contrast, the main role of staff departments is to support the line departments in their effort to make profits for the organization.

Thus line positions are generally the training grounds for future leaders in the organization. Now, there's nothing wrong with accepting a staff position or spending your entire career in a staff position—*if* that's what you want and *if* you know that it's not likely to be the path to the top. The only exception is taking a staff position in order to gather some vital experience that you can use in order to be more qualified for a line position. However, it can be an illusion to think you are really moving up just because you have had some promotions within a staff department. You may be moving up within that particular staff department, but are you really moving up in the organization? Remember, a staff vice president might have decision-making authority within his department, but normally even staff vice presidents only *recommend* to line vice presidents, who make the final decisions.

Keep in mind that the line departments, which are the profit centers, control the organization and have the real power. They are the key decision makers. If you are on a track to the top, you will want to focus on line positions. The powerless are often relegated to quasi-powerful positions in staff departments. In the past, this has all too often been the case for women who have been smoke-screened into believing they were really advancing in their careers by being promoted to the position of staff vice president.

THE FALLACY OF ACHIEVING GOALS

Many of us are afraid to set goals because we then feel some sort of obligation to meet them or live up to them. This is not necessary. Yes, that's right. You do not need to achieve your goals; *you just need to have them!* This takes tremendous pressure off many people who are afraid of the heavy commitment they are making when they set a goal.

Many people, in fact, don't set a goal unless they are *sure* they will achieve it. The fallacy is not in having goals but in believing that you must *achieve* them. Achieving your goals is temporarily pleasing, but the joy soon wears off. The real excitement and joy for most people is in the process of striving to *attain* the goal.

I make this point about the fallacy of goal achieving because I have counseled many professionals who thought they should only set goals that they believed they could achieve. Such thinking is too self-limiting. Worse yet, as I said, achieving the goal is *not* what is important. *Working* to achieve the goal is what is really important. By working toward a goal, you will find yourself much more likely to (1) set high goals, (2) invest your best efforts in attaining them, and in the process (3) be more likely to accept the challenge that may result in your achieving the goal.

Not succeeding doesn't require that you be unhappy any more than achieving your goals means that you will be happy. You are never your successes or your failures. You are always you, no matter what the outcome of your actions. With this in mind, look at setting goals as a wonderful adventure in which you will, of course, do your best to achieve the goal—knowing that your real challenge is investing and committing yourself to the *process* of completing the goal.

YOU HAVE MANY TALENTS—YOU CAN
HAVE MANY JOBS

In past generations, people had one job; they did it well and generally for their whole life. They even expected their children to follow in their footsteps to do that same job. Many of us have grown up looking for that perfect job we were meant to be doing for the rest of our lives. We rationalize that until we find that job, we are just marking time.

Fortunately, we have transformed to a great extent our traditional view of the job we should be doing. People are now starting to recognize (and even be counseled) that everyone is capable and talented enough to do many jobs in their working career. Such a notion will help keep you professionally excited and vital instead of stagnated and bored.

We should recognize that through our own individual maturation process we will have different needs at different times in our lives. You may have the need for a greater intellectual challenge in your work, a need for more responsibility, a need to manage and lead others, or a need to make lots more money. Those needs can be the impetus for having a new career in a totally different industry. Those needs may no longer make it acceptable to be employed by others. Instead, you may decide to go off on your own and become an entrepreneur.

If you accept the fact that your work needs will inevitably change, you will feel less apprehensive about planning future goals. After all, you are not making commitments cast in concrete. Changes in your career goals are part of a natural evolution.

So you may have thought as you looked at the sample track-to-the-top chart, "There is no way I would be willing to spend a year in a sales position because I just know that I wouldn't like it."

You could be wrong. In a few years you might be very interested. In fact, you might actually love the area of sales. Yet based on what you think and feel today, you may block your own career mobility and not take a necessary career risk because of the inflexibility of deciding today what you will and will not be interested in doing five or ten years from now. It's the same thing you may have gone through as a kid when you hated eating spinach. As an adult, you may have grown to love eating spinach.

Moral: Don't assume you *know*. All you know is that today you have a feeling or belief about a particular thing. Tomorrow it could change drastically. Factor that unpredictable part of human nature into your career planning and know that you can plan a goal without being required to achieve it.

CHARTING YOUR TRACK TO THE TOP: A TEN-YEAR CAREER PLAN

I have heard career counselors talk about planning out your career over 20 or 30 years. And while that may be appropriate for some, I happen to believe that it is a bit impractical and of limited value. Most people don't really plan out each year. And there are too many contingencies and variables that will occur that they can't even anticipate.

What I believe offers you much greater value and practical use is creating your own track-to-the-top chart: a ten-year career plan. Here you can organize a plan that has some continuity and that you will have a greater likelihood of fulfilling. After all, ten years is much easier to grasp as a unit of time than imagining what plans you'll make in 20 or 30 years. You can review ten-year plans and create additional ten-year plans.

Take a look at the ten-year career plan exercise on page 328. Ask yourself what your goals are and how you are going to achieve them. Even thinking about that can be intimidating. Yet if you begin by looking at your track-to-the-top chart and giving some serious thought to what you believe your ultimate goal is (knowing that it may very well change), you can then lay out the various *positions* that are most likely to bring you to that goal, all the while using specifically planned completion *dates* for achieving that goal.

In addition, as you begin doing this exercise, you will have to begin thinking about the actual *methods* you will use to achieve those goals (which we will discuss shortly). And you will want to consider an *alternative career move* if you don't achieve the position you are working toward.

Lastly, you will want to examine the potential *obstacles* in your path, or what I call "stops and blocks." Knowing in advance what these may be will help you prepare for them, and, at the very least, you won't be shocked if and when they occur. Best of all, being aware of the stops and blocks in your career path will maximize the possibility of your coming up with a strategy to work around them or at least not waste valuable time over a no-win block.

With this general overview in mind for completing the ten-year career plan exercise, let's go through each of the components to give you an even clearer understanding of how to diagram your future career goals.

TIMING

You can begin by writing down what you believe today is your ultimate goal. I hope many of you want to be president of your organization. But if your goal is being a lawyer, doctor, plumber, or certified public accountant, that's fine, too. And if you have always imagined taking a long trip to Europe, you can also put that in your ten-year plan. You may want to plan on having children, going into your own business, or anything else you have always wanted to do. Just put it in your plan. I have started you out with calendar quarters in the exercise, so that you have a sense of urgency rather than feel that you have a whole year in which to begin. If you at least plan the first year in calendar quarters, you'll feel a much stronger focus toward your goal direction.

If you don't have the faintest idea of what your ultimate goal is, be creative and start from year 1 and see if you can imagine where your career would take you and toward what ultimate fantasy conclusion it might lead you. Just make a plan, using every year of the ten years.

HOW LONG IS TOO LONG IN ANY POSITION?

At my seminars and workshops, people often ask me how long they should stay in any given position. My own rule of thumb is *do not stay in any given position for longer than three years.* This is a good rule for anyone, especially someone who is aspiring to climb the ladder to the top. You should be able to learn just about anything you need to learn by being in a position for that long. If you stay in such a position much longer than three years, management may brand you as being unpromotable, figuring that you have found your niche and are satisfied.

That is why, as you pay attention to your career clock, you should continually publicize your interest for a promotion to a particular department or position (see Chapter 9 on publicity and visibility). And you must be sensitive to being passed by for a promotion. This may be management's way of saying, "You are fine where you are, but we have better talent than you to promote." If this is the case, you may have to leave and work for another organization where your star has a more realistic likelihood of shining.

One of the biggest mistakes I observe business and professional people making is that they do not pay attention to their career clock. It becomes much too easy for them to stay where it is comfortable and familiar. And while it can be painful to leave friendly colleagues and an organization where you may have worked for years, this is precisely where being a true risk taker can make or break your career. So as difficult as it may seem, if you want to advance your career rapidly, you must be willing to leave your current organization if you are not growing through meaningful responsibilities or through new job promotions.

YOUR POSITION

By looking at your track-to-the-top chart, you can begin planning your career by listing positions that you will work toward attaining. Find out from people currently in that position how long it took them (and what experience they needed) to get to that position. This will help you develop more realistic timing for when you might be able to occupy such a position. Also, work with your manager on establishing your career goals and the specific positions you are interested in. You might even invent a position and attempt to show management why there is a need for it as well as why you are the perfect candidate to fill it.

DEFINING YOUR JOB VERSUS BEING DEFINED BY IT

Many people look at their current position and responsibilities and realize that their position has evolved greatly. In many cases, your current job is totally different from the original job you took when you were hired. The result may be that you are actively carrying out what were once major responsibilities of the manager, even though your official title is still assistant to the manager.

Often people in such a dilemma not only don't have their rightful title but are not getting paid accordingly, either. This is called self-exploitation. You are allowing yourself to be exploited when you let your manager add the major responsibilities of others onto your position when you aren't receiving commensurate raises or title promotions.

Not surprisingly, I have worked with and counseled hundreds of people who are resentful over having increasingly more work and responsibility assigned to them with no additional pay or title change. If this happens to you, remember, you are allowing others to exploit you. The first step in changing this is to define your job—don't let it define you.

The following exercise will help you to define your job. Begin by taking your original job description and writing down the major responsibilities. If you don't have a job description, you have made one of the cardinal mistakes: *Never, ever take any job unless you have a specific job description of what your duties and responsibilities will be.* Be suspicious if your new employer doesn't have a job description. Exploitation begins with only vague references to what you will be doing. This is utter nonsense and is totally unprofessional. After all, it is in the interest of both parties to be clear on what is expected. If necessary, before accepting the position, establish in writing with your new employer what your specific responsibilities will be in this position. You should also have some standard of measurement to determine how well you are doing, so that judging superior performance is not totally subjective.

Write down your manager's idea of what your job description is. You may be amazed at how most managers lose a perspective on the disparity between what they hired you to do versus what they now think you are doing versus what you are *really* doing! Finally, write down the specific responsibilities you are currently handling—what you actually *do* in your job.

If you are like many people who do this exercise, you may find out that you clearly have many more responsibilities than when you were originally hired. And if you have not been given some special recognition in the way of raises or title promotions, you have been defined by your job.

By contrast, when you define your job, you are periodically assessing your current job responsibilities every quarter. If you are noticing additional duties and project assignments, you should be the one to speak to your manager about getting a title that represents your new responsibilities more fairly. Or ask for a salary increase that is indicative of your heavier work load and responsibilities. This exercise will help you take total responsibility instead of telling others how you have been exploited.

Exercise: DEFINING YOUR JOB VERSUS BEING DEFINED BY IT

Directions: From your original job description, write down the major responsibilities. Next write down your manager's idea of what your job is. Then write down what you actually do.

YOUR OFFICIAL JOB DESCRIPTION

_____

_____

_____

_____

_____

YOUR MANAGER'S IDEA OF WHAT YOUR JOB IS

_____

_____

_____

_____

_____

WHAT YOU ACTUALLY DO

_____

_____

_____

_____

By defining your job, you may be able to make a great case for why you are now ready for a promotion, based on having acted in that capacity despite not having the official title. This exercise may also show that while your official title has been assistant, actually you have been carrying out the responsibilities of a manager.

Patrick found this to be the case when he did this exercise. He then confronted his manager about this, and she said, "Sorry, but that's just the way it is." Patrick, in turn, wrote up a new résumé and next to his formal title of "assistant" he wrote "acting manager." He listed the managerial responsibilities that he had carried out during his time with the company. He then began working with several executive searchers. And he told them with great confidence that although he did not have the formal title of manager, he did have the actual experience.

Patrick's awareness of what his job really was (as he defined it) was instrumental in his ability to make prospective employers believe that he was, in fact, a manager, not just an assistant. It eventually lead to his finding an excellent management position with another company.

So if you do feel exploited, this exercise may be the start of your taking responsibility for your career and even parlaying your "acting job" into credit for the job as if you had the title.

By doing this exercise and discovering that you ought to be promoted to a job with the title covering the responsibilities you have, you are in a position to make a presentation of why you expect to be promoted to that position, along with the money that goes with it. Or you can go to a personnel agency and say, for example, "I was hired as a staff person, but I'm really working as the acting manager in my position. My responsibilities are such and such. I'd like to talk with you about getting that formal position in another company and the salary that goes with it."

Define your job; don't let it define you. Otherwise, you will be doing a lot more and not being paid for it.

METHODS TO GET THERE

When I ask most people how they expect to get from position A to position B, they say they will "really work hard." That's great—but it's an insufficient promotional strategy of how they expect to get there. And it's no more reassuring than having a runner tell you that he plans to win a race by running hard. To achieve your planned career goals, not only must you work hard, but more important, you must be willing to "work smart." That means having some specific methods in mind for achieving your goals as you plan your career moves. There are many options; here are a few that I'd like to suggest you consider as you fill out the ten-year career plan.

METHODS TO ADVANCE YOUR CAREER GOALS

1. Be promoted to the position

2. Make a lateral move to a line or staff position

3. Get additional education

4. Change companies

5. Return to your original organization

6. Use executive search firms

7. Answer ads

8. Join trade associations and network organizations

9. Become an entrepreneur

1. BE PROMOTED TO THE POSITION

This is everyone's favorite method. However, if you expect to move from one position to another via a promotion, remember that to be promoted, you must not only demonstrate your worthiness through achievement, but you must also make your promotional interest known to your manager and others in the organization. Also make sure that you pay attention to potential obstacles to your promotional opportunities (see the list of "stops and blocks" on page 319).

2. MAKE A LATERAL MOVE TO A LINE OR STAFF POSITION

I have seen people refuse an opportunity to move from a staff to a line position because it was "just a lateral move" or because they were offered very little additional money. This shortsighted thinking ignores longer-term career strategy, which suggests that moving laterally from a staff to a line position can be an excellent way to position yourself for a decision-making leadership opportunity in the future.

There are some instances where to get position C, you will need to move from line position A laterally to staff position B. Even though position B is a staff position, it may be in an area of expertise you will need to be qualified for promotion to position C. While there are certain dangers in spending too much time in staff positions, one method for advancement is going from a line position to a staff position, or vice versa.

3. GET ADDITIONAL EDUCATION

Sometimes to be seriously considered for advancement in an organization, upper management will ask you (or make known indirectly via a hidden rule) to get an MBA or other advanced degree. Or they may require you to enroll in a university-sponsored management training program, such as the special executive program run by Harvard University, or to attend certain technical courses or seminars. So, if you are in a low-level marketing position and are planning one day to be director of marketing and you know that all directors of marketing have an MBA, you had better plan on getting this degree to advance your career.

By the way, many companies become ecstatic hearing that their young executives are working on their MBAs. Even if you aren't sure that you are totally committed to obtaining the degree, consider taking one of the electives that are a part of an MBA program. This might not only be educationally valuable to improving your job expertise, but it will also allow you to publicize the fact that you are "doing MBA graduate work." This will most likely make you competitive with companies that advertise "MBAs preferred." It may seem cosmetic, but psychologically it puts people on notice that you are seriously interested in getting whatever education is required to advance your career.

4. CHANGE COMPANIES

In many organizations, especially if your upward mobility is blocked (for example, if there are no vacancies in positions you would like to be promoted to), the best method for advancement is to change companies. I have known executives who were well regarded in their organization but understood that at the present time there were no promotional openings. These individuals found the appropriate promotional opportunities with other companies, sometimes direct competitors. However, they had an implicit understanding with their original company: "Get the right experience and come back in a year or two and we will find a position for you. Or we will call you when one opens up."

Keep in mind, in this case, that this is nothing more than an informal, nonbinding understanding. If you're a great upper management prospect or someone with special talents, you can often move up the ladder by changing jobs, with the medium-term intent of returning to your original company. Make no mistake, *the quickest way to climb the organizational ladder is by moving around from company to company*. You can average a new title every 18 months to two years.

Be aware, however, that job-hopping is viewed negatively by most employers. Usually, someone who has had more than one job in a year or a different job every year for a period of several years is considered suspect of job-hopping. However, if you change jobs every

18 months to two years, it is easy enough to let prospective employers know that you have planned your career and experiences so that you can be on a track to the top. Let them know what your ultimate goal is so that they can see that it was careful planning, not job-hopping.

One other point to accent: Whenever you change jobs, the first organizations to consider working for are your current company's competitors. A certain machismo is alive and well in today's organizations: Companies love to steal each other's talent—even if, in reality, they didn't steal you because you elected to join them. The fact that you came from a competitor carries with it the notion (which may really be a fantasy) that "you know what's really going on at XYZ Widget Company, and once you join up, you'll tell *all!*" Practically speaking, by working with competition, you can often step right into a position because you know the organization and the industry so well. This is a prime method of advancing your career.

5. RETURN TO YOUR ORIGINAL ORGANIZATION

As I mentioned, in some organizations you can establish an implicit understanding that you are leaving only to gain experience elsewhere. Once you do, and once your old company has the right position, you expect them to let you know about the opening. If you are well regarded, there is a lot of power and prestige in leaving and then returning. When you come back, your arrival may be treated like that of General MacArthur—"Hail to the conquering hero returning . . . "

6. USE EXECUTIVE SEARCH FIRMS

Once you are in your new position, one of the first things you should do (and, incidentally, probably the last thing most people do) is update your résumé. Send it out to at least five of the best executive search firms in your city (or nearest large city to you). You never know when you may get that magical call from an executive searcher who may offer you a "position you can't refuse." (By the way, any time you receive any publicity or visibility, send a copy to each of the executive searchers.)

Executive searchers are the wild card in your career. As you may know, they differ from typical personnel agencies in that they usually are retained by a particular firm, often exclusively, to fill a specific position. A personnel agency may not have any exclusivity for the job they are trying to fill, because many other personnel firms have the same opportunity to fill that position. Whoever fills it first gets the commission.

Another distinction of executive search firms is that they tend to be retained to fill higher-level and higher-paying positions than personnel agencies. Executive search firms or personnel agencies will keep your résumé confidential and can be an extraordinary source of information on what is happening in your company and industry. A good placement counselor can give you excellent advice on what career moves to make to advance you toward your ultimate goal.

Most people make the mistake of contacting a search firm or a personnel agency when they are frustrated or upset or ready to be fired from their position. This puts a severe pressure on them and can jaundice their otherwise levelheaded thinking. A much more favorable time to be in contact and establish a relationship with an executive search firm is when you are under absolutely no pressure or have no serious interest in leaving your present company. This is an excellent career advancement method.

7. ANSWER ADS

Again, most people do this when they are totally stymied, frustrated, or about to be fired. They then become like a wounded animal backed into a corner. Avoid this by making it a daily practice to go through the *Wall Street Journal* and your local newspaper. Both usually list the largest variety of executive and professional jobs on particular days. Look through the want ads and consider replying, especially to jobs where you *don't* think you have a chance of being considered.

I knew one colleague who said to me that he would never leave his job unless he could advance at least two levels and make at least 25 percent more than he was currently making. Those types of ads were the only ones he answered. He answered no more than one a week on the average, and since he wasn't particularly motivated, he would send the ad and only his résumé. He really didn't want to put out too much energy. Again, his attitude was, "If they want me, let them come and get me."

After nine months, he got a call and went on an interview with another company. He came back in shock. He had just been offered a senior-level vice presidential position and a 35 percent increase in pay.

My point: By regularly watching for career opportunities (even ones you think are over your head), you can advance your career by leaps and bounds. Best of all, you can do it with no pressure and minimal effort.

8. JOIN TRADE ASSOCIATIONS AND
NETWORK ORGANIZATIONS

By being a regular member (as was discussed in Chapter 14), you will hear about positions opening up and special career opportunities. It is not uncommon for executives in a trade association to establish excellent contacts, even with competitors. One executive may tell another, "If you ever want to leave your company, let us know because we'd love to have you. We'll find a spot for you."

Thus, if you are looking for a particular promotion and don't get it, put out feelers to see if any of your network contacts know of a similar position elsewhere.

9. BECOME AN ENTREPRENEUR

Many times, people plan out their careers expressly for the purpose of gathering the experience and competence they will need to start their own businesses. I know one executive, Maria, who always knew that she wanted to run her own clothing boutique. So she took a retail position with a major upscale department store chain. She took positions in buying, merchandising, and advertising with the chain. All her experience was geared to the day when she would open up her own retail clothing store.

Maria did it and became fabulously successful, eventually hiring some of the best talent from her former department store chain.

USE A SYNERGISTIC METHODS APPROACH

I have listed only nine methods to consider. There are certainly other methods to advance your career. When you plan out a position you want to work toward obtaining, don't feel obligated to pick one method; instead, use a synergistic approach, a combination of parts to equal more than the whole. No one method, obviously, will guarantee your securing the position you are planning for. Choose several methods to focus on to achieve the position you want.

For example, throughout the ten-year plan, you may be using executive searchers as well as networking contacts. The key is to have various methods in mind to maximize the likelihood of your achieving your subgoals and your ultimate goal. Don't leave your career to fate or the fantasy hope that you will be lucky and get the next position just by being there.

YOUR ALTERNATIVE CAREER MOVE "IF YOU DON'T GET . . ."

As Robert Burns pointed out, "The best-laid schemes of mice and men often go astray." And since your ten-year career plan represents your best attempt to plan out your career, it only stands to reason that you may not attain the position you have planned for or you may not do so in the particular time frame you had planned.

The big question in such a case is, "What is your alternative career move if you don't achieve your objective?" The purpose of your filling in this particular column is for you to seriously consider what, if anything, you will do as a countermeasure to not attaining your specific timed goal. You may not choose to do anything other than to wait, perhaps, one more year to achieve the position you had planned for. However, the key is that you *choose* consciously to consider what your alternative career move will be. Don't make a decision "by indecision." That just isn't the stuff that winners are made of.

The alternative career moves may very well include the methods to advance. For example, if the position you would like to be promoted to is unavailable because someone else is occupying it, you may want to consider a lateral move elsewhere. There, at least, you can accumulate experience in an area that will benefit your career in the interim. Or you may decide to leave the company and find that position elsewhere. Again, use this "alternative move" column to plan your contingency career moves (which, of course, are always subject to change and revision). In many cases it may be wise to let influentials, especially your current manager, know what your alternative career move will be if you don't get a particular promotion.

Rachel was considered a rising star in her organization. She had held a staff position for the last two years and was told by several upper-echelon executives that she would be seriously considered for a supervisory position that would be opening up soon. When it did, someone else was given the promotion. Rachel let her manager and several of her upper-echelon contacts know that as much as she loved the company and the people she was working with, if the company couldn't find a similar management position to promote her to within the next six months, she would be looking for a similar position in another organization.

Notice that Rachel was not threatening about it. She was just assertive and smart to set a limit, six months. This put upper management on notice that unless they wanted to lose a prized team player in whom they had invested a great deal of training and grooming, they had better take her career plan seriously. Of course, if Rachel did not get offered a promotion within the six months, she would be smart to say no more about the consequence she had issued. Instead, she should silently begin looking for a position elsewhere, unless she has some reason to believe sincerely that a promotional opportunity was just around the corner.

OBSTACLES TO YOUR UPWARD MOBILITY

Many factors besides your experience, competence, and expertise are responsible for your getting or not getting promotions within the organization. These factors include everything from the politics of your organization to timing, logistics, and plain old luck.

As you decide to advance your career, it is vitally important for you to be savvy to the obstacles that may be in the way of your achieving your career goals. Assess the "stops and blocks" to your career. Otherwise, you may very well succeed only in deluding yourself that you will attain a position that you should have known you would never get in the first place. Keep in mind that these career obstacles are constantly changing. In other words, a block may not be prevalent while you are in position A, but when you are promoted to position B, you may automatically face a block that you will have to surmount.

In diagramming your future career risks, being aware of these various obstacles will make the difference between having career momentum or career stagnation. Here is a list, followed by discussion, of stops and blocks that I have seen stall some of the most promising careers. Be aware of their existence and know that it is your responsibility to devise a strategy to counter the obstacles in your career path.

STOPS AND BLOCKS

1. No vacancy
2. Being over-qualified
3. Improper grooming
4. Discrimination and stereotyping
5. Insufficient background or expertise
6. Image problem
7. Lack of support
8. Indispensability
9. Unkept promises
10. Acting titles
11. Being passed by
12. "Going nowhere" positions
13. Positions off the beaten track
14. The staff trap
15. The dinosaur organization

1. NO VACANCY

This block is the simplest to discover. All it takes is looking at the position you want, seeing who is in it, and evaluating your realistic chances of getting that position. How young or old is the current occupant of that position? How well is he regarded by upper management? Does he appear to aspire to the next level up, or is he planning to be in that position for years to come?

As simple as it is to determine whether people have a shot at the positions they want, it is just as amazing how many people are simply "waiting for Godot." I could never figure out what such people were waiting for, because a quick assessment would reveal that they would have to wait for many years (and ironically, even if they did, waiting that long would in and of itself disqualify them, assuming that they are not frustrated to death first). Apparently, it's human nature for people to just wait and hope that something will come along or that something will happen. But when it doesn't, many people are very upset.

So check your organizational chart, and consider your competitors and how many of them there are. Set your own personal limit for how long you will give yourself to attain a particular position, knowing that if you don't get it, you will implement an alternative career move. Remember, if there are "lifers" in the position you want or too many young stars like yourself, you may have to wait too long to get the opportunity to prove yourself.

2. BEING OVERQUALIFIED

This is a very special block because it presents a dilemma both to you and to your employer. Many times an individual has a strong background and experience that appears to exceed the scope and responsibilities of the position the individual is seeking. Sometimes this is so evident that management is likely to ask, "Why on earth would you want a position that is so likely *not* to challenge you professionally?" The logic of such individuals may be either that this is the only position they would feel comfortable taking or that they want the position for a very short period of time, believing that they can quickly leapfrog to the next position.

Management's fear of your being overqualified is that the position won't challenge you and once frustration sets in, you will want to make a change or quit. Also, striving to attain a position for which you appear to be overqualified invites suspicion and doubts about your ambitiousness and your motivation to stretch yourself to your professional limits.

Of course, being overqualified may be a catchphrase management is using to discriminate against you and obscure the real issue, which is their not wanting *you* to get a particular position.

Being overqualified is in the eye of the beholder. If there is a sincere perception that you already have more than sufficient expertise to handle a position, your motives and staying power in that position will be suspect. So find out the perception others have about you and the position you want *before* you run a publicity campaign to get that position. If you suspect that you are truly being discriminated against, consider leaving and working somewhere where you don't have to face bigotry and discrimination.

3. IMPROPER GROOMING

Many times people in the organization think they are genuinely working toward a particular promotional opportunity when in reality they don't even have a chance because they have not had (a) the proper visibility to get that position, (b) the right sponsors to support them, (c) the necessary prior experience, (d) their manager's support for the position, (e) the perception by upper management that others in the organization will cooperate with them, or (f) sufficient charismatic leadership for higher-level responsibility.

The bottom line is, they are not ready, and just about everyone knows this except them! So make sure that you periodically get assessments from your manager and other influentials on your state of preparedness to move up to the next level or position you desire.

4. DISCRIMINATION AND STEREOTYPING

Guarding against this block can often be accomplished by looking at the organizational profile you prepared in Chapter 2. If you can see that historically the company has never had women or minority individuals in certain positions, beware! This is especially true where there is tokenism, which is nothing more than the organization's recognition that for political or legal reasons they had better get at least one woman, Jew, Hispanic, or black into a higher-level position.

If this is the case, you may be duped into believing that management is receptive to minority members in positions of authority when in reality those few people in token positions are nothing more than cosmetic executive fixtures whose career path has already been predetermined by upper management. There will be plenty of hidden agendas that will reveal the organizational attitude toward the kind of people who are likely to be discriminated against.

Perhaps a bit more subtle than discrimination is another form of prejudice called stereotyping. This is a tendency of management to look at your role or desired position as being inappropriate for you. For example, Samantha graduated with a technical degree in automotive engineering. Yet because she is a woman in a predominantly male organization, she was never perceived as being a competent automotive engineer: "After all, how much could a woman know?" The fact that she knew a great deal did little to change the stereotypes held by some of the more traditional or chauvinistic men. It is questionable as to whether she will ever receive fair acknowledgment and sincere consideration for a promotional opportunity.

5. INSUFFICIENT BACKGROUND OR EXPERTISE

Often because you have stayed in one position or department too long or have lots of experience in only one area, you may be regarded as unpromotable or promotable to only a narrow range of positions. The key is to find out what kind of background and experience you need to qualify as a serious contender for the next position you want. Find out the background of the current position holder. Don't set yourself up for the disappointment of not getting a promotion only to find out that you just didn't have the right background or experience to begin with. And remember, as a general rule of thumb, that management puts far greater value on your having had diverse work experience than it does on your having specialized for years in one functional area.

6. IMAGE PROBLEM

Ira is technically a very bright guy. However, he dresses like a nerd. And he loves to play practical jokes. Despite his sincere interest in moving up the ladder, he is insensitive to the fact that he has a poor image among coworkers, subordinates, and superiors. They don't take him seriously. He is not perceived as leadership material. He is viewed as being "just fine where he is." (See Chapter 6 on charismatic leadership style.) You must have an image that inspires people's confidence and trust if you expect to be promotable. Style is just as important as substance in the real world.

7. LACK OF SUPPORT

Grant is currently a manager with a very aggressive and abrasive style of leadership. He seems to get the work done, but most of the people in his and other departments shy away from him. It's obvious that because of his poor "people skills," he doesn't get the cooperation necessary to produce results in the most efficient manner. In fact, some of the people in the organization actually subvert his efforts—that's how much he is disliked. Grant is encountering great difficulty getting promoted because management sees that his aggressive leadership style does not inspire help, support, or cooperation.

If management doesn't perceive you as a leader who can get cohesive support and production not only from people over whom you have authority but also from people over whom you have no line authority, you will not be seriously considered for higher leadership positions.

Another form of lack of support is of a more political nature. You may have formed unpopular liaisons with people out of favor, or you may in the past have been unsupportive of other people's projects. Upper management may then see you as having no connections and no likely prospect of getting the cooperation from other managers whose departments' support would be necessary for you to produce results in a new position.

8. INDISPENSABILITY

You may have heard the old adage "The irreplaceable man gets fired." It's true: many people who thought they were irreplaceable or indispensable find themselves abruptly fired. Upper management made the judgment that it was too demoralizing or too threatening for anyone in the organization to have such a swelled head or such a bloated sense of his own value. This can certainly happen to stars who have an overexaggerated sense of their own worth to the organization.

In contrast, the real stop or block for many people is that they are regarded as being indispensable to their immediate manager. For example, Erin was a very able staff analyst. She had told her manager, Gwynn, that she wanted to be considered for a promotion to one of several positions. However, to Gwynn, Erin was almost an alter ego, a competent and talented individual who made the department and Gwynn look fantastic. Gwynn rationalized, "One day I'll recommend Erin for a promotion, but for now she's too valuable for me to let go!"

In effect, you can become such an asset to your manager or to someone else who is benefiting from your superior performance to the point where the other person, out of self-interest, will seek to justify reasons why you aren't ready or why the time isn't right. In reality, you are a prized possession.

If you are in such a position, you must set time limits with your manager. And you may have to issue a consequence of action you will need to take if no promotional opportunity is forthcoming.

9. UNKEPT PROMISES

It is extremely important to your career advancement that you work for and with people who have integrity and who keep their word. This may sound elementary, but I counsel hundreds of people who are incredulous that their manager duped them or promised something only later to develop amnesia about what was said.

Usually, I ask these naive people, "Have you ever known of any instances where your manager did something similar to someone else in your department or to someone in another department?" I am usually told, "Yes, but we had a very special relationship. I never dreamed he would do it to me!"

So here's another rule of thumb: If you see your manager take advantage, not keep his word, develop amnesia with others, or do anything you consider dishonest to others, be assured that your turn will come one day, too!

A manager's word, and his ability to be responsible for keeping it, must be a major consideration before accepting a position. Any promises that affect your career, such as future raises or promotional opportunities, should be put in writing by you or your manager (see Chapter 10). This is the best-known cure for "manager's amnesia," a disease that attacks the memory of opportunistic and expedient managers who promise now and worry about delivering later.

10. ACTING TITLES

Watch out for a position where you have all the responsibilities without formally getting the title or the money that goes with it. This is one of the oldest cons used to exploit people by giving them the illusion and promise of the title while getting the same work from them as from someone who had formally been bestowed the title and the accompanying salary.

Now that you know about such a ploy, you can only allow someone to exploit you if you accept an "acting title" position with the promise "If you take on the responsibilities of this position and do a great job and prove yourself, in four or five months I'll do my best to get you the title and the money that go with it." Your reply ought to be, "I have a better idea. If you have the confidence to give me all the duties and responsibilities of the position, give me the title and the money that go with it. And if in four or five months I haven't done an excellent job in this position, fire me."

The only exception whereby you would accept an acting-title position without the title and money that go with it is when you have set a time limit. In doing this, you ask your manager to put in writing that at the end of the five months you will either get the formal title and money or you will be released from the responsibilities of the "acting job." Managers who are not willing to agree to one of these two options are telling you in advance that they are up to no good and interested only in exploiting you for their own self-interest without any regard for you.

11. BEING PASSED BY

When you are waiting for a promotion and find that management has chosen someone else instead, it may be time to reevaluate your stock in the organization. It may be a legitimate case of the organization having too much talent, or you may actually have been "neck and neck" with the other candidate and lost out. In that case, you may want to wait longer. If you are continually passed up for promotions, however, particularly by others who appear to have less experience or competence than you, it is time to acknowledge that you have reached a dead end in your organization. You may have to consider changing jobs. If you stay in the same position too long, you will be branded as unpromotable and probably not considered on any career track to the top. You are better off finding an organization that will let you play in the game instead of sitting on the bench withering away.

In many of the organizations I have worked for, the hidden rule was that if you were passed up for a promotion more than once, management was subtly letting you know that your future is very limited and that if you want to advance, you'll have to do it at another company.

12. "GOING NOWHERE" POSITIONS

These are positions that inherently carry no upward mobility with them. And anyone who paints some rosy picture about how "in this position anything is possible" is deceiving you or giving you a false expectation. The most classic case of this happening repeatedly is the position of secretary. While there are certainly many instances of secretaries going on to higher positions of authority, the numbers of those who do are small in comparison with the numbers of secretaries who go nowhere. Most secretaries remain secretaries. Many of them, encouraged to believe that their secretarial jobs will be launching pads for management trainee positions, become disappointed and embittered once they realized they have been misled.

Years ago, with the tremendous discrimination that women faced in trying to get into management positions, a secretarial position might have been a realistic track to a management position—perhaps the only path. However, in the 1980s and beyond, this is simply not the case. Many other options are now available.

Keep in mind that in a secretarial position (as with other "going nowhere" positions), it is in the interest of a manager, for example, to keep an experienced and competent secretary almost as an indentured servant. And unlike staff, for whom managers can be held responsible for developing for higher promotional positions, managers have no such responsibility with secretaries. Upper management generally recognizes that it is an end-of-the-line position. Being a secretary is certainly a great career for someone who wants to stay a secretary, but realize that there is no track to the top from this position.

There are many other "going nowhere" positions, and it's fine to hold them as long as you are not laboring under the false belief that you have a great opportunity to advance from there.

13. POSITIONS OFF THE BEATEN TRACK

Sometimes positions evolve or are created out of a special need or by a very powerful person that are not on any recognized organizational chart. Such a position may be temporary, lasting as long as the person in power who invented it. If you are in a position "off the beaten track," you may find it frustrating when you try to move up from there and encounter no recognition for your position.

Such was the case for Burt, who had a manufacturing position. His manager, the vice president of manufacturing, got a bright idea on how to work more closely with the sales department. The VP was interested in having one of his manufacturing people keep an eye on the sales force and any problems they were having with manufactured goods from his plant. So he made Burt the sales production analyst, the first one in the company's history!

Burt was excited about the position because he was interested in breaking into the sales area. After about a year in the job, Burt made some inquiries in the sales department about positions he could apply for, based on his recent experience. He was told that he was in manufacturing and had no experience in the sales area. His sales production analyst position was an oddball job that was strictly a figment of his manager's imagination (and ego). Burt found out the hard way that his position was on no sales track.

Beware of departments that develop their own liaison without having recognition and credibility from the organization's upper management or key influentials in other departments.

14. THE STAFF TRAP

As already mentioned, staying too long in staff positions makes it increasingly difficult to be accepted for an opportunity in a line position. You begin to be stereotyped as a support person instead of a decision maker for a profit center.

15. THE DINOSAUR ORGANIZATION

One of the worst stops to your career advancement is working for an organization that is antiquated in its thinking, its product line, its marketing, or its image. Imagine what it would be like to be working for a company that manufactures horse and buggy whips, when you know full well that the future is in that "new-fangled contraption" called the car.

Yet there are a number of companies and organizations whose extinction is imminent or working for whom brings you no credibility. (How would you like to tell people you had a marketing position developing the Edsel?) You may find that the biggest obstacle in planning your career is continuing to work for your present organization.

This is another reason why networking and being a member of your industry's trade associations will often give you advance news on trends and forecasts for the future and some valuable opinions from executives who know what is happening at the top in many organizations.

A company also can be a dinosaur and face extinction if it keeps losing money for its stockholders. This could be another factor in considering whether you want to try to advance your career in a more progressive organization.

Exercise: TRACK TO THE TOP—YOUR TEN-YEAR CAREER PLAN

Directions: The chart on the opposite page is for you to write out your ten-year career plan. What are your goals? How are you going to get there? Keep in mind that a goal is an achievable accomplishment with a specific date of completion. "Upper management" is not a goal; "vice president of operations in two years" is a goal.

SHOULD I STAY OR GO?

In diagramming your future promotional strategy, ultimately you will come to a basic question: "Should I stay or should I leave?" It seems very risky to make such a decision. Especially since it rarely will be 100 percent clear what you should do.

I often counsel people about whether they should stay at their current company or move on. And in so doing, I find that many people are waiting for overwhelming evidence to help them make their decision. In reality, you may find that the reasons to stay or leave might be 60 percent one way and 40 percent the other. You would think that this should be sufficient to make a decision, but for many people, it isn't. So be realistic when you make your decision. Don't look for extreme benefits for staying or leaving as the justification for taking action. You are taking a risk—but if you make a decision with a 60 percent confidence level, the odds are that it is a good decision.

USING A DECISION MATRIX

To help you make such decisions simply, use a form, similar to the one shown on page 329, called a decision matrix. Lindy must decide

YOUR TEN-YEAR CAREER PLAN

TIMING	POSITION DESIRED	METHODS USED TO GET THERE	ALTERNATIVE CAREER MOVE	STOPS AND BLOCKS
1st Qtr.				
2nd Qtr.				
3rd Qtr.				
4th Qtr.				
Year 2				
Year 3				
Year 4				
Year 5				
Year 6				
Year 7				
Year 8				
Year 9				
Year 10				

Ultimate goal: _____

whether to stay with her current company, knowing that her next promotion will involve a relocation to another city, or leave and find a position with another company.

In a decision matrix, you analyze the decision question by listing the pros and cons. You subdivide them into short-, medium-, and long-term factors. This way, you can get a clear picture on what variables are most important to you. You are more likely to approach the decision analytically and objectively rather than emotionally and subjectively. Also, when you lay out your pros and cons in this format, you are more able to show people what factors you are considering and thus better able to get their input.

Note that in Lindy's case, she not only had to decide whether to take a risk regarding a major move but also had to take a risk of finding a new job if she elected not to accept a relocation promotion.

With the pros in mind, Lindy saw that the short-term benefits of staying with the company and relocating were money, status from the new title, and more job knowledge. The medium-term benefits were that she would further her career goals and knowledge. The long-term benefits were security with an established company where she had accumulated power through a somewhat lengthy tenure.

On the negative side, the cons in the short term were related to the trauma of relocating to a new city. The alternative was going through the search and interviewing process of finding a new job. In the medium term, she would have to accept additional relocating to advance her career. In her current company there was the predictability of knowing what her career track would be. Since she is creative and spontaneous, this bothered her. In the long term, Lindy was unhappy about the constant uprooting that she would go through if she stayed with her company. She also foresaw salary limitations. Her ability to establish a marital relationship and family would suffer as a result of the traveling and relocation that her track to the top in this company required. And she would miss her family and friends from the city where she was working and in which she loved living.

DECISION MATRIX

"Should I stay with my current company, which I like but which requires eventual relocations, or shall I find another job elsewhere?"

	PROS	CONS
SHORT TERM:	Salary increase Significant promotion Opportunity for increased responsibilities	Trauma and adjustment to a new city Leaving means job search and interviewing Temporary lifestyle adjustment Have to leave current city I love
MEDIUM TERM:	Further my career goals Valuable learning and growth Greater job satisfaction	Staying means additional relocation and uprooting Total predictability of future
LONG TERM:	Secure company Like the people Increase my power in the organization through lengthy tenure	Constant uprooting Limitation on earning capacity Negative impact on establishing marital relationship and family Will miss friends and a city I love

This decision matrix helped Lindy to make her ultimate decision, which was to plan on leaving her current company and begin a job search for a position that might involve traveling but not relocating. What is important to realize about Lindy's process is that her decision matrix revealed the differences between how she thought intellectually and objectively versus how she felt emotionally and subjectively.

In making such decisions, people are frustrated by what they think they should do versus what they really want to do. A decision matrix will help you discover the most important factors for you. Most of the internal conflict I observe in the people whom I counsel stems from their trying to live by the needs and shoulds of others— friends, family, or colleagues. In reality, they should be listening to themselves and their own needs.

In Lindy's case, this matrix showed her that there was no clear-cut decision for her to make. In other words, she didn't get caught up in looking for a black or white answer. Instead, she saw only that there was risk associated with whatever decision she made and that the most overwhelming factor to her in making the decision to leave her company was her recognizing her need to have roots and stay in a wonderful city and environment she loved. She had already traveled to most of the major cities in the country, including the one to which her company was considering relocating her. All other pros and cons were dwarfed in importance and subordinated to her main need: to stay in her current environment.

In diagramming your future, there is no question that there will be many uncertainties to contend with. That is the nature of being in the world of work. And it is a fundamental part of anyone who is seriously planning to advance in a career. Become aware of some of the typical pitfalls and obstacles you may encounter, and really look at the methods that you will use to advance in your career. Examine alternative choices you can make. These choices will then be based on prudent calculations, which in turn will maximize the chances of climbing the ladder and having a successful and fulfilling career.